D1715773

The Life and Legacy of Stephen Olford

John Phillips

Stephen Olford

The Life and Legacy of Stephen Olford

The Biography of
Stephen F. Olford

John Phillips

THE LIFE AND LEGACY OF STEPHEN OLFORD
© 2006 Olford Ministries International

All rights reserved.

This is an updated and revised edition of the book, *Only One Life*, published in 1995.

No part of this book may be reproduced or transmitted in any form or by any means, electronic or mechanical, including photocopying and recording, or by any information storage and retrieval system, without the prior written permission of the publisher, except in the case of brief quotations embodied in critical articles or reviews.

Unless otherwise indicated, Scripture quotations are taken from the King James Version of the Bible. Scripture quotations marked "NKJV" are taken from the New King James Version®. Copyright © 1982 by Thomas Nelson, Inc. Used by permission. All rights reserved.

ISBN-10: 1-879028-20-4
ISBN-13: 978-1-879028-20-3

Library of Congress Control Number: 2006925779

Printed in Canada
10 9 8 7 6 5 4 3 2 1 Printing / Year 10 09 08 07 06

Preaching has to change from shallow sermons on popular subjects to sound, expository presentations on the nature of God, the exceeding sinfulness of sin, the redeeming work of Christ, the need for radical repentance, the call to total discipleship, the daily infilling and anointing of the Spirit and the joy of Christian service and sacrifice. The art of expository preaching is almost unknown. It has to be revived, that the faith of men should not rest in the wisdom of the world but in the power of God.

Stephen F. Olford

Col 2:20.

CONTENTS

Preface

PART ONE – THE MAN

1. The Boy 15
2. The Believer 29
3. The Husband 41
4. The Father 53
    Testimony of the Parent 54
    Reminiscences of an Elder Son 71
    Reminiscences of a Younger Son 76

PART TWO – THE MINISTER

5. The Soul-Winner 85
6. The Traveler 95
7. The Evangelist 127
8. The Pastor 151
    Duke Street Baptist Church: Richmond 154
    Calvary Baptist Church: New York 163
9. The Communicator 191
10. The Teacher-Preacher 207
11. The Contender 227

PART THREE – THE MENTOR

12. The Counselor 241
13. The Man 263
14. The Dreamer by Stephen F. Olford 281
15. The Afterword by David L. Olford 291

Chronology 305

The Published Works of Stephen F. Olford 337

Notes 341

PREFACE

My first glimpse of Stephen Olford was casual. I had been sent to the missionary home called "Hebron" on Stow Hill in Newport, South Wales with a parcel from my parents to his parents. I rang the bell. The door was opened by a young man I had never seen before. It was Stephen, the Olfords' eldest son. He stood there dressed in casual clothes, including a turtleneck sweater. I remember it because I had never seen a sweater like that before.

I came to know him better over the next few years – as well as a shy lad in his early teens like myself could know a dynamic, outgoing popular leader in his early twenties.... He and his family attended our church while he started a young people's ministry in town. He was a born leader, and like so many others, I gravitated into his orbit.

During the next half-dozen years Stephen – apart from my parents – became the most formative, long-range influence in my life.... It all came to fruition when, at age 18, I was drafted into the British Army. At once Stephen Olford's teaching crystallized. Sitting in a train on a cold winter's night, destined to be inducted the next day into barracks life, I made a decision. I would let it be known I was a Christian and I would establish the habit of a daily quiet time, using the simple method Stephen had taught.

Later I was sent to Palestine. In those days Palestine was still a mandated territory of the British Empire. I was stationed on Haifa docks and thus had more freedom than was usually granted.... Much of my spare time was spent in the local Gospel hall, an indigenous, friendly little church on the lower slopes of Mount Carmel.

This church had no recognized pastor and very little in the way of ministry. I was invited to preach. I was a greenhorn if ever there was one – but I had one asset: a supply of Stephen's sermons. I became an immediate hit with that congregation! It was there I learned how to preach. I modeled myself on Olford's style of having three alliterated main points, each one supported by three more alliterated subheadings. When I had exhausted my supply of his sermons I was thrown back on God! Still, if one had to have a temporary substitute, one could not have had a better model. During the next year and a half I organized a "Young People's Christian Fellowship," in tribute to Stephen Olford, and we saw a number of people (mostly British soldiers) profess faith in Christ.[1]

It was with these words that Dr. John Phillips began the first edition of Stephen Olford's biography, *Only One Life*, published in 1995. What began as a student-teacher relationship would grow over the years into a life-long friendship. Their mutual appreciation for each other allowed them to minister together on several occasions. Out of his deep respect for my father and as a "labor of love," Dr. Phillips graciously offered to write his biography. This incredible offer was accepted with enthusiasm and sincere gratitude by my father and all the Olford family. What a blessing!

On August 29, 2004, my father, Stephen F. Olford, went home to be with his Lord. As my mother and I reflected on my father's life and legacy in the months that followed his death, it became clear to us that his story did not end in 1995. In fact, the final decade of his life was gloriously significant and productive. An updated edition of his biography would add the final chapter of a life lived to the glory of God.

My family and I would like to thank all those involved in the production of this book. First and foremost, we extend our heartfelt gratitude to John Phillips for sharing his time and giftedness as an author to write my father's story. Secondly, we would like to thank the board members, friends and staff of OMI for their unwavering dedication to continuing the legacy Stephen Olford set before us. Thank you also to Anita Bosley for her coordination and editorial assistance on this new edition. We also offer our thanks to Karl

Schaller, Jeanette Lee, and Jeff Lane of LegacyRoad for their expertise in bringing this project to fruition.

Finally, Ellen and I and Jonathan and Catherine would like to thank our mother, Heather Olford. Throughout her marriage to our father she was his true helpmeet – a perfect partner in every sense. She has been the model of a godly woman in a Christ-centered marriage, committed to ministry and service to our Lord.

As I mentioned previously, Stephen Olford's story did not end in 1995. And, with the continuance of Olford Ministries International, it could be said that my father's story did not end in 2004, but continues on for the glory of God.

David L. Olford

Part One

THE MAN

Stephen Olford at an early age.

CHAPTER 1

The Boy

*It pleased God, who separated me from my
mother's womb, and called me by his grace, to
reveal his Son in me, that I might preach him.*
Galatians 1:15-16

It was David Livingstone who put Africa back on the map. He had
gone there originally to evangelize, but when he saw the horrors of
the slave trade he went back home to tell the world what was really
going on. Later he returned as an explorer, hoping to find the secret
sources of the Nile!

David Livingstone was the first Protestant missionary to reach what was
to become Angola. He sliced through the heart of the country in 1854 in his
historic trek across Africa from east to west. In 1886 Frederick Stanley
Arnot, a pioneer Scottish missionary associated with the Plymouth
Brethren, followed. This was the Africa which beckoned a young man in
England and a young woman in the United States. Nor did it beckon in vain.
The lure of Angola and Chokweland drew them to its dark heart.

The A-Chokwe were a proud and independent people. They plundered
the trade caravans. They considered themselves princes of royal blood. They
disdained work, especially manual labor. They cut their teeth into a V-shaped
point, carried knives, and swaggered in pride of place and race.

They "are reputed to be descendants of the Jaggas, a fierce tribe of
cannibals which invaded Angola from the north in the seventeenth
century. They spent their time in murder and pillage, continually drinking,

dancing, and feasting on human flesh. They worshiped a huge image encircled by elephant tusks, each with a human skull stuck on its point. On the death of their chief, two wives, with limbs broken, but still alive, were buried with him."[1]

Stephen Olford's father, Frederick Ernest Samuel Olford, was born in Plymouth, England on July 12, 1889. He was born again in his teens as one night he joined the throngs of people going to Soldier's Hall to hear the great American revivalist Reuben A. Torrey. He had sat spellbound on previous nights as the one-time lawyer, and close friend of D.L. Moody, unfolded the Scriptures in a pungent, logical, and persuasive way. Young Fred had already made a profession of faith but he had not yet made it public. He would never forget what happened that night.

Torrey's song leader, Charles M. Alexander, had just finished singing and the crowd had evidently been moved. Dr. Torrey stood up, visibly stirred. He gazed out over the great crowd before he preached. He issued a challenge: "Is there anyone who will stand up for Christ?" Frederick Olford stood up. Torrey pointed to him and said, "God bless you, young man."

Fred Olford was already making a name for himself as captain of a local rowing crew. He was an apprentice to a shipbuilding firm already marked for success. He knew that night, however, that God had touched him; he was no longer his own. His first response was to go back to the other members of his rowing crew, bring them to the crusade, and see all eleven of them saved. Thereafter, "Peter and his eleven," as they were nicknamed, became a familiar sight preaching in the open air and leading people to Christ.

Shortly after his baptism, at the age of 16, Fred heard the Macedonian call ringing across the seas from distant Africa. It was the sight of a ruined harvest that tilted the scales.

Fred had been preparing for a career in engineering. His studies were behind him and a promising career lay before him. Thoughts of the mission field stirred him, however, from time to time, but his prospects in business were alluring. An inner battle was already underway.

About this time he accompanied his mother to Cornwall for a short holiday. His relatives were gentleman farmers, and the Olfords planned to stay on their estate for a few days. One evening, Fred was standing at the window of his room looking out at a field of golden grain. The wheat was ready for harvest. The setting sun, the peaceful countryside, the gentle evening breeze, all breathed an atmosphere of peace and calm.

Then it happened! That night a freak storm broke with inescapable fury. The thunder roared, the lightning blazed, the wind blew, the rains came. When Fred Olford looked out of his window next morning it was on a scene of desolation. The harvest field was flattened—ruined!

Fred called his mother. Together they gazed at the ruined harvest.

"Mother," he said, "this is it. It's Africa for me. I dare not disobey this call. I must not be late. I must go and reap for God." There and then on his knees, his mother beside him, he yielded himself to the Lord of the harvest for the ripened fields of Central Africa.

He plunged into preparation. He took training in medicine at Livingstone College in London in 1912. The next year he went to Portugal to learn Portuguese (in those days Angola was a Portuguese colony). On June 28, 1913, he left for the mission field. He wrote the following dates in his Bible:

Sept. 1, 1912	Livingstone College
April 23, 1913	Portugal
June 28, 1913	Left for Central Africa
July 18, 1913	Arrival at Lobito
Aug. 1, 1913	Arrived at Capango
Nov. 2, 1914	Left Capango
Nov. 16, 1914	Arrived at Luma-Cassai
May 15, 1917	Married

Bessie Rhoden Santmire was born in Buffalo, New York on January 22, 1893. Her early life was touched by sorrow. She was only seven when her mother died, so she was taken to live in the home of her married sister in nearby Blasdell. When she was nine her sister led her to Christ. Like the young man in England, of whom as yet she had never heard, Bessie was associated with a group of Christians known as Plymouth Brethren.

When Bessie was about sixteen years old she felt that God was calling her to the mission field. In 1914 the local brethren wisely advised her to get some experience. They directed her to "Sister Abigail," a well-known local lady who cared for a number of helpless patients suffering from arthritis. Through this experience Bessie received some basic training in nursing. Meanwhile Central Africa was calling.

Early that same year Bessie attended the Toronto Bible College. Her studies were cut short, however, when the way opened for her to accompany missionaries Leonard Gammon and his wife, first to England and then to Portugal and Angola. In England she took some training in midwifery; in Lisbon she studied Portuguese. Then in 1915 she and the Gammons sailed for Angola.

The trip eventually led them into the interior. In those days African travel was primitive and rough. Both the men and the women walked, with the women taking an occasional ride in a hammock. It took a week, traveling 25 miles a day, to reach the base missionary station at Bie. From there Bessie and some other missionaries pressed on through wild country to Luma-Cassai.

First home at Luma-Cassai, Angola.

It was there that Bessie, the American from Buffalo, met Fred, the Englishman from Plymouth. Their courtship, by the very nature of the case, was clandestine. Bessie recalled: "Mr. Olford had seen my photograph. He had a feeling that we were to become more than friends and co-workers. For the sake of the nationals, however, it was not etiquette for us to be seen together, so we wrote notes and passed them to each other in hymnbooks! This went on for months."

It was a dog that finally did the trick. Bessie said, "One day a dog came up behind me and pushed me over. As I fell I dislocated my kneecap. Mrs. Taylor and Miss Smith tried for some time to reset the kneecap but eventually Mr. Olford had to be called. He had heard of the accident and was studying his medical books. Soon, with the necessary knowledge gleaned, he put my kneecap back in place. He made a crutch for me, and it was then that I thought him wonderful!"

Two years after Bessie's arrival at Luma-Cassai, Fred Olford and Bessie Santmire were married. Bessie said: "Though we had never been out together or spent an evening alone until after our wedding, God brought us together."

Their son, Stephen Frederick Olford, was born in Kalene Hill in Northern Rhodesia on March 29, 1918. Fred Olford's knowledge of basic medicine, and the experience he had gained on the mission field, caused him to anticipate that the birth of their first baby might be accompanied by complications. Rather than take a chance, he and Bessie made up their minds to make the thousand-mile trek from Angola to the British colony of

Northern Rhodesia. Fred walked every step of the way while Bessie was carried in a hammock by A-Chokwe men.

Stephen arrived safely. He was carried all the way back to Luma-Cassai on the head of an African tribesman. By the time of the return journey, however, rains had caused the rivers to rise. There were no bridges, of course, so the rivers had to be waded. What was more, they were often infested by crocodiles. When they came to a river Stephen's father would march ahead, firing shots into the water right and left to frighten away the fearsome reptiles.

When the Olfords arrived back at their station they were warmly received by the tribesmen. The birth of Stephen had broken the ice of caution and suspicion. "Now the white man is really one of us," they said.

Stephen recalled: "My parents took me into villages all around Angola to break the barriers of suspicion, unbelief, and hostility. My father would come to a village and sit down with the chief. Then he would call my mother to bring me. She would hand me to my father who would then hand me to the chief. The chief, in turn, would pass me from hand to hand all around the village. I became 'a peace child.' Those Africans loved their children. They would say: 'If this white man is prepared to hand his child over, then he is a friend. We will listen to what he has to say!'" Stephen later commented, "I was handed out as life. I was handed back to my mother as 'abundant life,' having collected a due ration of lice!"

Stephen had many reminiscences of his boyhood days in Africa. It was not unusual to find a snake nestling at the bottom of a boot. Once he was badly stung by a scorpion. Another time a leopard leaped through the window of their home and devoured a pet dog. On another occasion a lion broke into the mission compound and killed the family's favorite cow.

Perhaps one of the most dramatic and memorable experiences happened very early one Christmas morning. Stephen had no present to give to his parents. Suddenly it occurred to him that a good fat goose would be a pleasant surprise and, at the same time, would provide a delicious meal for the festive table. So rising before daybreak, he picked up his shotgun and stealthily left the house before anyone could see him. As he opened the gate of the mission compound it squeaked—no oil! That little incident was to prove critical an hour or so later. Down to the rice fields he hurried to catch the first flock of geese as they flew in to feed. Then it happened! The birds were overhead, swooping down in perfect range. He chose a fine looking gander and fired. It dropped instantly; but better still, the spread of shot winged another bird that also dropped but was struggling to get away. Young Stephen, keenly aware of the price of cartridges, decided to give chase, instead of shooting the wounded bird. In his haste, he misjudged a jump and landed in a marshy bog, sinking down to his chin. He struggled to find a foothold, but all in vain. Reluctantly he plunged his gun into the bog to try and save himself, but that also failed. Panicking he cried out, "Lord, save me! Please, Lord, save me!" It was like Peter of old.

Just then a voice shouted to him, "Tivi!" (That was his Chokwe name). Stephen looked around and saw João, the compound boy, running toward him. João had heard the gate squeak and had jumped from his cot in time to see Stephen headed for the rice fields. He knew that Stephen was courting danger, so he had followed at a distance. But now it was do or die. Watching his footing carefully and leaping with speed, he reached the sinking lad. Taking a new beautiful print cloth that was wrapped around his body (a Christmas present from Ngana—white man) he quickly twisted it into a makeshift rope and threw it to the boy. Stephen grabbed it and João, with dexterity and strength, rescued Stephen from certain death. The boy, the gun, and the geese were recovered. But as Stephen has remarked on many occasions since, that experience dramatized the gospel to perfection! Jesus laid aside the garments of glory and came to men and women sinking in the bog of sin; and in answer to their cry of faith, lifted them from death to life! In the words of Stephen, "I have never forgotten that experience. It was the best Christmas I ever celebrated!"

On another occasion he was lost in the bush; but to his distraught family's immense relief, he eventually showed up at camp safe and sound. The date of this event was indelibly impressed on the memory of his tutor Nellie Sawyer, who noted it in her diary—August 10, 1934.

At times Stephen accompanied his father to outlying villages where he saw witchcraft, idolatry, superstition, and raw paganism firsthand. Once he sat with his father at a campsite as tribesmen ate meat plucked off human bones.

Stephen remembered how once a witch doctor was determined to wipe out the missionary family. He approached the Olford home, gun in hand, announcing his intention of shooting each member of the family. Inside the house they could hear the man shouting even as they prayed. Stephen's father rose from his knees and, unarmed, walked out to the veranda. Protected by the promises of God, he addressed the demented man: "I rebuke you in the name of the Lord Jesus Christ, the Son of God." The witch doctor stopped in his tracks, dropped his gun, and fled. Twenty minutes later Mr. Olford was called to the hut where the witch doctor lay dead. There was no natural cause of death; the only explanation was God.

On another occasion Stephen and his brothers, Paul and John, accompanied their father on a visit to a tribe that had never heard the gospel. They watched a man going through a ritual of witchcraft. The marks of demon possession could be seen in the distorted features of the man's face. They watched him plant his idols and go through his incantations as he worked himself up into a frenzy. Stephen and his brothers were very frightened. Then the youngest boy accidentally kicked over one of the idols. The witch doctor was furious and cursed him.

Suddenly the witch doctor fled into the bush. Presently he reappeared and began to perform superhuman feats. He jumped into a fire of blazing logs, picked up the heavy logs, and threw them into the air, scornful of the leaping flames. As the logs fell to the ground, some of them battered his body; yet he seemed to feel no pain. His skin was burned, and the pungent smell of burning flesh hung heavily in the air. Men tried to grab and hold him, but like the demoniac in the Gospels, he simply flung them aside. He had the superhuman strength of ten men.

Stephen sent someone to get his father. The missionary soon summed up the situation. Pale, but resolute in his faith, he lifted up his voice in prayer: "Lord Jesus Christ, who died to conquer the devil, by the value of the precious blood You once shed, in Your Name and Your power, I command the demons in this man to be cast out." Instantly the witch doctor collapsed like a punctured balloon.

After a few moments the witch doctor cried out, "Ngana, have mercy on me! Have mercy on me! The demons have gone!" Stephen observed that his father immediately knelt with the man and very quietly talked to him about Christ and asked him to receive the Lord Jesus into his life. "That man," Stephen recalled, "became one of the greatest saints I, as a boy, ever knew. We stayed there three days while my father washed the poor man's wounds, put medicine on him, and comforted him, and then counseled him how to live the Christian life."

Still looking back on his boyhood days, Stephen remembered an incident that led almost directly to his conversion. While he was being carried across a fast-flowing river one of the carriers slipped and the hammock overturned. He was almost pitched into the water. The only thing that saved him from death was the fact that his jacket caught in the branch of a tree. He was terrified. He realized in that dread moment, young as he was, that he was not ready to meet God.

There was an element of the miraculous in these boyhood escapes from death. Looking back we can clearly see that Stephen Olford was "a chosen vessel," separated, like Paul, from his mother's womb, for the gospel. Satan's attempts to cut short that life were foiled time and again by a higher hand.

It was the same with both Charles and John Wesley. When Charles was born, he was premature and appeared to be stillborn. He neither opened his eyes nor cried. Indeed, for some time there was no sign of life at all. Eventually, however, his mother detected a faint heartbeat. She wrapped

A-Chokwe tribesmen

the tiny form in soft wool and laid him down, making no attempt to feed him. He remained seemingly lifeless for several days. When the moment came that, according to the ordinary course of nature, he should have been born, the baby opened his eyes and cried. Thereafter he was just like any other newborn. He was destined to give voice in music to the great Methodist revival.

Young John Wesley likewise had a close brush with death when he was six years of age. His father, Samuel, earned the wrath of some of his recklessly extravagant parishioners by his bold denunciation of their sins. On two occasions they tried to set his house on fire. On the third occasion they succeeded. About midnight the rectory went up in flames. The father's cries of alarm woke the numerous members of his family. The door was locked, however, and it took precious time to open it. Some of the children climbed through a downstairs window. Some ran out through a little door into the garden. Mrs. Wesley had a narrow escape, literally wading through the flames to safety. Her clothes were burned but she miraculously escaped injury.

John, however, had been overlooked in the panic. His father heard him crying in the nursery, but the stairs had been destroyed and the boy could not be reached. In the meantime the little boy climbed on a chest by the window and cried for help. Two neighbors ran to the house. One climbed onto the shoulders of the other, reached up, and pulled the boy from the burning windowsill. The next moment the window fell in. John Wesley, so greatly used of God in later years to usher in the Methodist revival, never forgot his boyhood brush with death. Later in life he had a picture painted to commemorate the event. On the margin of the painting he wrote the words: "Is not this a brand plucked from the burning?"

Shortly after his narrow escape from death by drowning, Stephen celebrated his seventh birthday. That night his mother conducted family devotions around the hearth fire. She read the opening verses of John 14: "I go to prepare a place for you . . . I will come again, and receive you unto myself; that where I am, there ye may be also" (2-3).

"Boys," she said, "if Jesus came back tonight would you be ready to go?"

She pressed a little further. 'Do you think Father would go?" The boys agreed that he would.

"Would Mother go?"

"Yes."

"Would Pedro, the cook-boy go?"

"Yes."

"Would João, the compound boy go?"

"Yes."

"Would you go?"

Stephen could still visualize the finger pointing to him. He toyed for a few moments with a piece of rag he happened to have in his hand. He did not answer. His mother was too wise to press the point. She prayed for her boys and bundled them off to bed.

That night Stephen tossed and turned upon his mattress. The pillow seemed to be stuffed with bricks. About twelve o'clock he felt indeed that the midnight cry had sounded. A sense of dereliction came over his soul. Suppose Jesus had come! After a few moments he decided to find out if his parents were still there.

"Mother!" he called. There was no answer. Desperately now, and in sheer terror, he called again: *"Mother!"* Then he heard running footsteps coming nearer and nearer through the sprawling building. Ah! It was Mother!

"What's the matter?" His mother felt sure that a hyena or a leopard had broken into the house. Instead, she found a very frightened little boy.

"I thought Jesus had come and I had been left behind," he said.

It did not take long after that. Out came the Bible. Paul's great words were read: "That Christ may dwell in your hearts by faith; that ye, being rooted and grounded in love, may be able to comprehend with all saints what is the breadth, and length, and depth, and height; and to know the love of Christ, which passeth knowledge, that ye might be filled with all the fulness of God" (Ephesians 3:17-19). "Christ in you, the hope of glory" (Colossians 1:27).

There and then Stephen received Christ into his life. He prayed the sinner's prayer:

> Into my heart, into my heart,
> Come into my heart, Lord Jesus.
> Come in today, Come in to stay,
> Come into my heart, Lord Jesus.
>   Harry D. Clark

His feet were now on "the path of the just . . . as the shining light, that shineth more and more unto the perfect day" (Proverbs 4:18).

Looking back, there seems to have been something inspired and prophetic about the passage of Scripture which Bessie Olford used that night with her seven-year-old son. For in those verses is the message of the indwelling Christ—a message destined to loom so largely in Stephen Olford's preaching, and the message that explains his extraordinary authority and success in the ministry.

Stephen was baptized when he was fourteen. To create a baptistry the Luma River was dammed up. Several hundred Africans gathered to look on at this spectacle of a white boy, the missionary's son, being baptized. This was a real event! They had been watching his life. Stephen said: "For a whole year I had lived under the searching eyes, the disciplining eyes, the haunting eyes, of the twenty-four elders of that local assembly of believers in the bush." His baptism marked a significant milestone.

Leonard Gammon, one of the missionaries, went into the water, followed by the young white boy. Stephen gave his testimony. Then seven A-Chokwe men followed—first a disabled man, then the others, including one old man. Then came two women. One was Chenda, wife of João, a very bright Christian.

Stephen's father gave a gospel message, and though the heat was intense there was rapt attention. After the baptism there was a brief time for a change of clothes and a hasty meal. Then there was a breaking of bread service at the school. Seventeen people were added to the church that day—the ten who had been baptized, and some others who had backslidden but now showed signs of repentance.

The boyhood days came and went with surprising speed. There was always something to do. Stephen's great responsibility was the truck. He was assistant mechanic and like working with his hands. He enjoyed carpentry, riding his bike, playing tennis, and walking on stilts. He liked taking care of his gun and enjoyed shooting game for the dinner pot, especially if the wild animals and snakes were plentiful and menacing enough! He kept a pet katoto (a small, monkey-like creature) which would run around the table and hide in Stephen's pocket. Once he brought it to school where it jumped up on the blackboard, much to the amusement of the teacher and his classmates. Every Wednesday night was Father's night to drill his boys in Bible study, and each one was expected to bring a Bible question for discussion.

Another person who had an influence on Stephen's life was his tutor, Miss Nellie Sawyer. She first met the Olfords at a missionary conference in Bath, England, in July 1930, and after the conference her parents invited the Olford family to come and stay in their home. "I was drawn to the whole family as soon as I met them," she said. "I came to know the boys quite well during their stay. Stephen struck me as an intelligent and interesting boy. When I heard that Mr. and Mrs. Olford had a great desire to take the whole family back to Africa if they could find a tutor for the boys, the call came to offer myself for this work." Nellie Sawyer had just graduated with honors from Bristol University with a B.S. degree.

She went to Africa with the Olfords and their boys Stephen, Paul, and John. Later David and Walter Gammon, who were on the same local mission station, also came under her wing. The school was a large room in the Olford home. The school day ran for about five hours a day, Monday through Friday. Each morning began with Bible study. Miss Sawyer followed the syllabus of a typical English school in those days. Portuguese was added due to the colonial status of Angola.

As the boys grew older, Nellie changed her method of teaching. The boys were given set assignments to be completed in a week with a certain amount of help from her. The plan worked well. Sometimes they had to deliver short lectures. "Stephen always had good marks," she recalled. Sports, physical education, and even missionary field trips were included in the learning process.

One day, when Stephen was fourteen, he and Nellie visited a nearby village to invite people to come to Sunday services. That day eight boys and one man professed salvation. On other occasions he and his brother Paul would visit villages to hold meetings. Thus, early in life, Stephen learned how to lead people to Christ.

Two of Stephen Olford's Scripture exams have survived from his boyhood days: one dated July 26, 1934 and the other April 15, 1935. It is interesting to see what a good grasp of Scripture Stephen had, even as a teenage boy. Asked at age 16 to "either give an account of the ministry and arrest of Stephen or give a summary of the address of Peter on the Day of Pentecost, along with the effect of that sermon," Stephen chose the latter. He displayed a skill in sermon analysis, a competent knowledge of the facts, a way with words, and a clear, bold, and ornate handwriting. He wrote:

PETER'S SERMON

On the Day of Pentecost, when the Holy Ghost had come upon the disciples, there [sic] were able to speak many languages. Many people from far had assembled in Jerusalem to the feast. Now when the people heard the disciples speaking in different tongues, some were astonished, but others mocking said, "These men are full of new wine." Then Peter stood up with the other disciples and preached to the people. His "theme" was "Jesus as Christ and Lord." He refuted the charge of being drunk, reminding them that it was only the third hour of the day and it was impossible. He showed them the prophecy of Joel, the prophet. He proved that Jesus Christ was the Lord by the works that were being manifested at that time. He took them back to the time when David foretold the Messiah's Kingdom after His death and resurrection. He showed them that himself and the other disciples were witnesses of the Lord's resurrection. That God had raised Him from the dead. The same One whom they despised and rejected had become the head of the corner. He showed the people their state, or "What must Israel do?" Then telling them of Jesus' love, and that if they believed and were baptized they would be saved. When Peter had ended his sermon, the people were pricked to the heart, and that day three thousand souls were added to the church.

How many sixteen-year-olds in our Sunday schools today could display such a grasp of Scripture? Thankfully (for the rest of us) he made some interesting spelling mistakes in his essays! When asked to name some Old Testament prophets and tell what he knew of them he chose to elaborate on Elijah and dismissed him to Heaven in only seventeen and a half lines! It was also amusing to find in one of his exam papers that Pilate was "King of Judea!"

The overall impression one receives from reading these exam papers is that a solid and effective Bible knowledge was already part of young Stephen's boyhood heritage. Indeed, the man who was to be was already present in the boy that was.

Then, in the spring of 1935 Stephen and his brothers pored over an atlas and plotted out the route their ship would take back to England, noting all the expected ports of call. They left in late May, arriving in Southampton a month later. Stephen was now seventeen years old; his boyhood days were over.

The Olford family on their return from Africa, 1935.
Fred, Stephen, John, Paul, and Bessie

CHAPTER 2

The Believer

*I have been crucified with Christ; it is no
longer I who live, but Christ lives in me; and
the life which I now live in the flesh I live by
faith in the Son of God, who loved me and
gave Himself for me.*
Galatians 2:20, NKJV

Seventeen-year-old Stephen Olford disembarked from the ship and
stepped into a foreign world. Now he would be exposed to an even
more savage place than any he had known in the Angolan jungles.
It was all the more dangerous because its savagery was masked by
sophistication. Many a time he had seen Satan as a roaring lion in Africa.
Now he must meet him on the college campus and in the sports arena as
the old serpent. Like Moses, he could no longer be hid at home (Exodus
2:3), given the personal protection of his parents, shielded from the
perils and pitfalls of life in a world of sin. Those days were over.

What could his parents do? All they could do was pray and remind
the Lord that this boy belonged to Him. All they could do was put him by
faith in the bulrushes and then besiege the throne of grace. Over the next
few perilous years lies the shadow of a praying mother in England and a
praying father in far-off Angola. Their prayers met and mingled at the high
court of the universe. Those prayers were heard and answered in due
time. But first Stephen learned for himself what a deceptive and
disappointing place this world really is. When we ask for bread, it gives a
stone. When we ask for fish it gives a scorpion. It is a thief and a robber.
The young prodigal will leave his father's covenanted home, full of desire

to taste and see that the world is good. Instead it will leave him dishonored and destitute and desperate, looking into a pig pail in a cold and inhospitable land. Lot could have told Stephen what to expect. Solomon wrote a book about it. But Stephen was not listening.

He soon enrolled in a course in mechanical engineering at the Devonport Technical College. There he encountered the materialism and humanistic philosophies and psychology of the age. His faith was to be sorely tried.

At this stage, Stephen intended to go back to Africa, but not as a missionary. He had seen enough of what he called, "the trauma and trial and tears of missionary life." He wanted to get a degree in engineering and return to the west coast of Africa to take up a position, which had already been offered to him.

At college, one of his professors took every opportunity to explain away his faith in terms of behavioral psychology. He scoffed at Stephen's testimony of his conversion as a lot of nonsense. Doubts began to find lodging in Stephen's heart.

About this time Stephen's father returned to Africa, faithful to his call, to introduce the gospel to a tribe in the upper reaches of the Cassai River. Stephen knew the area, having charted the whole pathway with his father with pedometer and compass. He had seen that savage tribe. He and his father had been the first white people those Africans had ever seen. Stephen said good-bye to his father, but not good-bye to his father's prayers.

About this same time, Stephen was mishandled by a local church. He had expected to see in the believers the same quality of godliness he had seen in his parents. Disappointed and disillusioned, he turned his back on the church and became a thoroughgoing backslider. It was to be the world for him.

At school he began working on his thesis and chose carburetion as his practical experiment. He developed a carburetor which could vaporize gas faster than ordinary ones. To test his work he took up motorcycle racing where he won many prizes and quickly became a notable figure in the sporting community.

Many a night he would come home late and climb the stairs of their little home in stocking feet, see a door ajar, and his dear mother on her knees, praying and sobbing her heart out for her backslidden, wandering boy. But willful and determined to go his own way, he continued until God said, "This far, and no further."

One night Stephen was coming home from a motorcycle race. He had three beautiful silver cups in the pack case of his motorcycle—a tribute to his prowess on the track. He was riding high, wide, and handsome. Life was good! He was a winner. Suddenly, his front wheel skidded on an icy patch. He was thrown off his cycle right onto his head. Suffering a severe concussion, he lay there for some hours on the icy road before he was picked up and rushed to the hospital. Pneumonia quickly set in. The doctors held out little hope and sent him home to die. "He has two weeks to live," they told his mother.

"Those weren't the days of antibiotics," Stephen said, "I lay on my bed fighting a tremendous battle. On the one hand, I knew the right way; on the other side I was so rebellious. I was going to dig in my heels right down to death. I wouldn't see any of the pastors who came to visit me.

"It was one afternoon, deep into that fortnight—two weeks to live— that my mother came in and dropped an envelope on my bed and quietly slipped out again. I looked down and saw my father's beautiful handwriting. He was writing to me from Africa where it took three months for a letter to get to England, and another three months for a letter to get back to him, so he wouldn't have had a clue of what was happening to me. He hadn't received any news of the accident; it was impossible to send a telegram in those days. But away there in the bush he had a burden on his heart, and so he wrote these words: 'My son, this is of the utmost importance: "Only one life, 'twill soon be past, only what's done for Christ will last." ' "

Stephen recalled that those simple lines smote him like a sledge-hammer. "I was crushed," he said, "I knew he was right. 'Only one life, 'twill soon be past; only what's done for Christ will last.' After a few moments of deep struggle I capitulated to the sovereignty of Christ. Though I wasn't allowed to move, I slipped out of bed, fell on my knees, and prayed, 'Lord, You have won and I own You as King of kings and Lord of lords.' I added a little postscript—a kind of cowardly postscript— 'Lord, if You will heal my body, I will serve You anywhere, at any time, and at any cost!' God answered that prayer."

Three weeks later Stephen was recuperating on the south coast of England. All his friends were inquiring about him. He had made local history. He recalled what happened next. "I was walking on the boardwalk, along the seaside, on a bright, sunny morning when I was stopped by a wonderful missionary, a Mr. Barnes from Barbados. He said, 'Are you Stephen Olford?' I said, 'Yes.' He said, 'I've heard some amazing stories about you. What are you going to do with your life?' I said, 'I've committed it to the sovereignty of Jesus Christ. I'm going to go anywhere, at any time, at any cost for Him.' He looked at me. 'Aren't you going to return to engineering?' I replied, 'No! That is one of the biggest battles I've fought in recent weeks, but I've settled it. I'm not going back to engineering. I'm going into the ministry.' "

The wise old missionary put Stephen's resolve to the test. Hundreds of people were thronging that promenade. Near where they stood were two big whalebones embedded in concrete. It was a local landmark. The missionary issued his challenge. "Are you prepared to kneel down right here and tell God what you have just told me?"

"I am," Stephen said. Then and there, to the amusement of the passing crowds, Stephen knelt down and prayed: "Lord Jesus, I want You to take over my life for any time, in any place, at any cost."

This decision was the end of a career in engineering. It meant training for the ministry. Stephen already knew he was being called to be a preacher. He went back and told his professor. The man exploded, "You are a fool, Olford! You are almost through. You are one of my most promising students." Stephen replied, "I know, sir, but this is what it is costing me to decide for Christ." Suddenly tears welled up in the professor's eyes. He said, "Perhaps, Olford, I'm the fool. Good luck to you. God bless you."

To prepare himself for the ministry, Stephen Olford first enrolled in St. Luke's College in Mildmay, London. He also did some external advanced work via correspondence.

———

I was twelve years of age when I first met Stephen Olford. His family had settled in Newport in South Wales. As commended missionaries with the Plymouth Brethren they attended the large, local assembly of believers and lived in the missionary home, owned by the group. The shadow of World War II hung like a pall over the land. I had been raised in that assembly. My father and one of my uncles were prominent members. I had heard good preaching all my boyhood days. My own father was a gifted expositor of the Word, in great demand locally as a conference speaker. Able men occupied the pulpit of our assembly every Sunday. Old Mr. Barnes, the man who accosted Stephen on the Teignmouth boardwalk, was a frequent and popular preacher—but I had never heard a man like Stephen Olford. His gift for alliteration, his exegesis of the text, his illustrations, often drawn from his African days, his passion and authority, his emphasis on the indwelling Christ—all this was fresh and fascinating. I often wondered where he had learned to preach like that.

He learned at the feet of venerable Dr. W. Graham Scroggie. From St. Luke's College Stephen went to the Missionary Training Colony, where Dr. Scroggie was the visiting professor of homiletics. He addicted Stephen to expository preaching. Dr. Scroggie wrote such books as *Know*

Your Bible, an analytic study of each Bible book, rich in outlines and alliteration; *The Unfolding Drama of Redemption,* a masterly survey of the Bible, abounding with helpful maps, charts, and commentary; and *A Guide to the Gospels,* one of the best books on the Gospels ever written. He was a gifted homiletician and a popular Keswick speaker. This was the man who drilled Stephen Olford in pulpit oratory, content, and style. It is not difficult to trace the skill in alliteration and exposition, which was to become the Olford hallmark, back to the training he received as one of Graham Scroggie's disciples. Stephen said, "Even after I finished that schooling, he took care of me and was my mentor. He came to hear me preach and critiqued my sermons."

The Missionary Training Colony was far more than a preaching campus. Classroom training was put to practical tests designed to prove endurance. Here Stephen learned how to cook, pull teeth, suture a wound, even take apart and reassemble a Model-T Ford. Here too he learned to trust God in a deeper way, and God never failed him. He received a lesson in trust during the early days of his training for the ministry.

He recalled, "I had to possess a certain sum of money before being accepted by the Missionary Training Colony in Highfield Hill, Upper Norwood, London. Every penny of this amount had to be prayed in! Miraculously, financial support came in from all quarters. The stated figure, however, was not complete as I came to the deadline date, and my faith was beginning to fail. So I dropped on my knees and told God that I was in His hands for the future, and if all the money did not come in, I would take it that this was my guidance not to go to the Missionary Training Colony.

"I had hardly finished praying when the doorbell rang. I ran to the door to see an envelope come through the letter slot. The postmark was Angola, Portuguese West Africa. My heart sank. Of all places, this was the last place from which to expect money. But I was wrong! I opened the envelope to find the exact amount required. The accompanying letter was from some of my dear African friends who, having heard of my desire to train for the ministry, had butchered an ox, sold the meat, and had sent the proceeds to help with my education. Their gift arrived on the right day and in the exact amount to make up the deficit." Sometime later, Stephen's African friends sent him the tail of the ox to prove the authenticity of their act of love for their old pal Tivi. Stephen told that story ever since!

——

Anyone who has seen Stephen Olford's library knows what an important part books have played in maturing his convictions. He named people and books that had greatly influenced his life. First and foremost were his parents. Then there was the evangelist Harold Wildish, whose impact on the island of Jamaica still lives on. His call to consecration and service, demonstrated in his life and communicated in his preaching, had a lasting effect on Stephen. Then there was Harold St. John, saint, scholar, and able Bible teacher. Stephen said: "To sit at his feet and hear the Word of God expounded, and to watch that same truth translated into Christian living, was something which convinced my young mind that Christianity really works." Another great influence was businessman A. Lindsay Glegg. Stephen added, "His sanctified common sense and statesman-like advice over the years taught me much of the secret of balance and realism in the Christian ministry." There were others—Graham Scroggie, of course, and Capt. Godfrey Buxton, who was the founder and principal of the Missionary Training Colony. His Bible readings every morning were rich, searching, and practical. He was a man who manifestly lived what he taught. Then there was Dr. G. Campbell Morgan, Dr. W.E. Sangster, Professor James Stewart, and Dr. Martyn Lloyd-Jones.

In terms of books and written sermons there was a host of classic authors: John Owen, John Bunyan, John Calvin, C.H. Spurgeon, Handley C.G. Moule, Horatius Bonar, F.B. Meyer, Andrew Murray, Alexander Whyte, and Alexander Maclaren. No wonder Stephen Olford's messages were so thoroughly sound in doctrine, so evangelical, so authoritative, so "God-conceived, Christ-centered, and Spirit-controlled."

Another dimension was yet to be added. When the children of Israel came out of Egypt they were first redeemed by the blood of the lamb. Then they crossed the Red Sea and, in type, were brought positionally through death and burial to resurrection ground. In the strength of that experience they could have gone on to conquer Canaan, but they failed to do so. Thus it was that, later, they had to cross Jordan. This was really a reconfirmation of the truth that they had already passed through death and burial to take their stand on the resurrection side of death. This second experience was made necessary because of their failure to make good on the first one.

A similar situation often arises with Christian believers. At conversion we are identified with Christ in His death, burial, and resurrection. We confess this truth publicly in water baptism. But like the children of Israel, many of us fail to make good in practice what we declare to be our position. As a result, some great crisis experience becomes necessary at a later stage in our spiritual pilgrimage. We experience what some call "a

Photo by G. P. Abraham

*The speakers and council members
of the 1952 English Keswick.*

*(From left, Back row) Rev. Wm. Still,
J. Taylor Thompson, Dr. H. J. Orr-Ewing,
Rev. Alan Redpath, the Bishop of
Barking, Rev. G. B. Duncan,
Rev. M.A.P. Wood, Preb. Colin C. Kerr,
R.A. Laidlaw. (Sitting) Rev. H.H. Martin,
A.W. Bradley, Fred Mitchell,
Rev.A.T. Houghton, Dr. W. Graham
Scroggie, Dr. Wilbur Smith, C.H.M. Foster,
P.S. Henman. (In front) M. Burch,
Stephen Olford.*

second blessing." It is not, of course, a new conversion. It is a new and more mature commitment to Jesus as Lord. It opens up Canaan. We enter into the rest, the resources, and the realities of all that we have in Christ. It is often accompanied by new power in the ministry.

When Stephen Olford dragged himself off his deathbed, dropped on his knees, and cried to God for mercy, longing for the Lord Jesus to be made real in his life, God met him. "For the first time in all those years," he said, "I experienced the realization of the glory and wonder of an indwelling Christ. I suddenly became aware that this broken, battered body of mine was a habitat, a dwelling place for the Son of God. And oh, the peace! Nobody told me. I didn't have a Bible open before me, but the wonder that this body of mine was the very dwelling place of the Son of God was so overwhelming that I just stayed there on my knees. Eventually I dragged myself onto my bed, and a wonderful peace came into my heart. Glory to God!"

He went, Elijah-like, in the strength of that heavenly food many days. In time there followed his tremendous ministry in Newport, in the church, among young people, and above all, with the troops embarking for the front line in France. In the end he was drained and exhausted. As the war came to an end he found himself emotionally depleted, physically ill, his vocal chords shot to pieces, and his soul spiritually dry. He wondered if he would ever preach again.

He said, "Somebody gave me a biography of D.L. Moody, and I read it through and it moved me profoundly. I read a biography of F.B. Meyer. One was an evangelist, one was a pastor, but their experience was just the same. I said: 'Lord, what did they have that I don't have, because I'm dry, absolutely dry?'

"I went into hibernation at a bed and breakfast flat, cancelled all my commitments, took two big suitcases of books, way back from the early writers and the Puritans—John Calvin, John Owen, Martin Luther—right up to Campbell Morgan, and modern books. *Veni Creator* by Handley Moule was a book that mightily moved me. So did A.J. Gordon's book on *The Ministry of the Spirit*. I had a little attic, all alone. I pored over those books day after day, hour after hour. At last I laid all those books aside and I began to study Ephesians 5:18 on being filled with the Holy Spirit. I had a cross-reference in my Bible to 2 Corinthians 3:6, 17: 'The letter killeth, but the spirit giveth life. . . . Now the Lord is that Spirit: and where the Spirit of the Lord is, there is liberty.' This can be understood, where the Spirit *is Lord*—that is, where He is given His true deity and sovereignty—there is liberty! And God set me free!

"I went down and paid my bill. The lady asked, 'Is the food bad?' I said, 'No.' She then inquired, 'Why are you leaving?' I told her my story. She stood there with tears streaming down her face. She said, 'You talk like someone who came out of the Welsh revival.' 'Well,' I replied, 'God has revived my heart.' I picked up my books and I went into Cardiff. I remembered that on that very date I was supposed to preach at a big youth rally but I had canceled out. A colleague of mine was preaching instead. I slipped into the meeting; I couldn't help it. I put my bags down and sat there. Then someone spotted me. When it was known I was there I was called up to the platform. I said, 'No, I'm not going to preach!' I meant it. Finally I said, 'If you don't mind I will tell the people what has just happened!' I gave my testimony. We were there until 2:00 a.m., leading souls to Christ."

That was just the beginning. From there Stephen Olford went to Hildenborough Hall. This was a conference center established by evangelist Tom Rees where hundreds of young people converged for holiday making and biblical teaching. Stephen spent the whole week sharing what he had learned from the Word of God concerning the work of the Holy Spirit in a believer's life—and there was revival! "At the end of that week who should arrive from the United States but Torrey Johnson, Chuck Templeton, Billy Graham, Cliff Barrows, Stratton Shufelt, and one or two others. As was the custom, there was a testimony meeting on the last night. Then to close the program, I preached on Ephesians 5:18. God came down in power. Tom Rees said, 'All who want dealings with God, who have not already come into blessing, go into the chapel. We are going to give Stephen Olford twenty minutes to rest.' I sat there with my head bowed.

"Suddenly I sensed a presence before me. I looked up and I saw this handsome, tall young man, Billy Graham. I can visualize him now in his light suit, sporting an impossible tie! He said, 'Why didn't you give an invitation?' I said, 'An invitation has been given. In twenty minutes I'll be meeting with all those who really want to know how to be filled with the Spirit. Why did you ask?' He said, 'I would have been the first to come forward. I don't know anything about this in my life.'

"He was unable to stay. He was going down to Wales. We made a date to meet in the Welsh town of Pontypridd, in Taff Vale, only eleven miles from my home, where Billy was having some meetings." In the book *My Most Memorable Encounter with God,* Stephen recounted:

> I found that Billy was seeking for more of God with all his heart; and he felt that I could help him. For most of two days we were closeted at Pontypridd's hotel with our Bibles open, turning the pages as we studied passages and verses. The first day Billy learned more secrets of the "quiet time." The next, I expounded the fullness of the Holy Sprit in the life of a believer who is willing to bow daily and hourly to the sovereignty of Christ and to the authority of the Word. This lesson was so new to me that it

cascaded out, revealing bright glimpses of the inexhaustible power of the love of God.

Billy drank it in so avidly that I scarcely realized the heights and depths that his spiritual life had reached already. At the close of the second day we prayed, like Jacob of old laying hold of God, and crying, "Lord, I will not let Thee go except Thou bless me," until we came to a place of rest and rejoicing. And Billy Graham said, "This is a turning point in my life; this will revolutionize my ministry."[1]

"Billy had been trying up till then to preach to the Welsh people. His sermons didn't last for more than fifteen or twenty minutes. The biblically-literate Welshmen would say, 'That's a good introduction, but let's hear the sermon, man.'

"That night, however, it was different. It seemed as though God had brought people from everywhere. The church was packed. Billy preached on Belshazzar and, before he was anywhere near the end of the sermon, people were pouring out of the pews, kneeling, broken at the altar.

"I went home that night in my old Ford car. I woke my father up at two o'clock in the morning. He said, 'Where on earth have you been?' I said, 'Sit down.' At the kitchen table I told him the story. 'Dad,' I said, 'the world is going to hear from that young man!'"

In the strength of that second (or was it third?) blessing Stephen Olford went on. It was at the heart of all he stands for as a believer. He summed it up like this: "While I believe I received the Holy Spirit at the time of my conversion as a young lad, I did not understand the meaning of the fullness of the Spirit until I was past twenty-one. Then I discovered it is possible for the Holy Spirit to be present without being president, to be dormant without being dominant, to be resident without reigning. The Holy Spirit can be quenched and grieved in a believer's life. But when sin is exposed and self is executed, the Holy Spirit can fill to overflowing and anoint with authority and power. This experience I entered into after much agony of heart, study of the Scriptures, and appropriation by faith and obedience."

He added: "The supreme discovery of my life has been that the Holy Spirit is in a believer's life; that the fullness and anointing of the Holy Spirit are not only blessings to be experienced, but imperatives to be obeyed. I found out that the Spirit-filled life is normal Christian living and anything less is falling short of the glory of God, a missing of the mark.

Moreover, to attempt to serve, either in prayer or in preaching, without the anointing of the Holy Spirit, is to offer the Almighty the fleshly efforts of Cain, instead of the spiritual sacrifices of Abel."

*The wedding picture of Stephen Olford
and Heather Brown, June 30, 1948
in Lurgen, Northern Ireland.*

CHAPTER 3

The Husband

The Lord God ... made ... a woman, and
brought her unto the man.
Genesis 2:22

Little did Stephen Olford know as he stood dockside in Belfast, Northern Ireland, watching the Ulster Monarch steam into port, that aboard that ship was one who would eventually win his heart. He was staying as a guest of the parents of Lilian Brown and had been asked to travel with her to meet her sister Heather at the ship and escort them home. He had known Heather as evangelist Tom Rees's pianist, and had appreciated her dedication to the things of God. But he little suspected, as he stood there—twenty-eight years of age and still unmarried—that the wife for whom he had prayed was on board that boat. As for Heather, she was wondering who would meet her. Little did she think it would be Stephen Olford. Still less did she imagine she was destined to become his bride.

——

Stephen Olford's standards on love, courtship, and marriage were very high. He was a very eligible young man: handsome, talented, full of personality. Some years before he met Heather Brown he had settled the whole issue of dating and flirting. His personal convictions about such things were based on his study of the first wedding performed on earth.

Having created Adam, and having brought the animals to him to name, God awakened in Adam a sense of lack; something was missing. Every animal had its mate, but there was none for him. Most likely Adam would not have analyzed his vague feelings this way for he had never seen a woman in his life! It was God who saw that it was not good for man to be alone. Having become aware of an area of need in his life, Adam went to sleep in the will of God, confident that God would supply that need according to His own "good, and acceptable, and perfect will." So we read that God caused a deep sleep to fall upon Adam. As he slept in the will of God, a wonderful thing happened. God went to work and created the woman who was perfect for him in every respect. Then came the awakening. Adam looked into the face of the woman God had made for him and had brought into his life.

Commenting on this revolutionary discovery, Stephen Olford said: "I decided I was not going to do any exploring to find a wife; I was resolved to leave all that to God. The amazing thing is that when you sleep in God's will, He puts a protection around you. Many young women could have broken into my life between the ages of twenty-three and twenty-eight, but God kept them at a distance while I gave myself to the work to which I had been called."

What happened next is illustrated in a letter the Olfords received years later from John and Vera Jones, friends of theirs from Newport days. They wrote of being aboard a plane flying to the States when they suddenly discovered they were sitting alongside a couple who were on their way to visit Stephen and Heather Olford! John Jones wrote: "I was almost speechless as memories of wartime in Newport came flooding back." He recalled the gospel crusade conducted there by Alan Redpath near the end of the war. He wrote: "Alan Redpath's slogan was 'Come Along but Not Alone.' I shall never forget the sense of despondency that settled on every eligible female in the Christian community in Newport when one night Alan announced, 'I was at a meeting in Belfast last week and Stephen Olford came along—and he was not alone!' It was the first intimation that an Irish lass had stormed and taken the citadel of Stephen's heart."

Heather Brown was born in a small town near Belfast in Northern Ireland. Her father was a linen manufacturer. The Brown home was known for its generous hospitality toward the Lord's people. Heather, her two sisters, Lilian and Grace, and her brother, Billy, knew what it was to frequently sit down to a meal with missionaries. The stories they told stirred her heart. The impression she had of Christianity was one of serving the Lord.

As part of her education, Heather was given every opportunity to study piano with the best teachers available. She loved playing, but deep in her heart she had no desire either to be a concert pianist or to teach music. The inward struggle as to what to do with her life was still going on when the Second World War broke out. Heather took a job with the government, helping to resettle evacuees and refugees who arrived in Northern Ireland.

A few months before, the English evangelist Tom Rees had come to her area for a gospel crusade. One night he preached on Romans 12:1-2 and the message struck home to Heather's heart. Some years earlier, when she was ten years old, Tom Rees had conducted services in her church and Heather had come under such conviction that she returned home and asked her mother to pray with her. She was saved that night. Now the arrow of conviction struck again. That evening she yielded to the Lord's demand that He be enthroned absolutely in her life.

Not long after this she received her call. Tom Rees was going to open a young people's conference center on the outskirts of London to reach the youth of Britain. He was launching giant rallies in the Royal Albert Hall and in Central hall, London, and he needed a pianist and remembered Heather Brown. Thus it was that, across the Irish Sea, Heather received an invitation to come to England to join Tom Rees and his wife, Jean, to be responsible for the music side of his ministry.

It was a thrilling ministry to which she had been called. I remember Tom Rees conducting a city-wide crusade in Newport. I can still see that handsome, polished, and eloquent evangelist as he held us spellbound with his gospel message. He could tell a story! He could make you laugh and sober you up in a moment. At times he would burst into song, with the appropriate verse of a hymn if that helped illustrate his point. He had a rich, resounding voice. He also knew how to draw in the net. I can still see the people coming forward to receive Christ. I can still hear the choir singing the haunting words of a chorus as people were leaving: "You'll never know real peace till you know Jesus."

Tom Rees would stand for no nonsense in his meetings. I attended a crusade he and Robert Laidlaw (the millionaire New Zealand businessman, evangelist, and author of the widely used booklet *The Reason Why*) held in Cardiff during the war. The place was packed. At one point Tom Rees invited people to give one-minute testimonies. One man stood up and launched into a major production. Tom Rees simply burst into song, beckoning the entire congregation to join him and drown the fellow's droning!

This was the man Heather was to join as a pianist. She recalls: "The rallies were blessed with spiritual results. Hildenborough Hall became a haven for many who wanted further teaching and training."

She recalls something else as well. "Prior to my leaving Northern Ireland Tom Rees made a tour of various cities and brought with him another preacher named Stephen Olford. They came to my hometown for a week of convention ministry. I was the pianist for those meetings. Night after night my heart was touched by the powerful expositions and by the challenge to growth and maturity in the Christian life."

During this time, Stephen shared with Heather his convictions, based on Genesis 1 and 2, concerning love, courtship and marriage. "It was a truth I needed," she said. So she, too, went to sleep in the will of God, little knowing that He was forming and fashioning her to be Stephen Olford's helpmeet a little later on. "Stephen Olford came to Hildenborough Hall to speak on several occasions," she said, "but even though my life was always challenged and blessed, I never for a moment thought of him except in terms of a powerful preacher and a man of God."

Then came the day when Heather Brown boarded the Ulster Monarch (that plied the channel between Liverpool and Belfast), and stood on deck watching the port close in around the ship. She was coming to Belfast as Tom Rees's pianist. He, in turn, was to be song leader for the Belfast convention, convened for young people, to be held in the 3,000-seat Presbyterian Assembly Hall. Since her home was in Northern Ireland she had been released from her other duties to enjoy a few days with her family before getting caught up in the convention program. Who would be there to meet her? One of her sisters, perhaps, or her Dad? To her surprise, it was Stephen Olford. He, too, was to be part of the convention and had left early for Ireland. And, of all places, he was staying for a few days at her parents' home! What did she feel when she saw that handsome, smiling face? We have her word for it that she was thrilled—but only because she thought that the two of them would be able to compare notes about the forthcoming convention to see if music and message could be appropriately matched.

Stephen took up the tale. "I went to Northern Ireland," he said, "to speak at a series of youth rallies. Evangelist Tom Rees was to be the song leader. He had accepted the invitation on one condition: he must be allowed to bring his own pianist, Heather Brown. It happened that the place where I was to stay was the home of Heather's parents, as a result of some change in the arrangements. I learned that their daughter was arriving on the channel steamer the very next day.

"It has always been my practice, when involved in special meetings, to read from the Psalms and the book of Proverbs. Some time before, there had been a restlessness in my spirit and I had canceled some meetings and gone away to pray. One morning, in my daily, consecutive reading, I read Proverbs 18:22: 'Whoso findeth a wife findeth a good thing, and obtaineth favour of the Lord.' God used that verse to still my restlessness. Now He was using it again to awaken me, as He had Adam."

One morning Mrs. Brown said to Stephen, "You know, Heather's coming tomorrow. She's going to play at the youth rallies."

"Next thing, I was at the dock with Lilian to meet Heather! We loaded up her luggage and took her home. We only talked briefly for she was very tired, having traveled through the night.

"A day went by," Stephen recalled, "and then Heather's sister, Lilian, arranged for an outing for four at the beach—Heather and Stephen, herself and a young minister. That day, however, there was a death in the parish and the young minister was called away to comfort the bereaved; so Lilian dropped out, which left Heather and me to go alone."

Stephen continued, "We started to talk as we drove the 60 miles or so to the beach. Then she made the most amazing statement. She said, 'You know God has called me out of college and out of social service into evangelism, and I believe God's ministry for me is Christian work for the rest of my life. But,' she added 'I am burdened because Britain does not offer the kind of training I want. I have been eager to go to America, if at all possible. I should like to attend Moody Bible Institute to go deeper into the Word of God and, above all, to study in their famous music department. Could you advise me at all about this?'"

Stephen was transfixed. "She did not know anything about my diary or that I was planning to go to America. I asked her what dates she had in mind. The dates she mentioned were identical to the ones I had in my diary. As we drove along there was a clear and unmistakable witness in my spirit that this was God's partner for my life. Unknown to me there was a similar witness in her heart.

"We stopped the car. That place marked by a row of trees on the way to Portstewart is a sacred place for us; we visit it every now and then. I said, 'I think we ought to pray about this.' I bowed my head. I prayed about her training, and her future. Then before I finished that prayer I added, 'And, Lord, thank You for giving me Heather.' Then she burst into prayer and said, 'Lord, thank You for giving me Stephen.' That's how we proposed! We raised our heads, we rejoiced in Christ, and our hearts were one. For the first time in five years I kissed a girl—a girl with whom I was deeply in love, and as far as heaven was concerned, we were engaged then and there. This was confirmed on our return home, when I asked and warmly received the hand of his daughter Heather from Mr. Cecil Brown, her father and my very dear friend. There had been no dating, no courting. God brought us together. We recognized His guidance and never once questioned it."

Heather said, "Neither Stephen nor I knew how things would work out for us, when we would be married, where we would live, but the joy of knowing God had brought us together made the future so bright that, without funds or security, we were publicly engaged to be married.

"We decided to go to America on the Queen Elizabeth with Stephen's father, Frederick Olford, who had arranged for preaching services in the United States. The year was 1947. Stephen was booked to be with Jack Wyrtzen, with Youth for Christ, and with the Moody Bible Institute for almost a year of preaching and traveling. While he did that I was to study at Moody Bible Institute where I was enrolled as a special student. It was a wonderful year, though I was homesick—especially for Stephen who was all over the United States and Canada in meetings. Stephen traveled some 34,000 miles doing evangelistic work, much of it with Billy Graham and Youth for Christ. He only turned up in Chicago once in awhile. But the Americans lavished love, hospitality, and kindness on me."

Heather's studies and Stephen's travels were interrupted when he became very ill and had to undergo surgery at Mayo Clinic. His presence at Mayo Clinic in Rochester, Minnesota was a sovereign provision of God Himself. Stephen's illness was serious and the required surgery dangerous. But God was in control. Arriving at the Clinic, Stephen was referred to a certain Dr. Carl Morlock, a famous internist and a brilliant diagnostician. As his name was called in the waiting room, Stephen went into Dr. Morlock's office with not a little apprehension! After all, this was his first "doctor's visit" in America. But he needn't have worried. Dr. Morlock stretched out his hand and warmly welcomed Stephen with these words: "I am sure delighted to meet you. Come right in and sit down. I can't tell you what your ministry has meant to me!" Apparently the doctor had heard a number of Stephen's messages on the Word of Life broadcast from Times Square, New York City! Stephen had been pinch-hitting for Jack Wyrtzen who had been hospitalized with a broken hip sustained while water-skiing at Word of Life Camp in the Adirondacks.

From that moment onward, Stephen Olford and Carl Morlock established a friendship that lasted throughout the years. Stephen often referred to him as "the beloved physician." Under his vigilant eye the surgery was performed and the aftercare graciously provided. Heather, who was summoned from Moody Bible Institute to Stephen's side while he recovered from surgery, was graciously hosted and comforted by Dr. Morlock and his wife Katherine. As soon as Stephen was able to travel, he and Heather proceeded to Wheaton, Illinois, where Dr. and Mrs. Joseph C. Macaulay welcomed them. Those were precious days of recovery and rejoicing in a home of understanding and generous hospitality.

In May 1948, Stephen and Heather sailed home to Britain, cheered not only by the goodwill and well-wishes of the many friends they had made in the United States, but also with suitcases full of all kinds of gifts that enabled them to get a good start in their married life.

The wedding took place at Lurgan, Northern Ireland, June 30, 1948. Heather's joy was tinged with sadness because her father was not able to give her away, having been incapacitated by a heart attack. Apart from that the wedding was one of "joy unspeakable and full of glory." Joyce Silcox, Heather's close friend, came from England to sing their favorite song: "Only One Life to Offer" and Stephen's dear friend, Alan Redpath, preached the message.

The Olfords began their married life in Newport, a very new place for Heather. It was there that Stephen had ministered all through the war years, and had started his Young People's Christian Fellowship. One and all were eager to catch a glimpse of the Irish girl who had successfully taken Stephen's heart. It was living there that gave Heather the opportunity to know Stephen's much-loved parents. Knowing them gave her a new understanding of her husband's tremendous missionary heritage.

About two years later, Stephen and Heather moved to Cardiff, the capital city of Wales. One reason for the move was to be closer to Stephen's father and mother—especially since Jonathan MacGregor, their first son, had put in an appearance on July 17, 1952. "He actually arrived," Heather recalled, "when Stephen was away speaking at the English Keswick Convention." There seemed to be something symbolic about that. Keswick meant much to both Heather and Stephen with its emphasis on full salvation. Both had entered into the truth of the Spirit-filled life. Heather recalled that "it was when Stephen taught me that the Spirit-filled life is not the higher life or the deeper life but the normal Christian life, made real in a daily walk with God, that my life was changed and matured."

The first years of the Olfords' married life were spent in crusades and conventions. In October 1953 Stephen was ordained by the Thames Valley Baptist Association and became the pastor of the Duke Street Baptist Church in Richmond, Surrey, England. His travels continued, but were offset by the demands of a resident ministry, which enabled him to spend more time at home.

There were so many definite advantages to a more settled ministry. For Stephen, it meant he could preach more consecutively through Bible books and the great doctrinal truths of the Bible. Also he could develop his own follow-up programs for new converts, often the missing link in itinerant evangelism. For Heather, it meant that she would see more of her husband.

There were fears, too. It was the first time she would be a pastor's wife. She said: "I am a retiring, private person. Suddenly I realized that even though I had spent at least seven years in evangelistic ministry I had managed to hide behind a piano and do some counseling if called upon, but then I would disappear as quickly as possible and head for home as soon as my duties were done. Now my life would change." The fishbowl life as a pastor's wife, always on trial, always being watched, always expected to do this or that or go here or there or to be someone she wasn't scared her.

Then there was the high example set by their predecessors, the Redpaths. Heather weighed the future and decided to commit it to the Lord. Her sole desire was to serve the Lord and the man the Lord had given her.

The Olfords soon settled down to life in a busy church in a London suburb. For Stephen, the adjustment was relatively easy. Besides, he had an unwavering faith in God's sufficiency. Heather was grateful for a lovely parsonage. Her baby, Jonathan, was only a few months old. Her desire to be a model wife and mother, and a helpmeet to her husband in his church activities, while not disappointing the members of the church, might well have caused tension. But Stephen soon set her mind at rest. He assumed his rightful role of leader in the home. He dispelled her fears. "Heather," he said, "Your first task is to be my wife and then be mother of our children. Then you can use the home as a haven of hospitality. After that, if there is opportunity you can use your musical gift and exercise your ministry to the women and engage in visitation. But your husband and your home are your primary area of responsibility." That settled it. She rested in the wisdom of her husband, in the will of God.

The years came and went. On May 2, 1956, their second son, David Lindsay Olford was born. From time to time Stephen was away crusading, but for the most part he was at home—the busy, anointed pastor of a growing church and head of a growing, contented family.

Then came the call to New York. There followed a time of heart searching and waiting on God. The "great door and effectual," which stood ajar in New York, was tempting, but by now the Olfords had worked their way well into the hearts of the Richmond congregation. Heather says, "I was ready to go to New York long before Stephen finally gave his answer. I felt there would be greater freedom in the States to reach the world—especially through radio. Calvary Baptist Church in New York aired its morning service every Sunday and that had a tremendous appeal to me. New York was a city comparable in size to London. In England the B.B.C. was a state-owned monopoly and no such opportunity existed." It appealed to Stephen too. Still, he was in no hurry because the important thing was to know the mind of God. Heather confided that she had a secret hope that, perhaps, if Stephen could reach the world by radio from a big-city pulpit he might not have to go away so much.

There were many letters and phone calls back and forth across the Atlantic, and nearly a year went by before the decision was finally made. On a memorable morning in August 1959 the Olfords arrived in New York. More adjustments had to be made in the life of the family, some of them monumental. Their boys, now seven and three, had always known the security of home, church and neighborhood, of a lovely manse, a garden, and parks. Calvary Baptist Church was a big inner city church in the heart of

Photo by Paul Bartley Photography, Inc.

Heather, the woman of Stephen's "dreams," and his
"sweetheart and companion for fifty-six years."

Manhattan where it was associated with a large hotel, which it owned. Schools were different. Life was different. Indeed, Heather is to be highly commended for the innovative and creative ways in which she made a hotel suite a home away from home. With two small sons, she had to think up all manner of surprises to keep the boys happy, exercised and entertained while they were young. Later, God wonderfully opened the door to send Jonathan first—and later David—to Stony Brook School on nearby Long Island. This fine Christian boarding school provided both lads with a solid education and the best available preparation for the college days that were to follow.

Meanwhile enormous demands were being made on Stephen. But with all the busyness, he never allowed work and ministry to invade the sanctity, security and spirituality of his home. Heather, too, worked hard at being all that a wife and mother should be. She saw her chief ministry to be that of relieving her husband of concern for the children. When they were younger she did not even attempt to do much in the church. The hotel was near Central Park and she would often take the children over there to play. It was safer in those days.

As for Stephen, he established a golden rule. Sunday was King's Day. On Sunday all was for Jesus, King of kings and Lord of lords. Monday was Queen's Day. "Each Monday," he says, "I gave first place to my wife. We might go swimming, play golf, attend a concert, or take a long walk. But always she and I took time on Mondays to talk, review the previous week and look and plan ahead. The whole secret was disciplined planning. So in matters of money, children, study, appointments, and preaching we went through the week, writing down what had to be done. I told her about people I had to see; she told me what she had to do. We were interested in each other and each other's lives. I told my wife I loved her and that she was everything to me." He added, "Any man who does not have a happy home life does not have the right to stand behind the pulpit."

Before he went to bed each Monday night Stephen had something else to do. "I give myself an hour or two alone with God and with a blank sheet of paper. Then I plan my entire week, hour by hour. That time with God was key to me. No matter how late it got. I never left my desk until the week was completely mapped out. Some of my plans were splintered by the unexpected, but I had my plan. I knew where I was going and I made the necessary adjustments. First thing next morning I was up and having my quiet time with God. The busy week had begun."

Heather was never forgotten. She knew she reigned as queen in Stephen's heart. Once when preaching to a group of pastors, Stephen put it like this: "The most vulnerable person in the ministry is the pastor's wife. A preacher spends much of his time with women. They are the majority in your church. It is frequently the women who come for counsel and help. You don't know what that does to your wife. You need to study 1 Peter 3:7 where Peter, a family man, says: 'Husbands. . . dwell with them with understanding'" (NKJV). That is why, with Stephen Olford, as surely as Monday follows Sunday, Queen's day follows King's day.

——

"It is fifty-six years since that great day in June 1948," said Heather, "when Stephen and I committed our lives to each other. I just have to praise the Lord for the way He led us. Our marriage motto was experienced in every area of our lives—'together with God' (1 Corinthians 3:9a). We were partners in our love relationship. Who would not want to be submissive and loving to a man who was loving and caring? Of course, life has its ups and downs, but the law of adjustment always worked to help us grow in our understanding of one another's needs and desires.

"Looking back over the years, my heart is deeply moved as I think of the ministry the Lord gave us in our life together; and even though my first responsibility has been to my Lord and then to my family, I have been fulfilled and rewarded as I have seen God direct, plan, and use Stephen in ways far beyond anything I would have ever dreamed of when I first became his partner.

"Transparency is a very important word in marriage and in ministry. With Stephen there were no cover-ups! At the same time we were never obsessed by an overwhelming sense of our defects so that we were constantly confessing our faults. We are all sinners, and there is no need for constant confession and cleansing, if we desire to walk day by day with our Lord; and this has to be the same in married life. But when Christ is Lord He rules and reigns over our hearts, minds and wills.

"Living with Stephen made me want to live for the Lord Jesus Christ and serve the Lord and also to be the best helpmeet to the man God brought to me to be my husband. I have been blessed!"

*The Olford family around the piano
in their New York apartment.*

CHAPTER 4

The Father

*Fathers, do not provoke your children to
wrath, but bring them up in the training and
admonition of the Lord.*
Ephesians 6:4, NKJV

S tephen Olford and Heather Brown were out for an afternoon stroll
through the streets of Lurgan, Northern Ireland. They were not yet
married but, perhaps, just to get the feel of what it would be like they
were pushing a baby carriage before them occupied by Heather's newest
little cousin. Stephen seemed very taken up with the baby. Presently, he
exclaimed:"What a sweet child!"There was a long pause. Then ever-practical
Heather replied: "Yes, but what a responsibility!" Commenting later on the
incident Stephen said:"I never forgot those weighty words, and subsequent
events proved the validity of Heather's words. Parenting," he added, "is a
responsibility. This is true of the mother—but even more so of the father."

The Bible is full of examples of fathers who were failures. David
pampered Absalom and set him a bad example; the results were tragic. Eli
failed to discipline his two sons; the result was the disgrace of his name
and the defeat of his nation. Isaac spoiled Esau, and Rachel favored Jacob;
the result was a divided home. Parental failure seems to have been the
rule rather than the exception in the family histories recorded in the
Bible. Rare indeed is the Abraham of whom God could say: "For I have
known him, in order that he may command his children and his
household after him, that they keep the way of the Lord" (Genesis 18:19,

NKJV). But even Abraham had one rebellious son, Ishmael, who grew up to be "a wild man" (Genesis 16:1-16).

TESTIMONY OF THE PARENT

Stephen Olford noted two key factors in his own acceptance of parental responsibility: one was his background; the other was his Bible. The influence of his father came immediately to Stephen Olford's mind as he thought of his own boyhood days. "I owe more than I can ever express to my parents," he said. "Father was a role model in every sense of that term." His father's devotional life made an early and a deep impression. He was a man who walked with God. "I can remember tiptoeing past his study at daybreak, and hearing him pray as he knelt at the window that overlooked the rising smoke of A-Chokwe villages across the Cassai valley."

Frederick Olford "ran a tight ship when it came to family prayers after breakfast," Stephen recalled. All five family members—Stephen, Paul, and John, together with Mr. and Mrs. Olford—retired to the living room where devotions followed a precise pattern. A hymn was played on the little organ (a gift from Sister Abigail of Buffalo, New York) and everyone sang all the stanzas. Then came the reading of the Scripture and an exposition, followed by prayer all around, and finishing up with a hug from Dad and Mom. That was the daily morning routine except on Sunday, which was reserved for attendance at all the services of the local church.

Stephen related, "There was nothing boring about this—nothing to put us off. Father made sure that meeting with God was exciting! More, his devotional life came through in his preaching. I have known A-Chokwe warriors stand to their feet while he was expounding God's Word and cry out like men and women did on the day of Pentecost!"

Frederick Olford was both a friend and a father to his boys. "His love for us," Stephen said, "was not effusive, but it was effective. We knew that he loved us dearly. The A-Chokwe people knew this too.

"Father always reserved Fridays for us. With shotguns on our shoulders, when we were old enough, and provisions for the day, we went hunting in the morning. On our way back, we visited as many villages as possible to share the gospel and invite the people to the Sunday services. Father always had some surprise to spring on us before the day was over. He was 'a good sport!'" (In England, by the way, that is one of the highest accolades one boy or man could pay to another.)

Stephen Olford's father was a man with a mission. The people of Angola needed to be won for Christ. That was his vocation. It was evidenced in everything he did. Whether it was building churches, translating the Scriptures, performing surgery, teaching, reading, writing hymns, counseling

Photo by Archie Handford, Ltd.

The Olfords with Stephen's mother, Bessie,
Croydon, England 1963.

seekers, or hunting wild game, all was subordinate to his master passion—
winnings souls! He used "all means [to] save some" (1 Corinthians 9:22).

"I think of one occasion when a troop of monkeys invaded our region,"
Stephen says. "They invaded our garden, raided our fruit trees, and virtually
ate everything in sight. The men in the surrounding villages begged Father
to help them make war on these pests. Father gave in to their pleas. He
took up his position in the thick jungle where the monkeys were hiding in
the trees. Father was a crack shot. With his shotgun ready, he studied the
treetops looking for targets. Suddenly he heard a bloodcurdling hiss behind
him. He swung around and saw a deadly black mamba, one of the most
venomous snakes in the bush, poised to strike, swinging its head to and fro
ready for the kill. One strike and Father would be dead! At first, Father
froze, the very slight of that serpent turning his blood to ice. But he
breathed a prayer, he aimed, he fired, he scored a direct hit. The mamba's
head was blown off."

The sound of that shot brought the A-Chokwe men running, converging on Stephen's father from all sides. When they saw the headless, but still writhing, black mamba, they raised a shout of victory that reverberated throughout the forest. Then the drums began to beat, sending the news far and wide. Before long men and women by the hundreds were pouring into the mission compound where the black mamba was now hanging from a scaffold. "No one meets a mamba and comes away alive," said one of the chiefs. "This is a miracle which only Ngana's God could perform." Said Stephen Olford, "For days, Father preached to the people on the crushing of the serpent's head (Genesis 3:15), and scores of men and women came to Christ. That was my father!"

Stephen had an equally godly mother. He sums up her cardinal virtues as spirituality, service, and sacrifice. "If there was a spiritual need among the missionaries or nationals it was Ndona to whom they turned. She led me to Christ," he says, "She was a servant to all in the home, in the church, and in the villages. She was always serving." His most vivid memories of his mother, however, were of her sacrificial courage. "There was a time, for instance, when a lion entered the compound and killed our most productive cow. If others were killed too, there would be no milk for us or anyone else.

"The lion had left part of the carcass. This meant he would be back, probably the next night, for another meal. Father and Leonard Gammon, his missionary colleague, determined to sit up that night to shoot that lion. They chose a suitable tree and built a platform which gave them ample visibility and mobility for their guns. Everyone was warned to remain in their homes or huts until daybreak. Someone blundering around in the dark might be mistaken for the lion and get shot by accident.

"That night the weather changed and it became bitterly cold. Mother's heart went out to the two men shivering in the tree. So she heated up some soup, lit a lantern, and sallied forth in the darkness to bring some warmth and nourishment to the two men. There they were waiting for the lion. There she was, a potential target for the guns and prey for the lion! Little she cared about that! Mother was brave to a fault!"

We can picture her, lamp held high in one hand, a canteen of soup in the other, making her deliberate way to the tree. Then the wind blew out the lamp leaving her standing in the dark. All about her was the threatening blackness of the night. Somewhere in the bush a lion lurked. Up in the tree the hunters had their rifles ready to shoot, should there be a movement or sound.

"What did Mother do?" Stephen asked, "Go back? Not a bit of it! She waited until her eyes adjusted to the darkness. Then in the faint light of the stars she continued on to the tree, lustily singing Fanny Crosby's hymn:

> All the way my Savior leads me;
> What have I to ask beside?

Can I doubt His tender mercy,
Who through life has been my Guide?

"Mr. Gammon was deaf," Stephen continued, "but Father caught the strains of the hymn. Quickly he lit his lantern and climbed down the tree to receive the thermos of soup and escort Mother back home. Oh yes, the next night the lion was shot!"

Another favorite story saw his mother aboard a banana boat sailing from the west coast of Africa to Portugal. The trip was to last nearly a month and a half. On board that boat was a wretched man who had been dumped on the deck to die. All over his body were terrible, infectious boils. There he lay on a blanket in the stern of the ship, shunned by one and all. No one would go near him. His food was pushed to him with a stick.

"Mother discovered it," Stephen recalled, "and even though she had a husband and two boys to think about at the time, she prayed about it and decided to give herself to minister to this man. Every day she went to where he was, washed his sores, fed him until he was cured, and then she led him to Christ."

The example of Stephen Olford's parents left an indelible mark on his understanding of what parenting is all about. He had a great saint for a father and a Good Samaritan for a mother.

The Bible was also an unfailing source of guidance. "Soon after our marriage," he said, "Heather and I gave ourselves to a more intensive study of God's Word as it relates to the roles of father and mother. I knew what affect this had upon Heather. I can say without hesitation that she has been a precious wife and a perfect mother. Her sons have risen up to call her blessed" (Proverbs 31:28).

Stephen Olford delved deeply into such passages as Ephesians 5:15–6:4; Colossians 3:18-21; 1 Timothy 3:1-13; and 1 Peter 3:1-7 and others. As a result of these studies he made three resolutions that he sought to keep by the power of the indwelling Spirit of God.

First of all, he resolved *to live as a father*. Such statements as: "Be filled with the Spirit" and "Let the word of Christ dwell in you richly in all wisdom" (Ephesians 5:18; Colossians 3:16) deeply impressed him. "No one can live as a father," he said, "without being activated by the Spirit of God and dominated by the Word of God. Over forty-six years of married life have taught me that it is impossible to be a husband or a father without supernatural enablement. This is true, of course, of all Christian living, but it is especially true of one of the most demanding roles in human relation-ships—fatherhood and motherhood. I have found that the happiest days in our home life have always reflected my walk with God in the light of His Word and the conscious awareness of the unquenched and ungrieved Spirit in my life." It is no accident, of course, that the command to "be filled with the Spirit" and the corresponding command to "let the word of Christ dwell in you richly" not only result in a life of overflowing joy and happiness, but are both set in the context of living the Christian life at home.

Next, he resolved *to love as a father.* He was gripped by the statement "Husbands, love your wives, even as Christ also loved the church, and gave himself for it" (Ephesians 5:25). "It shook me," he said, "when I realized that this was a command, and failure to obey it was sin!" Needless to say, such agape love can only be generated and governed by the indwelling and infilling Spirit. This is a love that gives and forgives; love that loves unto death, love that overflows to everyone in the home. Steadfast, unconditional love like this produces an answer to every evil force that threatens joy in the home, kindness in the home, goodness in the home, faithfulness in the home, gentleness in the home, self-control in the home (Galatians 5:22-23).

We have seen already that Stephen submitted, for a number of years to the restraining ministry of the Holy Spirit in his life—so far as love, courtship, and marriage were concerned. That does not mean he was oblivious to the women in his life. He said regarding Heather: "In spite of the Holy Spirit's restraint on me, until God's precise time, I loved Heather at first sight, and that love has grown with every succeeding day."

That love spilled over to his boys when, in due time, they came along. He remembered looking for the first time into the face of Jonathan, his first-born. "He was a week early at birth. He arrived while I was a speaker at the great Keswick Convention in England in 1952. I was so overwhelmed by the news from 'Mother Brown' over the phone that several thousand people learned about it in a couple of hours! Indeed, so meaningful was the birth of my son that when the missionary call included those who were prepared to sacrifice their children for God's call to overseas service—I stood! I stood, despite the fact that at Keswick it was normally discouraged, as a matter of policy, for any speaker on the platform to do so.

"Then came my visit to Northern Ireland and my first glimpse of that precious little boy. I cried, and I cried! Jonathan gave us very little to worry about as a baby, except for a skin problem that kept him awake at night. But during the week I walked the floor with him while Heather coped on weekends."

In his regular Fellowship newsletter for December 8, 1956 (when Jonathan was four years old) Stephen wrote:

> This week we recorded Jonathan's voice on tape. He was enthralled. "Daddy," he said, "let me say something." We asked, "What will you say?" "Oh, the Lord is my Shepherd," he replied (he can repeat the psalm down to the words "for His name's sake," which

he always follows with a fervent "Amen!"). All was set and the signal was given for him to start. He peered down at the microphone and with a cherubic look on his face began: "Fuzzy Wuzzy was a bear, Fuzzy Wuzzy had no hair. Fuzzy Wuzzy wasn't fuzzy, was he?" Wasn't it Paul the apostle who said in Romans 7, "The good that I would, I do not"?

Jonathan trusted Jesus as Lord and Savior at an early age, following a service at Duke Street Baptist Church. "He loved to talk about spiritual things," Stephen recalled, "and often had me stumped!" One question he asked, which drove his father into a corner was: "How will we recognize people that we have never met when we get to Heaven?"

Jonathan thoroughly enjoyed his first term at school in England. He came home one day and before saying a word to either of his parents, he carefully positioned himself and then performed a double bow! It seems the boys at school had been practicing this genuflection for some coming event. Another time he came in to say goodbye to his dad who was leaving for Bible convention. Confidently he bade his father farewell with the words: "Goodbye Daddy, have a good *contention!*" Commented his dad, "mind you he was quite scriptural, for we are exhorted to 'earnestly contend for the faith.'"

After they moved to New York Jonathan had to cope with the public school system. "He was a sensitive boy," Stephen said, "and reacted dreadfully to rough behavior and tough teachers. Eventually, when he was old enough, we sent him to Stony Brook School on Long Island. There, Jonathan flourished in every way, to the immense relief of both his parents. We believe that parents must give their children the best home, the best school, and the best church."

Anyone who has been away from home can appreciate how much letters mean—especially when they are from loved ones left behind. As a father, Stephen Olford was diligent in writing to his boy away at boarding school. Here is one of the many letters he sent:

My dear Jonathan:

This is just a little note to assure you that our thoughts and prayers have been with you in these early days at Stony Brook. We were so grateful to God that we had such a pleasant day on Tuesday. It has been raining incessantly ever since, although there is a break today.

By this time you will have received your school case and wastepaper basket. The case I think you will find useful on rainy days to carry your books in; the wastepaper basket, I am sure, will match the color scheme of your room.

You will probably be phoning tonight and, unfortunately, I will be away in Columbia. However, I shall look forward to hearing news of you either through Mother, or by letter—if you have time to write.

You will be interested to know that we rededicated our renovated and refurbished bookstore last night. It was a wonderful occasion. David came to the ceremony and stayed for the evening meeting. We had a great crowd and a very blessed time.

I trust you are enjoying your studies and settling in with the other boys. Remember to have your Quiet Time and to give a good example, not only to Peter, but to the other lads who will be watching your life. I am sure you are going to have a great time at Stony Brook, preparing yourself spiritually, mentally and physically for all that God has for you in coming days.

Mom and David join me in sending you our warmest love.

Affectionately,

Dad

When Jonathan graduated from Stony Brook he went on to pursue studies at Springfield College in Massachusetts, one of the best schools in the country for training in physical education. Jonathan enjoyed sports and excelled in them. He believed that he could use sports as a means to an end. It would pave the way for him to reach into the lives of boys and girls he desired to win for Christ. He earned first a bachelor degree and then a master's degree in his chosen profession and did so with distinction.

Then came a major crisis in Jonathan's life. He, his brother David, three other boys (Robby and Ronnie Richardson and Paul Leonard), and two godly veteran missionaries (Mary Beam and Betty Cridland) went to Kenya, East Africa, on tour. They went not just to see that beautiful country, but to take a firsthand look at missionary work there.

On the way back the party stopped off in London and visited Westminster Abbey. Jonathan stood at the tomb of David Livingstone in that great national shrine. All about him were the tombs and statues of Britain's illustrious dead. He stood there staring at the text on that unpretentious stone slab which bore the name of the great explorer, emancipator, and missionary. The words of John 10:16 stared back at him: "Other sheep I have, which are not of this fold: them also I must bring." The word *other* struck a chord in the young man's heart. It was God's call—God's call to Africa— where his father had been born and where his grandfather had labored among savage tribes. Africa! He knew he had to go.

"Heather and I were with him all the way as he applied to the Africa Inland Mission and then went to Columbia Bible College Graduate School to prepare further for service abroad," Stephen said. "There God brought into his life a darling partner, Catherine Matthews. That's a love story all of its own!"

The wedding took place at the First Baptist Church in Columbia, South Carolina. It was Stephen Olford's joy and privilege to marry them. Then, as they left for their honeymoon he wrote to them:

> 19th November 1977
>
> Our dearest Jonathan and Catherine:
>
> This is to say a Happy Honeymoon!—and again to rejoice with you in the way in which God has led and blessed since the day He brought you into each other's lives.
>
> We thank God for a wonderful son, whose life and love and Christian testimony have eternally enriched our lives.
>
> We thank God for the precious gift of a daughter whose Christ-like character and charming personality have completely won our hearts.
>
> We thank God for your marriage in the Lord that promises all that our Heavenly Father has intended in partnership, parenthood and pleasure.
>
> From this day forward, you belong to each other and, therefore, *leave* one dimension of life to *cleave* to another (Gen. 2:24).
>
> While this is right and proper, we want you to know that until Jesus comes or calls, your father and mother are accessible, available and adaptable! *We love you*

Photo courtesy of the Billy Graham Center

*Jonathan and Catherine Olford on their wedding day,
November 19, 1977.*

dearly and desire for you both nothing less than God's "good, . . . acceptable, and perfect will."

Again, have a happy and holy honeymoon.

Yours affectionately,

Your Dad and Mom

Since then, Jonathan and Catherine have completed seven years of missionary work and presented their parents with three grandsons—Jeremy, Justin and Joshua! In 1993 Jonathan completed his doctoral work in Clinical Psychology to further equip himself for ongoing ministry at home and overseas. Jonathan and Catherine's years in Kenya opened their eyes to the great need for Christian Psychology applied to those in missions, in cross-cultural work, and to those Christians both in the United States and abroad that may be involved in vocational ministry.

Recalling the birth of his second son, David, Stephen Olford remarked: "David's entrance into this world was something else!" At the time Stephen was in Scotland for ministry near Gleneagles. He was sharing the platform with Mr. A. Lindsay Glegg, a man he describes as "the dearest man I have ever known, a father in Christ to me and a host of others."

Lindsay Glegg was a layman. He was also a powerful preacher and a most effective convention speaker. He was a low handicap golfer as well. He and Stephen were playing golf together at Gleneagles on that memorable May 2, 1956. "We were completing our round on the King's Course," Stephen said, "when a loud speaker, mounted on a jeep, announced my name. I dropped my clubs and hurried over to the jeep to learn that Heather had given birth prematurely to a baby boy who was not expected to live.

"The news was shattering. I left at once for the hotel to pack and leave by night train for London. As I threw things into my bag, Lindsay Glegg entered my room and asked for the latest news. I told him that I had phoned the doctor who confirmed that, because of a complication in the pregnancy, our little 'David' was in serious condition.

"Mr. Glegg put his hand on my shoulder and asked me to kneel. Then he offered a prayer that was Spirit-inspired (I have often wished that I could have recorded it). He claimed the life of David and thanked God for answered prayer! As I rose from my knees I blurted out through my tears, 'If the baby lives, his name will be called *David Lindsay Olford.*' With a twinkle in his eyes, and a confidence in his voice, Mr. Glegg announced, 'Stephen, his name is David Lindsay Olford. The child will live!'

"That 'prophetic utterance' has been more than fulfilled! The physical problems were soon overcome and baby David never looked back."

Young David was only three years old when the Olfords moved to New

York City to assume the pastorate of Calvary Baptist Church. Despite his tender years he did not miss much! "I remember having breakfast in our hotel room one morning," Stephen said. "In the rather confined quarters of our suite the boys were restless and irritable. I cautioned Jonathan for being rude to his mother. 'Remember,' I said, 'your mother is queen and I am king in this family.'" There was hardly a pause when young David shot his hand in the air and yelled, 'and I'm the Statute of Liberty!'"

When David reached school age his parents enrolled him in Trinity School in New York City. He had to travel by bus across Manhattan. This really concerned his parents—especially when they were told to give him "mug money" to ensure his safety. Thankfully, David survived this ordeal and prospered in his studies.

Like Jonathan, David trusted Christ at an early age and quickly grew in grace and in the knowledge of our Lord and Savior Jesus Christ. In fact he chose to attend the main services at Calvary rather than go to children's church. He took copious notes of his father's sermons in a shorthand notebook and discussed with his father points he did not understand.

Very soon he wanted to be baptized. He was only ten years of age so his father arranged for him to meet the elders of the church and give his testimony. They heard his testimony all right and observed the clear answers he gave to their questions. Finally the chairman said to him, "David, we are satisfied that you are saved and ready for baptism, but you are very young. We suggest you wait for another year or two." The boy listened carefully and then replied: "I am willing to wait so long as you promise me you will baptize me before Jesus comes again!" Needless to say he was baptized soon afterwards.

David was crazy about sports, all sports, but especially baseball. He was an avid Yankee fan. He had stacks of baseball cards and knew every man by name and fame. "This became embarrassingly evident during a holiday we had at Ocean City, New Jersey," Stephen recalled. "On Saturday he had watched the Yankees play and was more than impressed with his favorite catcher, Elston Howard, No. 32. Next morning we went to church. The church was full with New York vacationers. The only available seats were up front, so we were ushered in and seated in front of the pulpit. There we were—Dad, Mom, David, and Jonathan. Presently the song leader rose to his feet and without any preamble opened his hymnbook and announced loudly, 'Number 32.' Like a shot David was on his feet yelling, 'Elston Howard! Elston Howard!' I have rarely heard a crowd break into such laughter, and rarely have I seen Heather looking more crimson! That's our David!"

On May 2, 1970 Stephen Olford wrote this letter to David:

My dear David:

Happy Birthday! In spite of the fact that your mother and I are away in Spain I want you to know that we are thinking of you and praying that God will make this day a truly wonderful occasion. You are now 14 years of age—a genuine teenager!

It occurred to me in thinking about this that 14 is composed of two 7s. Seven as you know is the perfect number. There are seven colors in the rainbow, seven notes on the piano keyboard and recurring sevens in the range of biblical revelation. It is the number that spells completeness, harmony and wholeness. Now you are 14, which means double 7! So I am praying God's double blessing on you.

I want to tell you what a joy you are to your mother and me. Ever since you were born we have followed you with prayerful interest, love and high hopes—and you have never disappointed us. In early life you came to know the Lord Jesus as your personal Savior, and ever since then you have grown steadily and graciously in the knowledge of our Lord. The witness of the indwelling life of Christ has always been an inspiration to watch. Your ability to share your faith and to teach the Word of God has always made me feel that there is a divine plan ahead of you in which you train others for Christian service. In the meantime, there is a long way to go and this letter is to encourage you to plod along, to trust the Savior to enable you in your studies, to inspire you in your athletics and to use you in your Christian witness.

It is our constant prayer that you will be wonderfully preserved from all the evils that surround a schoolboy today. If the devil does not trip you up morally he will want you to use drugs or tempt you with other of his subtle seductions. But thank God, "greater is He that is in you than he that is in the world." As you read God's Word, claim the fullness of the Holy Spirit, and trust the mighty arm of the Savior you will be more than conqueror.

So bless your heart on this birthday! We love you and want you to know that. Have a great day, and we will celebrate when we next meet.

Yours very affectionately,

Dad

At Stony Brook, David won awards in every discipline he tackled. While he vacillated at times as to what to focus on for future studies, ancient languages and Biblical literature were his first love. He applied to Wheaton College in Illinois where he earned his B.A. and his M.A. before going on to Sheffield, England for a Ph.D. in Biblical Studies, which was awarded to him in 1985.

By the time David returned to the United States, Stephen and Heather were on their way from Wheaton, Illinois, (where they had served under the umbrella of the National Association of Evangelicals) to Memphis, Tennessee to establish a Center for Biblical Preaching. In the providence of God, David was on hand to facilitate the move and catch the vision to share in this new enterprise.

For David, however, something even more exciting happened. After all his years in Wheaton, Sheffield, and Cambridge, with exposure to every level of social life, God's partner for his life was being prepared in Memphis, Tennessee!

The charming and consecrated young woman who captured David's heart was Ellen Grogan, the daughter of Dr. and Mrs. Fred Grogan. Ellen graduated from Memphis State University and taught and coached at John Brown University in Arkansas. She served as Assistant Director of the Family Life Center at Central Church in Memphis. It was a perfect match as the engagement, the marriage, and the subsequent parenthood have proved. The couple has since provided the Olfords with two granddaughters, Lindsay Gayle and Stephanie Grace.

David became the Vice President of Encounter Ministries, Inc. and Director of Studies at the Stephen Olford Center for Biblical Preaching. In January of 1994, he was appointed President of Encounter Ministries. He writes for their publication *Anglos* and has compiled a book entitled *A Passion for Preaching*. David continues to lecture and teach at institute events and preaching workshops at the Center, around the country and abroad. "Without him," Stephen claimed, "our ministry among needy pastors would be impossible."

Anyone can tell that Stephen Olford is proud of his sons. "Yes, and without apology," Stephen said. "The father is called upon to love his wife and family until the last drop of blood. To me, this is not only a duty but a

Photo by Dennis Zanone

David and Ellen Olford lighting their wedding candle,
April 12, 1986.

sheer delight." It was in this very mood that he composed three stanzas in honor of David's birthday on May 2, 1990:

> David, our son, you are our joy:
> God's gift to us some years ago.
> No words of many can we employ
> To tell you how we love you so.

> We thank our God for who *you* are,
> And praise Him for your ministry.
> You have your gifts like any star
> And use them with rare dignity.

> God bless you, son, with many years,
> To serve our Lord with mind and heart;

And though life's path may bring some tears,
God will to you His grace impart.

Dad and Mom

Having resolved to live as a father and to love as a father, Stephen Olford resolved further *to lead as a father.* "Fathers," the Scripture says, "provoke not your children to wrath: but bring them up in the nurture and admonition of the Lord"; and again, "Fathers, provoke not your children to anger, lest they be discouraged" (Ephesians 6:4; Colossians 3:21). It is a divine demand made on fathers that they *lead.* Stephen Olford points out the tremendous force behind Paul's words quoted above. "The apostle is here addressing the common sin of fathers. It is possible to use paternal authority to abuse a child, break his spirit, and discourage all aspirations and expectations. Such cruelty to children is rampant in our land today."

The opposite of such abuse of parental authority and power calls for three clear leadership responsibilities. The first is *a caring leadership.* Stephen Olford said: "The word translated 'bring up' in Ephesians 6:4 is translated 'to nourish' in Ephesians 5:29. The Christian husband and father is to nurture both wife and children physically, mentally, and spiritually. The family must know that Dad cares. Although my boys are grown and married men, they still expect a hug and kiss from Dad. My boys knew that they could always count on their father all through their boyhood days and even today. It is possible to be accessible without being available. I can be in the same room with my boys, but so engrossed in the newspaper, in television, or in my hobby that the little fellows are totally denied the touch of the hand, the listening ear, or a wrestling match on the floor!

"By the same token, I can be available but not adaptable—'It's not the right time!' 'It's not convenient!' 'I've got the wrong clothes on!' and so on. Caring leadership takes everything into consideration and then makes a judgment in their favor.

"I remember being away from my church on sick leave. As always Heather and I phoned the boys to let them know where we were. No one else had that number. My elders and staff wanted it this way. One night a loud ring from the bedside telephone awakened me. It was two o'clock in the morning. I picked up the receiver and heard a familiar 'Dad!' at the other end. It was Jonathan from Springfield College. Before I could even ask 'why a call at this time of the night?' Jonathan apologized for the unearthly hour but added: 'Dad, I wanted you to be the first to know! I have just led my roommate to Christ!' My heart leaped for joy! I was glad to hear the news, but even more important than that, I was glad that my boy knew I was accessible."

Dr. Charles Stanley wrote in 1991 that "fathers spend more time watching a commercial four times a day than they do with their children all day (thirty-seven seconds a day). That shouts to a child, 'I am not worth anything to my Daddy.'" Children need our acceptance and love.

Then, too, there has to be *a correcting leadership*:"Bring them up in the nurture . . . of the Lord" (Ephesians 6:4). Stephen Olford pointed out that "this word *nurture* carries the idea of learning through discipline. It is translated 'chastening' in Hebrews 12. Modern psychology and philosophy in child-rearing scorn any form of discipline. What God says, however, overrides what man says (Proverbs 13:24). Needless to say, all discipline must be done in love, with reason and much prayer.

"Warren Wiersbe tells of a wayward girl who said to him:'I never knew how far I could go, because my parents never *cared* enough to discipline me. I figured that if it wasn't important to them, why should it be important to me?'

"Strange as it may sound, Heather and I never remember administering corporal punishment to either of our boys. Of course they were verbally cautioned and sometimes corrected. It was a little different with my father! He had a black ruler that we boys called 'sin'—(black as sin) that was used when necessary. I thank God for a father who cared enough to discipline when it was necessary."

Finally there has to be *a counseling leadership*:"Bring them up in the . . . admonition of the Lord" (Ephesians 6:4). Said Stephen Olford, "This takes in the whole sphere of instruction and inspiration. Much of this will be common sense advice and admonition. But, even more importantly, it will be the teaching of God's Word at family prayers, in regular conversation and those special sessions where children can let their hair down and talk and talk.

"Heather and I will be eternally thankful for our 'family summits'— especially during vacation times when our boys would pour out their hearts late into the night on every conceivable subject or problem. I would not trade those precious hours for anything in the world! Those were the times that made me a father. Any normal man can have children, but that is only a beginning. What matters is the spiritual impact of living, loving and leading in the home or wherever the family happens to be.

"When they were old enough, I always gave my Saturday mornings to my boys. Of course I tucked them in bed, when possible; of course I shared meals with them; of course I read and told stories to them, but Saturday morning was quality time. Like my father before me, I also thoughtfully planned some surprise to keep the boys guessing and stretching!"

One poem often motivated Stephen Olford to be the father he wanted to be:

> I took my little laddie once,
> And drew him to my knee,

And whispered to my little lad,
"Do you want to be like me?"

"Like Daddy?" said my little lad,
"I'm gonna be like you,"
I bowed my head in humbleness
And suddenly I knew

If my small boy would be like me,
There's one thing I must do,
The steps I take, the things I say,
Had better all ring true.

As in the night I lay awake,
While my wee lad slept on,
His words reechoed through my mind
Like some old haunting song.

"Like Daddy," that's the thought we need
To help to keep us straight,
Upon the way we fathers walk
Depends our children's fate.

Glen Wagoner[1]

In June 1991 Stephen was preaching on the subject of "Faithful Fatherhood" in Dr. E. V. Hill's church in Los Angeles. God came down in power and blessing. Hundreds came to the altar to rededicate their lives to faithful fatherhood. Later one man wrote Dr. Olford this letter:

> Dear Dr. Olford:
>
> I must begin by saying thank you, for your faithfulness to God's Word has resulted in my life being changed.
>
> Last Sunday you preached at Mt. Zion for Father's Day. The sermon touched my heart. I was one of the men who came down to rededicate my life. Before this sermon, my wife and I were considering separating. Our marriage for the past two years was crumbling. We spoke to counselors and ministers about the situation, but no solution. Everything seemed all right because we weren't arguing, cheating, or anything of this nature—just frustrated and unhappy.

But, praise God, this past weekend was the best of my entire life. Something changed in us. We're not only speaking, we are actually listening. For the first time since we dated together, we hugged, talked and enjoyed each other's company. When I looked into her eyes I saw a new woman. The woman gave a scent of confidence, peacefulness and beauty that she never had. We even began making plans about growing old together. For neither of us knew it could be this wonderful.

But this is not the end of [my] praise report. On Tuesday, I attended [your] Institute. My study and prayer life had dried up. My preaching (sermons) had no vigor. But praise God that has changed. It is 5:00 a.m. in the morning and I am reading the Scriptures and praying. Thank God!

Please pray for me, because these are only the beginning steps.

After receiving that letter Stephen Olford was more resolved than ever to give himself to his wife, sons, daughters-in-law, and grandchildren in a new "pledge of allegiance," using the words he found in a church bulletin.

A FATHER'S PLEDGE

I pledge allegiance to my home . . . to my wife . . . to my sons and daughters. I will honor my home and consider my trust in supporting it as a sacred one. I will do more than this. I will take time to cultivate friendship between myself and my family. I will not be too busy when they need me . . . even though it is only to catch a football or mend a doll's broken leg. I will love my children as only I can. I will compliment their mother's hours of care and concern. I will introduce my children to Christ and share with them the joys of Christian values in a Christian home.[2]

REMINISCENCES OF AN ELDER SON

As one reads the Scriptures in an attempt to understand the role of a father, it is difficult to come up with even half a dozen men who are

Jonathan and Catherine with their sons,
Jeremy, Justin, and Joshua (left to right).

portrayed to us as ideal fathers, though we can think of many women who are set before us as ideal mothers. The Olford boys were singularly blessed. They not only had a godly mother, but they had a godly father who considered ministering to his sons a task of equal or even greater importance than preaching to millions and pastoring a successful and growing church.

Jonathan MacGregor Olford was born July 17, 1952. He says: "My earliest memories are somewhat idyllic. I recall expansive gardens, lots of flowers, and the safety of a fence and bushes that seemed to surround a backyard as big as the great outdoors. Such was the life of a preacher's kid, living in a parsonage outside London."

Like most of us, Jonathan remembers where he went to school, and isolated events that he feels must have been related to his first couple of years at school.

By the time he was four or five years of age he had attended numerous Sunday school meetings, and Sunday services, where the "children's talk" was always the highlight, as well as some baptismal services on Sunday evenings. Even at that tender age he realized that some kind of decision was involved.

"I recall talking to my father," he says, "about what it meant to be a

Christian. I don't recall the content of the conversation, but I do recall making a commitment to Christ behind the kitchen door of our home. It was after a baptismal service, where the testimonies and my father's message on the meaning of asking Jesus into one's heart left an imprint on my heart and mind that called for a decision."

Jonathan recalls how his dad wanted to use him to illustrate a point he wished to make during a children's talk. He was not quite sure how effective the talk was that day, as all he can remembers is the part he played. The lesson had to do with our strength, as opposed to the strength of God.

At the appropriate time in his father's presentation Jonathan was summoned to the platform—"a somewhat terrifying experience" in itself—there to be bound with thread. His father wound him round and round with several strands of thread to illustrate the binding power of Sin—a few lies or falsehoods, for instance. He was able to flex his arms and break the strands. The lesson continued, showing that once we have engaged in sin it continues to bind us by its power. We may think we can escape its grip but it continues to wind its cords around us until we are held completely captive. So, despite the thinness of the thread, the continual winding of that thread around him finally immobilized him on the platform. He could no longer snap the threads that bound him.

Yet all was not lost. Through the power of prayer and the confession of sin, God could cut the cords of sin that bind us. A pair of scissors, shearing through the threads that bound the boy, illustrated the point. He was released from his imprisonment! He could be thus set free from sin! "In my memory," Jonathan comments, "the ministry of Stephen Olford has been, and still is, a family ministry."

Jonathan's life took a turn when the family moved to New York. "The adjustment to life in 'the big city' was a difficult one. On reflection, it must have been very hard for my parents as they endeavored to find a stable environment for my brother and me. Public school was extremely difficult. There were numerous fights and arguments and ridicule. I found my personal adjustment somewhat more difficult than simply trading in my gray flannel schoolboy shorts for a pair of blue jeans and sneakers.

"However, I recall that my parents believed me as I shared with them the atrocities of the day. That was extremely important to me. My own separation anxiety was quite traumatic but my father and mother accepted their responsibility, coming to one particular school regularly about ten o'clock in the morning to pick me up due to my nausea and vomiting. Life was not limited to the pulpit! The adjustments I had to make were important to them. I felt they were on my side."

Jonathan was taken out of that school and enrolled in another public school when the family moved to the east side of Manhattan. "This was not much of an improvement," Jonathan recalls, "so despite the limitations on their income, my parents put a priority on my education and on my well-being, and placed me in a private school with a decidedly European flavor. I am deeply grateful to my parents, who most certainly had their own adjustments and adaptations to make, as they were keenly aware of my needs and what it would take for me to 'survive.' I did reasonably well in my private school—except for languages—but that wasn't my parents fault; that was the fault of Mrs. What's-her-name!"

Once Jonathan completed the seventh grade he attended the Stony Brook School. "I still recall the day I went to Stony Brook to be tested and interviewed," he says. "I was terrified. I remember crying all the way home. As I look back I know that my parents' decision to send me to Stony Brook was in my best interest, but it was a terribly difficult one to make at the time. I did suffer from homesickness and my initial adjustment to boarding school life was not all that pleasant.

"I grew to love my time at Stony Brook, however, for it gave me much that has molded and directed me in my later life. It also provided me with the basis with which I fleshed out the things that were constantly and consistently discussed with my parents along the way—things concerning the direction of my life and where my interests lay.

"However, Stony Brook was not easy. I did not like being separated from my parents, and they did not like being separated from me. Both my parents and I recognized that it was for the best and in most respects I flourished at school—but to this day I still find goodbyes difficult; and the tears that form in the eyes of my parents suggest that it hasn't become any easier for them either."

The Olfords made many sacrifices to ensure their sons a good education in a private high school. "I am often asked," Jonathan says, "whether or not the sacrifices were worth it, since it meant the family was often apart. I did not have the enjoyment of my parents' presence at all my athletic events. It was difficult at times to get them on the phone when I needed a quick answer to some earth-shattering dilemma that required an immediate solution. However, what I have come to realize is that a family does not experience closeness based upon physical proximity.

"Speaking now from my current professional role, in which I am now deeply involved, I believe I know myself well enough to be unable to discredit this as denial or as pure rationalization, for I daily work with children, adolescents, adults, and families who, while they live under the same roof, seem to have little or no concept of intimacy.

"Would I have preferred to have lived at home and, at the same time, to have enjoyed the space, the sports, the friendships and the freedoms Stony Brook offered? My answer is a resounding yes! But this was not possible. My parents and I made a sacrifice, and the Lord blessed it. For despite the distance of sixty miles that separated us (which might as well have been five hundred miles since we had no car or transportation) our family was close, and the times at home were always special. There were times of family gathering and celebration—and they always made it so difficult to leave again."

Jonathan, on his own confession, did not leave his mark in the record books. But he did experience an appreciation for sports and for his own physical talents, and he did gain a love for people.

"I believe," he says, "both of these talents have something of a genetic predisposition, since both my father and my mother are giving people. As far back as I can remember we had people in our home. Sunday dinner was always an event, and many a missionary, church leader, or spiritual giant graced our table. At the same time, my folks were seemingly just as dedicated to the regular folk within the church and the community. They prayed for them. Indeed, I was privileged to see God answer my father's prayers for his constituents."

Jonathan comments on his parents' lifelong and continuing athletic activities. "My introduction to golf and tennis," he says, "were through my parents. We have enjoyed many foursomes on the golf course and doubles play on the tennis court as a family. My father's athletic undertakings with his sons had one trademark: to develop a competitive spirit coupled with a desire for and an appreciation of fair play.

"Even my father's interest in motorcycles (which of course predates my birth) I have shared. I have been an active and enthusiastic motorcycle rider for over twenty years. I still remember the first motorcycle I ever had—a small 65cc Harley Davidson. My father started it up 'to show me how.' He suggested that he ride it to the end of the block. If I remember correctly he came back somewhere between forty-five minutes to an hour later!"

During his high school years, Jonathan spent many summers in North Carolina where his father served as Director of the Ben Lippen Conference. "These years," he says, "gave my brother and me the opportunity to gain an appreciation of 'country life' and the finer things—such as box turtle hunts, swinging from vines in the woods, and poison ivy!

"It was here also that I recall sitting under my father's ministry. Perhaps it was my age, perhaps it was the moving of the Holy Spirit, perhaps it was many things all working together at one time; but to this day I remember the fascination I had with the Friday evening missionary message each week. I recall responding to an altar call for service 'any time, anywhere, at any cost' when I was about twelve or thirteen years of age. This was a key experience in my life. The Lord did, indeed, in due course hold me to that commitment. My wife and I served with the African Inland Mission for ten years, seven of which were spent at the Rift Valley Academy in Kijabe, Kenya, East Africa.

"It was the influence of my father's teaching, too, and the example set by both my parents within our home which gave me the impetus to pursue my undergraduate and graduate degree in physical education and sports medicine. My father was never one to pressure me or push me in the direction of the ministry or the pastorate. I chose a field that was far removed from 'following in my father's footsteps' into the ministry or becoming involved in 'the family business,' so to speak. But I did so in the full knowledge that I had my parents' blessing."

Jonathan sums up his relationship with his father and mother. He says, "As I look back I can see the mark of my father and my mother on my life as I have taken a variety of twists and turns along the path which has led me to where I am today. I was raised in a people-oriented family, a family that was committed to each other on both the human and the spiritual levels. I see my parents' influence indelibly marked upon my life's history.

"As I have already said, there was never any pressure to be anything. My interest in sports and my investment in young people led my wife and me to Kenya. My ongoing investment in people's lives brought us back to the United States for further training, this time in psychology. I am now in private practice. As President of Crisis & Consultation Services International (CCSI), a non-profit ministry organization, I am focused on supporting and training churches and para-church groups who are attempting to manage crises, traumas and suffering in their congregations, neighborhoods, communities, cities, and countries. My father and mother have served as models for my life of service, for a life of commitment, and for a life in which our own individual gifts and talents are invested to reach others for the Lord."

REMINISCENCES OF A YOUNGER SON

David Lindsay Olford was born on May 2, 1956 when his father was in his stride as pastor of the Duke Street Baptist Church in London, England. Now a grown man, with children of his own, he became his father's partner and right-hand man in Encounter Ministries, Inc. David gives us his own view of the man we only know as a friend or a preacher or a soul-winner or as a man we admired and loved. What a son thinks of his father— especially when that father is a public figure, and in the public eye as an outstanding Christian leader—is always a matter for history. Many a man has been cheered as a great Christian in the church, only to turn out to have been a veritable demon at home. It has been said that no man is a hero to

David and Ellen with their two daughters,
Lindsay and Stephanie (left to right).

his valet. Certainly no man is a hero to his son who does not earn the right to be a hero to his son.

Accessibility! Availability! Adaptability! These were the pillars of Stephen Olford's philosophy and practice of parenthood. How well did they work out when looked at from a son's point of view? "I always feel comfortable hearing my father discuss these three A's" David says. "They were the real characteristics of my father's relationship to me and with me and my brother.

"Preacher's kids" says David Olford, "have a somewhat dubious reputation. People realize that my father was, and still is, a very busy man and that he puts great priority on his ministry. So what about his kids?"

Looking back to his childhood, from the standpoint now of a man of fifty, David says, "My father was extremely busy during my childhood days. But as I grew up I did not live with the belief or feeling I was unimportant to my father, nor was that the case in adulthood."

The three A's had much to do with this. "I always felt I could be with my father," he says. "His study was not a fortress from me with the words *keep out* written over the door. I realize now that I had access privileges not true of many people. It wasn't just that I could enter my father's workplace; I knew I was both important and welcome. My father has always had an ability to focus his attention and that was true in his relationship with me. My father was accessible; I could be near him.

"He was also available; I could feel I was 'with him.' Adaptability was an important ingredient in the fathering I received, though I would not have called it that at the time."

Adaptability? Well, allowing David to throw his red rubber ball against the bedroom wall not only made noise, it also left definite marks on the wall! The Olford boys did not have a backyard in New York City. They lived both on the East Side of Manhattan and in midtown. On the East Side they lived in an apartment building, and in midtown at the Hotel Salisbury above Calvary Baptist Church. For most of their years in New York City home was on the "fourteenth" floor (actually the thirteenth) in both locations. Stephen Olford, as a wise father, made allowances for this. The bedroom, not to mention the rest of the apartment, were allowed to function as play areas. David remembers occasions when not only a rubber ball but also a baseball flew out of his bedroom window to land some thirteen or fourteen flights below!

Television viewing was allowed. True, in the sixties and early seventies television programs were not what they are today. Just the same, many conscientious parents wrestled with the problem of whether or not they should even have television in their home. "I was allowed to watch television," David recalls. He adds, "I was a pretty conscientious and eager student and I don't remember television ever getting in the way of school work or study. I don't remember specific regulations about television viewing nor do I recall a feeling of frustration over restrictions." Doubtless there were rules, but evidently they were reasonable and not irksome.

Always a conscientious student, David remembers with appreciation how his father would turn even a walk through the streets of New York into a learning experience. "A walk down 57th Street in New York, or along Fifth or Sixth Avenue, is not quite like walking on the beach or in the woods," he says. "But for this boy, growing up in the city, such walks were meaningful and interesting, not to mention a necessary break at times. Of course walks on the beach were fun experiences also. Accessibility, availability and adaptability communicated that I, as a son, was important to my father. I would probably not have expressed it in that way, but I think that is what was accomplished."

David Olford puts forward the word "inclusion" as another important word from his childhood. Some of his favorite memories are of meals shared with visitors to the Olford home. "Many people came through our church in New York, including well-known preachers. I often shared in meals or living room conversation with such people. These were times of exposure to men and women of God, times when truths my parents stood for were reinforced by the words and character of others.

"I'll never forget the radiant face, character, and life of Bishop Festo Kivengere. On arrival at our home (apartment) at 123 West 57th Street in New York, he captivated me. I remember Billy Graham visiting us and a conversation in the living room with him and members of the team. Preachers and evangelists, missionaries and leaders, friends and family, came through our home at different times. I was included in such times, and they were crucial to my Christian experience."

The joy of being included reached into other areas of young David's life. He was taken to a number of concerts at Carnegie Hall. "I remember hearing the American Symphony, and Van Cliburn with the Moscow Symphony. In fact, Van Cliburn was a member of our church. Such social occasions were not necessarily always anticipated with enthusiasm, but they left a great and positive impression."

One of David's favorite memories was when he attended the fifth game of the 1964 World Series with his father. "I was a Yankee fan through and through," he says. "I remember my father picking me up at school. I left my second grade class early that day, which in itself was unusual." He can describe with some detail the course of the game. His favorite player was Bobby Richardson, the Christian second baseman. He recalls the packed stadium, the old Yankee Stadium with the deep center field. He recalls going to many baseball games while growing up. "But the World Series was special!" he says. "I'm glad my father took me to that game. By the way," he adds, "the Yankees lost the series 4-3 primarily due to the tremendous pitching of Bob Gibson. But what a boyhood memory!" There speaks a fan! There speaks a man thoroughly appreciative of a father who took him to exciting events, a father who took time to build into his son memories of a positive kind.

The Olford boys attended boarding school from grades eight through twelve. Their parents saw to it that vacations were very special. Vacation provided time for lots of extras—time for play, for golf and tennis, time for long walks and conversations late into the night. David remembers the ranch-style home his parents purchased in the Poconos in Pennsylvania. "I remember the good times I had there," he says, "and the good times my parents had there. They went to the usual functions together, but they also played together, especially golf." The fact that his parents thoroughly enjoyed each other's company made a deep impression on David.

Going away to boarding school was not a traumatic experience for David, probably because his older brother had already paved the way and was there with him for his years at Stony Brook. The school made sure the boys were kept busy. "The last thing needed at a boarding school," David comments, "is a lot of free time to think about home!" The first night back at school after vacations usually found him homesick. "But once school started the next day I was totally involved in the responsibilities and relationships of that fine school." The fact that the school was only some sixty miles from New York City undoubtedly helped. Between vacations and occasional weekend breaks, the brothers were home quite often.

Because he was at boarding school his teen years were unique. He was not home every afternoon. He could not interact with his parents on a day-to-day basis. That only made vacation times all the more important. "I recall our many times of interaction and conversation," he says. "Sometimes these would grow out of Bible reading or devotions. But, however they began, I can remember discussing all sorts of issues and topics. My father's obvious openness to talk with us, as well as his wisdom, meant a lot to us. Openness was always encouraged." And his parents were always just a phone call away.

David's parents had a great influence on his spiritual life and development, something for which he never ceases to praise God. "I can remember asking Jesus into my heart privately at our apartment on York Avenue in New York," he says, adding candidly enough and in parenthesis, "I may have done this more than once as a boy." Milestones along the way are associated with Calvary Baptist Church and the Ben Lippen Conferences during his boyhood summers. "I was baptized at Calvary Baptist, my father standing by my side as I shared a word of testimony. The text he gave me on that occasion was 2 Timothy 2:1: 'Thou therefore, my son, be strong in the grace that is in Christ Jesus.'"

His most memorable boyhood spiritual experience occurred during a trip to Jamaica in the West Indies where his father was to speak at a Keswick Convention. David was 14 at the time. "It was a time of heavy conviction and tears," he says, "a time of 'soaking in' the truths that were taught. I remember standing to submit to the Lordship of Christ over my life. I remember talking to my father about what was happening. He wanted to know why I was crying." David cannot remember now what his father said to him. He is sure, however, that his father counseled and comforted. "I have been tempted," he says, "to see that experience as the time I really was born again. But I think it is better to view it as a deepening experience, when a 14-year-old understood more fully the Lordship of Christ, when the Holy Spirit made truths real to me in a new way."

David highlights another aspect of his father's spiritual wisdom. "I listened to many, many sermons in my early years and to many different preachers. I was presented with serious spiritual challenges at these times. By contrast, however, I don't remember my father pressing or pushing for spiritual decisions, one-on-one, at home. He did not force us to make decisions or cram the Bible down our throats."

David's memory of family devotions is a very positive one. He particularly remembers the times when the family was on vacation. Memory has faded as to the specifics, though he does recall the use of the Scripture Union Notes. Devotions were centered around the Word of God. Involvement and interaction from the boys was encouraged, and there was flexibility and variety over the years. The sad thing is that all too many children have negative memories of such times, of being forced to sit impatiently while the meal grows cold or of sitting afterwards when so many more interesting things beckoned. The trouble is that parents do not prepare adequately for family devotions; they get into a rut; they provide little or no scope or variety and employ even less imagination.

Many young people growing up in Christian homes develop resentment against Sundays in general, and church in particular. David Olford treasures positive and happy memories of Calvary Baptist Church. He remembers Sunday school teachers, Christian life conventions, and missionary conferences with pleasure. He loved the monthly baptismal services. He drank in the testimonies given by the candidates. He remembers most of all the love of the people. He remembers Adelaide Dobson, for instance, "who would arrive on a given Sunday, prepare and serve a fabulous meal, and then clean up afterwards and quietly leave, not wanting anything but the opportunity to serve." He adds, "I share these things because they are important to me. I share them because they indicate I did not resent church. I did not see it as something that was more important than me or that got in my way." Today David is an enthusiastic churchman himself, something he traces in part to his home and church heritage.

David's father continued to be an important influence in his life. He says, "My relationship with my father continued to deepen over the years. His role as father did not stop when I left high school. All the significant decisions of my life have been made with a desire for his counsel." David's choice of college and graduate schools, his decision to go on for his Ph.D., his involvement with Encounter Ministries, and above all, his marriage were decisions he made after seeking counsel from his father. He rejoiced in his father's continuing love, and personal interest in his life and activities. He adds: "Of course, my father's continuous love for my mother, and the unity they shared in life and ministry, is a tremendous example and model to me in my relationship with my wife, Ellen."

David is often asked if he really understood the greatness of his father. "I know what people mean when they ask that," he says. "They want to know if I realize, or realized when I was growing up, what an outstanding preacher and church leader he was. When I was growing up I did not realize this. Of course I respected my father, but I didn't compare him with other evangelical preachers. One reason is that I have always been around people who didn't know my father from Adam! All the way through school there were kids who didn't know my father, so I didn't grow up being known as the son of a great preacher.

"This situation continued in the later years of education. Some people knew of him and respected him greatly; others had not heard of him or only knew of his ministry from a distance.

"I knew he could preach, because I listened to him pretty regularly. I guess I knew he was an important person because of his leadership positions, but I did not realize how respected he was or how extensive his ministry was. These discoveries I made in later years.

"The more I work with preachers and pastors, and the more I hear and see firsthand of the blessing wrought through my father's ministry, the more I realize how great a man my father was. But as my brother said in his tribute to my father in the book, *A Passion for Preaching*,[3] if I felt that my father had not been 'Dad,' in the midst of his other responsibilities, I would not be too excited about his 'greatness.' If I felt he had dumped my brother and me, on the road to ministerial success, his greatness obviously would be minimal in my eyes. But, even as I realize more and more the many great qualities and gifts of my father, I also realize how important my brother and I were to him."

And today? David says: "He was the man who most influenced and still influences my life. He was my boss and my colleague. He was a great friend. Most importantly, though, he was Dad!"

Part Two

THE MINISTER

Stephen Olford, the evangelist
Winnipeg, 1950.

CHAPTER 5

The Soul-Winner

He who wins souls is wise.
Proverbs 11:30, NKJV

In the words of A. T. Pierson, "A light that does not shine, a germ that does not grow, and a stream that does not flow is no more an anomaly than a Christian who does not witness." This statement made a tremendous impression on Stephen Olford and he has used it over and over again in his preaching.

"Witnessing," he says, "is not a gift but an anointed lifestyle. Whether in silence or whether in speech, we are *all* witnesses. The big question is whether or not we are good or bad witnesses. However, within the witnessing community there is also the *gift* of soulwinning. As witnesses to our Lord Jesus Christ we are either sowers or reapers. Both are needed. Reapers have the *evangelistic* gift."

Stephen Olford testifies to the fact that God gave him this gift. However he maintains that it never manifested itself with any kind of authenticity until a work of grace had been done in his heart. On the contrary, there was a time in his life when even the thought of talking to people, publicly or privately, paralyzed him with fear. He was not only painfully shy, but completely indisposed to meeting new people. "Many a social occasion in our home was spoiled," he said, "because of my unannounced disappearance."

The fact that he was a committed Christian did not seem to make any difference. Indeed, in one sense it made him worse. As a saved person he knew it was his duty to witness for the Lord and, when possible, to seek to win others to Him. All that did, however, was bring him into bondage. "I have known what it is," he said, "to pray for courage and walk the entire length of a train giving out gospel booklets to anyone courteous enough (and, I thought, pitying enough) to take one. But I was glad when the task was completed!"

It was not as though he had not studied the subject of soul-winning. Indeed, he had read a wide selection of books searching them and hoping to find the secret of successful soulwinning.

Then God graciously stepped in. "He had permitted me to struggle long enough to convince me that I could do nothing about it. I was shy. I was bound. I was defeated. The fact was, I was a failure." Right from the start divinely-ordered circumstances were used to bring Stephen Olford out of the bondage of soulwinning in the flesh into the blessing of soulwinning in the Spirit.

He met an old friend he had not seen for years. In the course of conversation, his friend drew Stephen's attention to an incident in the life of saintly Oswald Chambers. When he was still a young man, Chambers was out for a walk with a deeply-taught Scottish divine. Presently a shepherd appeared from around the mountain track. He would have passed the two men with little more than a word of greeting but for Oswald's intervention. He left his elderly friend, approached the shepherd, and pointedly asked this stranger if all were well with his soul! Now, surely, this was an opportunity redeemed, a witness nobly done and boldly given. However, when Oswald Chambers rejoined the man of God he was met with an unexpected and sobering question, "Tell me, my friend, did you receive the Holy Spirit's permission to speak to that man about his soul?"

"That story started me thinking," Stephen said. "I began to see slowly, but clearly, that soulwinning is God's work. He must plan and carry it through from beginning to end. My business is to be in line with His will. Winning people to the Lord Jesus Christ is not a matter of trial or error but of being 'led by the Spirit'" (Romans 8:14).

Soon after this, Stephen was at a spiritual life convention at which a humble servant of God expounded John 7:37-39. Something that was said arrested him. "There is only one successful soul-winner, the Lord Jesus Himself. To try to copy Him is to fail miserably, for His thoughts are not our thoughts, neither are His ways our ways. If we would succeed in this great task of winning the lost to God, then Jesus must work in us and through us by the power of His Spirit. Mark His words: 'He who believes in Me, as the Scripture has said, out of his [innermost being] will flow rivers of living water. But this He spoke concerning the Spirit, whom those believing in Him would receive: for the Holy Spirit was not yet given; because Jesus was not yet glorified' (John 7:38-39, NKJV). Only as we believe in Him and allow Him to flow through us by His Spirit will men and women, whom He is drawing to Himself, respond. To the Spirit-led child of God, this will mean liberty, joy and blessing in the work of evangelism."

That evening Stephen Olford went home determined to cease trying and to start trusting. From that moment soulwinning for him was different. Not only was he delivered from shyness and self-consciousness, but he was introduced, as he put it, "to a level of soulwinning which is divinely directed and unspeakably joyous."

"I have failed many times since," he said, "but I have also known the reason and the way of restoration! It is only when He is in complete control of my life, that I can hope to share in the fruits of His labors."

He soon discovered that such surrender to the sovereignty of the Lord Jesus did not necessarily imply or guarantee on-the-spot decisions for Christ every time a person was approached on the subject. "We certainly are called upon to preach the gospel to every creature," he said, "but the Lord adds to His church only 'such as should be [or are being] saved' (Acts 2:47). This is a deep mystery, but it is a fact of Scripture and of personal experience.

"What happens is that as we witness in the power of the Spirit some soul is especially laid upon our hearts. Like Philip of old, we are compelled inwardly to go near and join ourselves to this or that person, as we learn from Acts 8:26-40. Sometimes this results at once in a conversion. Then there are other occasions when that honor is reserved for someone else. In either instance, however, the issue from the divine standpoint is certain and successful. What matters supremely is that we are 'led by the Spirit of God.'"

But what about people who reject the gospel? Stephen Olford bluntly said that that is none of our business. "Providing we have witnessed as faithfully as we know how, and have given the individual concerned every opportunity to trust the Savior, then to be sensitive to the divine leading we must go no further. It is God's work, and He will be glorified in the ultimate issue (2 Corinthians 2:14-17). Such an attitude keeps the Spirit-filled soul-winner humble, prayerful and increasingly aware of the fact that he is only the instrument to be used as and when the Master pleases."[1]

——

One of the greatest training periods in his early years was at the Missionary Training Colony. As a member of the student body he was sent out every Saturday night to witness to people at opposite ends of the social scale. The students referred to these spheres of service as the down-and-outs and up-and-ins ministries. They would leave the Colony at dusk every Saturday and work right through the night until dawn the next morning.

If the assignment was to the down-and-outers they went to London's famed Thames Embankment to hand out tracts and seek to win the derelicts to Christ. The students worked closely with the London Embankment Mission, which was a veritable haven for these unfortunates.

"We operated two by two," Stephen said, "so that we had both protection and backup for our soulwinning work. I can remember how amazed I was to talk to some of these men and to discover that quite a number of them came from wonderful homes and university training, but were now down and out.

"Approaching these people was an art in itself. Many times I was rebuffed and even threatened. On other occasions, though, with the anointing of the Holy Spirit and with well-chosen words, it was a sheer joy to share the Lord Jesus Christ and His power to save. Over the years of training at the Colony it was my holy privilege to lead many of these men to a personal faith in Jesus Christ."

The alternate ministry was to the up-and-ins. The two students would tour the red-light districts of London and, with God-given boldness, enter cabarets, vice dens, the backstage area of theaters and other similar places of entertainment. They would talk to people "stone cold" about the Lord Jesus.

"Even though I knew the principle that 'as many as are led by the Spirit of God . . . are the sons of God,'" Stephen recalled, "it was a step of faith to approach these people and discern whether or not they were in any way disposed to talk about spiritual things. Again and again we found that behind the façade of a clown, an actor, a dancer or a singer, there was a hungry, empty heart.

"I remember once being asked by a talented young actor, 'Whatever made you come to talk with someone like me?' The young man then went on to say that he was utterly amazed that anyone in the religious world— especially among the clergy—would ever care for the souls of the people in show business.

"My colleague and I had the opportunity to distribute thousands of tracts on such occasions, and every now and then had the privilege of introducing the Lord Jesus to hearts ready to receive and follow Him. This was valuable training and I thank God it paid off in the years that followed."

During the war years, in the 1940s, it was Stephen Olford's privilege as an Army Scripture Reader to lead soldiers to a personal faith in Christ at gun sites, on the street, and especially in a center he and his parents established in Newport, South Wales for the armed forces.

During the same period he led many young people to Christ in connection with the Young People's Christian Fellowship in the same town of Newport. My own life was one of the many impacted for Christ in this Fellowship. Many from that group went on to become distinguished servants of God in pulpit ministry at home and abroad.

"I recall one young man who walked out of a meeting where I was teaching the Word," recounted Stephen Olford. "He was obviously irritated and angry. I concluded my message and handed over the closing of the service to one of my teammates. Walking down the street in the darkness I believe I was led by the Holy Spirit in the right direction. Presently I saw this young man, Victor Roberts by name, leaning against a lamppost. It was wartime. The 'blackout' was rigidly enforced because of the danger of air raids. There was only a glimmer of light.

"I went up to Victor and said, 'I'm sorry if I offended you in anything I said tonight, but let's talk about it.' Quite a heated discussion followed, but I went on talking with him, trusting the Holy Spirit to give me not only the correct words but a loving, and patient spirit.

"Presently he blurted out, 'I am a coward. I just can't face the challenge and claims of Jesus Christ.' I immediately replied, 'I can understand that and I can identify with you. Without the power of the indwelling life of the Lord Jesus I would be a coward.'

"It was not many minutes after that that I led Victor Roberts to commit his life to Jesus Christ. In my mind's eye I can still see two men under a dimly lit lamppost trying to read the small print of a little New Testament I held in my hand. Victor Roberts went on to become a mature Christian and a very successful businessman who kept in touch with me right up to his death. He had a special interest in his fellow business professionals and had a wonderful ministry to them through luncheons and special events he held in the city of Liverpool."

In 1957 Stephen Olford was invited by Billy Graham to come to America to take part in the Madison Square Garden crusade in New York City. Because of a bad ear infection his physician advised him not to fly. So he booked passage aboard the *R.M.S. Carinthia* and sailed from Liverpool for the United States by way of Canada. As he boarded the ship he noticed a young woman on the gangplank who looked extremely lonely and sad. He learned the reason later on.

That evening, before going down to his cabin, he took a stroll around the upper deck. As he passed the bar on that deck he saw this young woman again. She was sitting there drinking with a number of fellows who were making sport of her. The Lord laid a burden for her on his heart. As he had his quiet time that night, his concern deepened and he prayed for this young woman. He could picture her in his mind. He imagined that she could just as easily have been a member of his church back there in Richmond (he was Pastor of Duke Street Baptist Church at that time).

The next morning was Sunday. He had been asked to preach at the Anglican service to be held in tourist class, but had excused himself because of ear and throat problems. Still, he attended the service and did lead in prayer. He did not know it at the time but this same young woman was in the audience.

A day or two later Stephen was passing through the main lounge of the ship on his way to get some writing paper. At the time he was in the midst of writing a book called *Successful Soul-Winning*, later published by Moody Bible Institute. A number of people were playing bingo in the lounge. Suddenly Stephen heard a voice say: "Come over here, stranger, and join us." He declined politely, explaining, "that's not my cup of tea" and adding that, in any case, he had work to do and had to go and get some stationery. It was the same young lady he had already noticed and for whom he had prayed. She did not want to take no for an answer. In a loud voice she asked him to explain why the game of bingo was not his thing.

There and then Stephen Olford gave his testimony to the people who were listening in on this unusual exchange. The bingo game was completely disrupted. "Some were serious, others were curious, while others were furious!" Having given his testimony Stephen rose to leave. The young woman followed him. She said, "Can I talk to you? I feel I must talk to you." An arrangement was made for a meeting the following morning in the lounge.

The hour arrived and the young woman, Beryl Gilbertson, was there. Stephen sat down and they began to talk. She explained that she was really running away from home. She was a brilliant radiologist and radiographer. However, she became involved with the wrong crowd; but first-class job or not, she had to get away. She had seen an advertisement in a Canadian paper and was now on her way to Montreal to take the position.

As she unfolded her sad story, Stephen told her that he had noticed her as she boarded the ship, that later he had seen her in the bar and that, furthermore, he had prayed for her. She was astounded that anybody would care.

"She looked into my face," he recalled, "and she said, 'I want to know the peace and joy that are obviously evident in your life. How can I know Christ as my personal Savior?'" Over a cup of broth he led Beryl Gilbertson to a saving faith in Jesus Christ as Savior and Lord. Each morning thereafter he discipled her. She became so radiant and alive in Christ she began leading souls to Christ.

"Subsequently she came down from Montreal to give her testimony at the Billy Graham Crusade in New York City, and met Billy Graham himself and all the team. On my return journey to England I went by way of Montreal to visit her. Her apartment was wall to wall with people waiting for me to address them. Most of them she had led to Christ herself since I had last seen her!"

Later Beryl Gilbertson married a find young man, Bob Adams, who took a government agency job that moved them to Pakistan, Panama, South American, and then to Africa. Everywhere Beryl went she established a Bible class and led scores of women to Christ. "To this very day I'm in touch with this couple and their lovely family and God has worked through Beryl's life in a most miraculous way. This is one of the joys of soul-winning!"

In 1960 Stephen Olford was invited to address delegates at the Baptist World Alliance Congress in Rio de Janeiro, Brazil. The subject assigned to him was "The Holy Spirit and Evangelism." He flew down with Billy Graham, his team, and a host of celebrities, including Martin Luther King— "with whom I spent two hours in very intense conversation on victory and unity in Christ!"

As the plane passed over Venezuela one of the engines caught fire and the plan had to make an emergency landing at the Caracas airport. A coup had taken place in the city so all the passengers were housed in motels around the airport. Because space was limited the passengers were obliged to be paired off and share rooms.

Stephen's roommate was a man named Thomas, the ambassador from Liberia to the United States. By the time the passengers reached their rooms it was very late. Stephen himself had taken something to help him sleep and he was feeling rather groggy! He was kept awake, however, by his companion who was phoning around the world on his privileged diplomatic credit card.

"When he got tired of that," Stephen recollected, "we started to talk and, of course, I told him that I was the pastor of Calvary Baptist Church in New York City and explained the nature of my ministry. He became intensely interested and the conversation led to the essence of the gospel. He was a prepared heart for a willing Savior! Not many minutes later he surrendered to the claims of Christ and we rejoiced together.

"Following the conference in Rio de Janeiro he became a member of Calvary Baptist Church in New York City. I followed him with great interest and prayer until he was transferred to Switzerland as ambassador to that country. Some years later I attended the Lausanne Conference with several thousand delegates. One afternoon I saw a little man moving towards me through the jostling crowd of delegates. It was Ambassador Thomas! He was still rejoicing in the Lord and thanking me for having been God's instrument to lead him into life more abundant."

Another travel incident that Stephen liked to recall took place on his way back from a preaching engagement. His plane had landed at LaGuardia Airport, where he took a cab to Manhattan. As the driver weaved his way through the traffic-laden highways of the borough of Queens, Stephen started a conversation. It did not take him long to detect a Jamaican accent!

"So you come from Jamaica?" Stephen inquired, to which the driver replied, "Yes, sir. I'm here trying to make some money and then get back home as fast as I can."

"Why? Don't you like New York?"

"No!" retorted the dissatisfied Jamaican, "this place is not only dirty, corrupt and cruel, it is a deathtrap. No one is safe in this city."

At this point Stephen Olford shared with him the fact that he was pastor of Calvary Baptist Church and had lived in New York City for many years!

"How could anyone be a Christian in a city like this?" exclaimed the driver. Stephen saw his opportunity and began to witness to him about a Savior who saves and keeps. Without warning, the Jamaican flipped back the meter flag, pulled his cab to the side of the road and pleaded, "Tell me more." In a matter of minutes that dear driver had prayed the sinner's prayer and was gloriously saved!

His only concern was how he could live a pure and holy life in such a filthy city. Stephen had the answer. He said, "I know your country well. I have been in Jamaica many times for meetings. One place I recall is Mandeville, where I spoke at a conference center on many occasions. Nearby is a well-known bog into which I was once thrown by a horse when out riding! I remember that in this rather smelly bog grew beautiful white lilies."

"You're absolutely correct," observed the driver.

"Well," explained Stephen, "just as lilies can grow in a bog, so a Christian can grow in a corrupt city like New York. God called Christians to live holy lives in wicked cities like Rome, Corinth, Thessalonica, and so on, and God has called you to live for Him right here in New York."

The man got the message, became a member of Calvary Baptist Church, and served his Lord faithfully for many years before returning to his own country.

On another occasion Stephen was conducting some meetings at Capernwray Hall, the Torchbearer's headquarters in Britain and the training center for the ministry of Major Ian Thomas. A considerable number of German young people were present and he was able to minister to them for the whole week. Many of them faced up to Jesus Christ, trusted Him, and yielded their lives to His lordship.

One person in particular caught Stephen's attention. His name was Hans Burki and he had come from East Germany. He was a dedicated Communist and, as such, he stood out conspicuously. A friend of his had extended the invitation and somehow Hans had gotten across the border and come to Capernwray.

He sat there with a steely face. His eyes seemed to be glazed as he weighed up in that intelligent, university-trained mind of his, all that was said throughout that memorable week. When there was humor in the meetings everyone roared with laughter, but not he. When there was pathos and a surge of emotion, he seemed to steel himself even harder. The week wore on.

Then came the last night. "I will never forget that Friday night," Stephen Olford said. "Somehow Heaven touched earth. The reasoned truth of the gospel of Jesus Christ broke upon his heart. At last Hans 'unsteeled' himself. God broke through into his life and he bowed the knee and was wonderfully converted."

Next morning everyone prepared to go home. Stephen was still in his room, having his quiet time, when there was a knock at the door. It was Hans. His face was absolutely radiant. He said, "I have come to say goodbye. I am leaving before the others. I'm heading back to East Germany and have to take a detour, but I wanted to come and say goodbye and also thank you."

Stephen invited him in. He recalled, "Hans sat on the edge of my bed, and I looked into his face and stated, 'So you're going back?'"

He reiterated, "Yes, I am going back. But first I came to thank you because I may never have an opportunity of writing to you. As you know our letters are censored and I doubt a letter would get through. I did not feel I could leave Capernwray without thanking you for leading me to Jesus Christ. I thought it through," he continued, "I settled it in my mind. I have opened the door of my heart to Jesus Christ, and He has come in. He is my Lord and my Master. But I know this—if Jesus demands anything He demands everything, and if He demands everything I am going to confess Him on arrival back in East Germany. And I know this, that as soon as my parents and my Communist group hear that I have yielded my life to Jesus Christ, that I am no longer a Communist, and am no longer going to have anything to do with them, I shall face possible death, and shall never see you again. I am going home to suffer for Jesus Christ."

"I had a word of prayer with him, but I never left my room for the rest of that day," Stephen said. "I bawled my head off. I prayed. I read my Bible. I wept again. I asked myself the question, 'Stephen Olford if you had been Hans Burki, would you be able to say that?"

It is no wonder that years later Billy Graham wrote in the Foreword to the book, *The Secret of Soul-Winning,* "Stephen Olford is not only one of the greatest Bible preachers I know, but one of the most successful soul-winners I have ever met . . . We have ministered together on three continents. He is unquestionably one of the most refreshingly radiant Christians I know. He exemplifies in his personal life everything the apostle Paul meant when he spoke of the fruit of the Spirit. He is . . . a man of great compassion, carrying a burden for the lost."[2]

God give each of us a similar passion for souls. May our daily prayer be:

> Lord lay some soul upon my heart,
> And love that soul through me;
> And may I nobly do my part
> To win that soul for Thee.
>
> Leon Tucker

*Stephen and Heather traveled to Japan on many occasions.
This picture was taken near Hakone, one of the regular
locations for Keswick meetings. Mt. Fuji is in the background.*

CHAPTER 6

The Traveler

In journeys often ...
2 Corinthians 11:26, NKJV

Preachers have often been travelers. Even the local pastor may have the God-given urge to preach beyond the borders of his parish or move to another church—if so directed by the Holy Spirit. The Prince of all preachers was always on the move. We read that, "He went through every city and village, preaching and bringing the glad tidings of the kingdom of God" (Luke 8:1, NKJV). We have only to count the number of times the word *went* occurs in the four Gospels to establish that Jesus was a traveling Preacher.

Moreover, He told His disciples to do the same. His commission was unequivocal: "Go ... and make disciples of all the nations" (Matthew 28:19); "You shall receive power when the Holy Spirit has come upon you; and you shall be witnesses to Me in Jerusalem, and in all Judea and Samaria, *and to the end of the earth*" (Acts 1:8, NKJV, italics added). In his *Word Studies in the New Testament* Marvin R. Vincent characterizes the evangelist as "a traveling minister whose work was not confined to a particular church." He was "a keeper of the apostles." An apostle, as such, was an evangelist (1 Corinthians 1:17), but every evangelist was not an apostle. In the *Didache* (also know as *The Teaching of the Twelve Apostles*, written about 100 A.D.)

it is prescribed that "an apostle shall not remain in one place longer than two days, and that when he departs he shall take nothing with him except enough bread to last until his next station."[1]

It is not surprising to discover, therefore, that Stephen Olford became a world traveler. Of him it can be said, "In journeys often." Throughout his life he was on the move for God.

Stephen recounted, "I don't know how many miles I have logged in my lifetime but, conservatively speaking, the figure is in the millions. To try and trace all these journeys would fill a book of its own; so a mere sampling must suffice.

"The first trip I ever made was as an unborn infant in my mother's womb. The journey for my birth entailed a thousand-mile trek from Luma-Cassai in Angola to Kalene Hill in Northern Rhodesia. Reference to this has already been made in chapter 1, but the story deserves more than a mere reference. To get there my father mapped out the trail, calculated the needed provisions, recruited the necessary carriers, and set off with chronometer, pedometer, compass, and gun. Each day was planned so that the men had time before nightfall to set up the tent, fetch water, cook food, and prepare for bedtime. My father walked the entire stretch. Mother was carried in a canvas hammock suspended on a pole held by two carriers with just a draped awning to shield her from the fierce afternoon sun.

"In due course the caravan arrived at Kalene Hill to a warm welcome from Christian Brethren missionaries and Dr. Singleton Fisher, who delivered me into the world almost to the expected day. As it turned out, the birth went smoothly; there were no complications—just cheers and celebrations! In due course I was dedicated and named Stephen Frederick. As soon as my mother was well enough to travel we started the long trek back to Luma-Cassai. It was April and the rainy season had started, making the swollen streams and crocodile-infested rivers more dangerous. As a precautionary measure, I was carried in a tiny cot on the head of the tallest African. One slip by him and I would have been the appetizer before the main course—all six feet of him!

"One night, when our protecting log fire had died down, a prowling lion pawed a hole in our tent just inches from my cot! It was a close call, but God mercifully preserved me. Later on in the journey there were some problems in feeding me. As there were no baby bottles in the African bush my ingenious father came to the rescue by using a punctured rubber ink container in his fountain pen, duly sterilized, to do the job.

"Finally, we reached Luma-Cassai. The rejoicing among the believers knew no bounds; but even more important was the impact upon the chiefs and leaders in the surrounding villages. Barriers were broken, hearts were softened, and freedom to preach the gospel of peace was not only enjoyed but exploited to the full.

"As a teenager, my most memorable trek with my father was a safari to find and chart the source of the River Cassai (in Angola). It was a memorable expedition because I was honored as the oldest son and also because I learned lessons that have served me well ever since. First-class carriers and interpreters were selected and everything we needed for rough travel was packed. Needless to say, we followed the course of the river and at times hacked our way through thick underbrush at a frustrating pace. Excitement was our daily diet! There was breathtaking scenery, heart-tingling scares, and mind-boggling statistics. Father was meticulous in tracing every curve in the river, registering every mile and recording every feature of interest and importance. Later all the research and maps were submitted to and accepted by the Royal Geographic Society of London.

"It was hard going, but every step was worthwhile. I came to know my father in a deep and intimate way. The Bible studies around the campfire at night, with the carriers and visitors we picked up on the trip, were so instructive and impressive to me at this formative stage of my life.

"We encountered tribes that had never seen or heard of a white man – let alone a missionary. I learned the validity of the anthropological argument for the existence of God. We met a chief one day who was out in the bush stalking game. He was as surprised to see us as we were to see him. Because he was not an A-Chokwe we had to use one of our interpreters to talk to him. Having established a bond of friendship with him, Father asked him a number of questions. Though technically an animist, he believed in a Creator-God. 'How do you know there is a God?' asked my father. Without a moment's hesitation the chief replied, 'How do I know that a deer walked over my newly-plowed garden this morning?' Then answering his own question he replied, 'I see God's hoof marks everywhere!'

"Father was so fascinated that we followed the chief to his village, where we camped for the night. Around his log fire, we talked with the elders of his village. Of course Father spelled out the story of the Bible from Genesis to Revelation. The chief was deeply moved and wanted to hear more; so we stayed on. In his own simple way, in concert with his men, he accepted the gospel – and later this was followed up by our evangelists from Luma-Cassai. But what struck me was the fact that this chief and his tribe worshiped their idols, using almost every sacrifice and offering mentioned in Leviticus. They observed (notwithstanding human imperfections) the Ten Commandments with the exception of keeping the Sabbath!

"Years since then I have come to understand the significance of such scriptures as: '[God] has put eternity in [man's heart]' (Ecclesiastes 3:11, NKJV); 'For the wrath of God is revealed from heaven against all ungodliness and unrighteousness of men, who hold the truth in unrighteousness; Because that which may be known of God is manifest in them; for God hath shewed it unto them. For the invisible things of him from the creation of the world are clearly seen, being understood by the things that are made, even his eternal power and Godhead; so that they are without excuse' (Romans 1:18-20); 'For when the Gentiles, which have not the law, do by nature the things contained in the law, these, having not the law, are a law unto themselves: Which shew the work of the law written in their hearts, their conscience also bearing witness, and their thoughts the mean while accusing or else excusing one another' (Romans 2:14-15).

"To me, the high point in all these discussions was the answer the chief gave to the profound question of how a mighty and holy God could communicate with weak and sinful man. 'How could God accomplish this?' asked my father. Walking over to an anthill, the chief knocked the top off with the heel of his foot. Instantly hundreds of ants scurried out and around their invaded home! Looking my father in the eye, the chief asked, 'How could I communicate with one of those little creatures?' Before Father could phrase his answer the chief broke in, 'I would have to become an ant!' In that one sentence he expounded those magnificent words of John's prologue: 'In the beginning was the Word . . . And the Word became flesh and dwelt among us, and we beheld His glory, the glory as of the only begotten of the Father, full of grace and truth' (1:1, 14, NKJV). To me, this journey was not only a lesson in cartography, but also in theology!

"We reached the source of the Cassai River and completed the objectives we had set out to achieve. Our skins were lacerated, our bodies were tired, but our hearts were glad. New tribes had been opened to the gospel and a young impressionable lad had been taught of God. This was a journey with a purpose, and the subsequent years have confirmed and crowned that purpose.

"My last journey in Africa, as a teenager, was from Luma-Cassai to Lobito Bay and then on to Southampton, England. The time had arrived to bring the family home for further education; so Father made the necessary arrangements to hand over his responsibilities and say the necessary farewells. It was a tearful time. I will never forget the send off. It was truly heart-breaking. I realized afresh what my parents meant to these wonderful A-Chokwe believers. In fact, chiefs, elders, and villagers surged around our compound during those final days weeping aloud and begging us not to leave. Finally, we made it to the nearest railway station, Vila Luso, and boarded the reserve carriage to make our journey to the coast. The engine was log-fueled and blew out such smoke, ash and soot that we could not afford to lower the windows without being showered and almost blinded! So we had to be content to

Dr. Olford, Rev. George Duncan, and Dr. Paul Rees:
speakers at Keswick conventions held in Japan in 1987.

swelter in the extreme heat. Again and again, the train had to stop to load up on wood and water. Of course we thought this was fun!

"The one serious concern we had as a family was the rather important matter of passage money for the tickets to board the *Balmoral Castle* to sail from Lobito Bay to Southhampton. Father had made the need known to his home church, but had received no reply. He had explained in his letter that we were traveling to the coast (Lobito Bay) because it was imperative to come home. The tickets for the train journey had been purchased and the reservations had been confirmed. No way could we change these arrangements after months of negotiation. This was Africa, 1935! What was more, we were told that we would not know the full price of the fares for the voyage until we reached Lobito Bay. That is just how it was in those days. But we had daily prayer meetings, as a family, for God's overruling and provision. So we planned to arrive several days before the *Balmoral Castle* docked. We stayed in simple living quarters during this period, so we spent most of the time on the beach resting and praying.

"Each day Father went to the post office in Lobito to see if there was any communication from England. Our faith was tested right up to the day of our planned departure. As he sat there praying, he heard his name being called. He hurried to the little window to see a smiling face. 'Mr. Olford,' exclaimed the excited official, 'I have a special mail letter for you.' My father took it eagerly and sat down to open it. There was a delightful letter from his home church and a money order enclosed. When he examined the amount, it was, to the last penny, what was needed for our fares on the Balmoral Castle! He hurried back to share the news with the rest of us and made us all kneel down and thank God.

"In a matter of hours, we were packed and aboard this magnificent ship—originating from South Africa, docking at Lobito Bay and headed for Southampton, England. In size it was one of the largest passenger ships of its day. It was named after the royal residence built by Queen Victoria in 1854 in Braemar, Aberdeenshire, Scotland. To the Olford boys, it was like a small town! It had everything including unusually wide decks that circled the whole ship.

"We quickly learned that we were traveling with royalty! Prince Arthur, Duke of Connaught (third son of Queen Victoria) was on board. Other distinguished company was the South African Cricket Team. In fact, as we weighed anchor and got under way, nets were put up on deck for cricket practice. I have never seen anything quite like it since. Wickets, batsmen, and some fielders and bowlers were used, as you would see at any normal cricket match. It was fascinating to watch—especially for the three boys. The team was to play England that year.

"Later on in the voyage something even more exciting was planned: a day's sports event, including running and sprinting. The latter had always been my strength since my school days at Wallingbrook School in Chumleigh, North Devon, England (when home on furlough). Naturally, I wanted to compete, but there was a problem. Before I left Luma-Cassai I had badly scalded my left leg just above the ankle. I wanted a last celebration with my African friends and volunteered to make some mandioch mush. In the process, I overturned the boiling mush on my leg. Father had been dressing it each day and it was slowly healing, but still very painful. So when I asked Father for permission to enter the 100-yard sprint (now 100-meters), the answer was an emphatic NO! But I persisted, and he made a proposal. He said that he would take me to see the ship's doctor and the final decision would have to be a medical one. The doctor looked at my leg, but also looked at my face. He could see that I was eager to compete. 'Oh,' he said, 'if I bandage it with plenty of padding, I will let you run; but only the race.' I was more than satisfied.

"The day came with a variety of events. I entered with a whole bunch of South African and British lads. The track was the widest deck on board. Prince

Arthur was present and fired the starting shot. I leaped into action and cleared the field and won! That evening there was a gala dinner where all the 'brass' was present, as well as the winners of various events and their families. At the conclusion of the meal and appropriate speeches and music, awards were presented. Of all the prizes I ever won in sporting events there is none I cherish more than the trophy and silver pencil handed to me by His royal Highness, Prince Arthur, Duke of Connaught! The wonder of that auspicious occasion, the thrill of the Prince's commendation, and the honor of receiving the prize still linger in my memory. Only one event will ever supersede that— please God—and that will be when I stand in the presence of the King of kings and Lord of lords to receive His 'well done, good and faithful servant!'"

"The immediate years that followed the family's return to Britain were busy with technical and theological training for a young man who, like Jacob of old, had to be 'crippled to be crowned.' As was observed in an earlier chapter, I had to learn that 'Only one life 'twill soon be past, / Only what's done for Christ will last.'"

——

"With my surrender to Christ 'to go or stay, come what may,' I traveled great distances and for long periods in the cause of Christ. Such was the 1947-48 tour of the United States and Canada.

"In the summer of 1947 I traveled to the U.S.A. with my sweetheart, Heather—to whom I had been recently engaged—and my father who accompanied us as chaperone. He was booked for meetings organized by the Christian Brethren. We sailed on the Queen Elizabeth and had the time of our lives! Heather was to proceed immediately to Moody Bible Institute in Chicago for special studies for overseas students while my assignments were under three auspices: first, with Word of Life; then Moody Bible Institute; and finally, Youth for Christ.

"I had met Jack Wyrtzen and his team in 1946 when he came to Newport, South Wales for meetings I had organized for him. Now we were in the U.S.A. at his Word of Life Camp in the Adirondacks. What a welcome we received!"

From Schroon Lake Stephen went to the Indian Park Bible Conference in Williamsport, and the Penn Grove Bible Conference in York, Pennsylvania. Looking at those early experiences, He was encouraged by the response of many to his preaching on "the deeper life" and to his appeals for men and women to come forward in clear-cut open confession of Christ. He was impressed by the splendid work being done by a handful of faithful men of God. He was also impressed by the Bible institute movement in the States.

Stephen Olford's mother had grown up near Buffalo, New York, so Stephen took advantage of the fact that he was in New York State to visit his mother's family. It took him fourteen hours by car to travel from New York City to the little town of Blasdell. Ever the evangelist, Stephen wrote: "During our brief stay in this place, we had the unique opportunity of meeting forty of our relatives at one time. This gave a real chance to witness to many of them who did not know the Lord. The impact made was evidenced by the number of them who attended a meeting at which I spoke."

A visit to Worcester, Massachusetts was soon followed by a visit to Camp Pinnacle in Voorheesville, New York. "One morning," Stephen recalled, "God broke through and the rest of the day was spent in confession, prayer, and with people getting right with God."

The next place of ministry was Providence Bible Institute, Rhode Island, for a Labor Day weekend conference attended mostly by young people. On Sunday afternoon Stephen Olford gave his testimony and called for a public declaration of consecration. Nearly two-thirds of those present took a public stand for Christ. Another meeting in the largest theater in Providence drew a thousand people and seventeen responded to the invitation.

At the beginning of September 1947 Stephen arrived in Chicago. Two things impressed him about this great Midwest metropolis—apart from the skyscrapers, the ceaseless traffic, the blinding lights (quite a change from Britain's wartime blackout) and the hurrying crowds. The first was that Chicago was known as Sin City, U.S.A. for its gangsterism, its political, commercial, moral, and religious corruption, and for its murders. One story, which went the rounds, concerned the mayor, who was head of a powerful political machine in the city. According to the story, he and two of his cronies were sailing on Lake Michigan in a small boat when it sprang a leak. It was decided that two of the three men would have to get out of the boat. A vote was taken to see who would stay in the boat, and the mayor won— by ten votes. The second was that Chicago was the capital for numerous Christian evangelical organizations, not least of which was Moody Bible Institute. Stephen was impressed by the school—especially by Moody's radio station which, even in those days, blanketed the entire city and its suburbs with the gospel.

While in Chicago for this brief visit, Stephen Olford had the providentially-arranged opportunity to preach in a liberal church. The previous speaker had been an advocate for atheism. "The Lord gave wisdom and grace," Stephen wrote in his diary, "and we had five grand conversions. The church was fairly shaken."

Next, Stephen went to Minneapolis to deliver three messages at the chapel hour at the Northwestern Schools (a complex of a Bible school, a liberal arts college, and a theological seminary). On the Friday evening there were 850 present. God broke in Stephen said, "Shall I ever forget the scene?— 400 men and women, broken and contrite, coming forward to consecrate their lives to the Lord. The confessions and prayers were something to be heard to be believed. God visited us in revival. Next day, and nearly all day at that, was spent in dealing with souls for salvation and consecration."

Beginning in October Stephen Olford was at the disposal of Youth for Christ while Heather remained at Moody. Stephen spent most of his time traveling Canada and the United States with Torrey Johnson, Billy Graham, Bob Evans, Peter Dyneka, and Cliff Barrows. "These were wonderful days of youth rallies, men's breakfasts, and other opportunities for preaching the gospel and ministering the Word. The meetings were larger, more representative, and possessed of greater potential than ever."

Meetings were held in Toronto, Smith Falls, Ottawa, Arnprior and Pembroke, all cities in Ontario within striking distance of the Canadian capital. The highlight was the Sunday morning service in Oswald Smith's famous People's Church in Toronto. The response to the call for consecration was overwhelming. The entire service was broadcast to a considerable radio audience—not at all the kind of thing one was used to in Britain.

Stephen Olford then returned to Chicago and Moody Bible Institute for an extraordinary week of meetings. "It was a holy privilege to serve with Dr. William Culbertson, its president." Stephen recalled, "We had revival. The Spirit of God swept through the campus. I prayed through the night with Dr. Culbertson and Dr. Philip Newell. Heather, my fiancée, was part of the whole experience."

The services at Moody were from 8 to 9 o'clock each morning with over a thousand students, some 700 staff members, plus faculty members. The meetings themselves were bathed in prayer.

"The first meeting made a grand start. The second was satisfactory. Then something just happened! It was God! I was closing the third address, with my own head bowed, when a spirit of conviction swept the place. Dr. Culbertson went to the podium and, with a broken voice, canceled all lectures and business for the rest of the morning and dismissed everyone to their rooms. Walking down the corridor to my own room I could hear the sobs, the audible confessions and prayers from the dormitories. Day after day there were endless interviews with students. The accumulated impact was tremendous."

Then it was on to the American West—Baker, Montana. Once again the sheer size of the country impressed the young English evangelist—twenty-four hours by train across the wide-open prairies and the Badlands, then driving through a heavy blizzard to Miles City; then on the plane to the far western cities of Spokane and Seattle; then down state Washington to

Portland, Oregon. "There," Stephen recalled, "we had a great Youth for Christ rally. Many souls found their Savior." Then back to Chicago by plane (eight hours in the air in those days).

November found Stephen Olford in Kansas City, in Manhattan, Kansas and in Grand Rapids, Michigan. "The people of this area," Stephen noted in his diary, "are Hollanders." Most belonged to the Reformed Church and tended to be somewhat suspicious of evangelism. Even so, God blessed. In one service seventy came forward in response to a call for consecration, and in the night service souls were saved, including a notorious drunkard.

Detroit, Michigan and the surrounding area came next—thirteen days of continuous preaching, interviewing and traveling. Over ninety people were saved and some three hundred surrendered to the Lordship of Christ.

"On the last evening," Stephen said, "a girl came forward to confess Christ. You can imagine my surprise and joy when she remarked, 'I refused to accept Christ when I heard you preach at the Beechwood Presbyterian Church in Newport, South Wales, but God sent you here (Detroit) to show me once again that the Christian life is the only one that matters!' It was, indeed, a classic case of casting one's bread upon the waters only to find it again after many days!"

Then it was back to Moody Bible Institute again. Stephen recalled, "I stepped up to the podium, remembering the revival experience during my previous visit. I had been invited to bring a special challenge on the need and burden of prayer. Hardly had I opened my mouth when I was conscious again of the same hush of the Holy Spirit, which had repeatedly fallen on my hearers earlier. On this occasion, some nine hundred young people reverently stood to their feet to confess their willingness to yield their lives to the indwelling Spirit for a special ministry of prayer in preparation for the coming Moody Founder's Week Conference scheduled for the following February."

In December Stephen traveled to Florida and the warm southern states. He left Chicago in the snow and stepped off the plane in humid, sweltering heat. It was another reminder to him of the vastness of the country he was in.

His first meeting was in Miami. "My!" he exclaimed, "what a meeting! God so convicted people we were there until well after closing time dealing with broken hearts and lives." One of the people who came forward was a popular nightclub singer. She told Stephen Olford that "she had long sought for reality, but had found nothing but an inner hunger, disappointment and disillusionment. Praise God, she found reality that night!"

On he went, to Palm Beach, St. Petersburg and the Tampa area. In each place there were "signs following" in the salvation of souls and in the hungry response of Christians. One afternoon Cliff Barrows took Stephen flying over Tampa. Back in 1947 flying was still an adventure, not the commonplace, everyday thing it is today. "He is an excellent pilot," Stephen continued, "and I felt perfectly safe. During that flight he invited me to take over the controls for about half an hour. After all, I was an engineer and his coaching was superb. I wrote to Heather and shared what had taken place, only to receive a letter back in short order with the sentence, 'Any more flying like that and I will return our engagement ring!'"

Jackson, Mississippi and Birmingham, Mobile, and Meridian, Alabama rolled by with the same accompanying evidence of the Holy Spirit's anointing. Though the services were smaller, the liberated preaching of the young evangelist resulted in conversions and consecrations everywhere. In Dallas he was able to speak to "thousands of pagan high school young people in a dozen different schools." Doors opened for him to speak both in open and exclusive clubs—all this in addition to the evening rallies where "the old, old story" proved itself still able to meet the heart needs of many.

The dawn of 1948 found Stephen Olford back in the Chicago area. He addressed a lunch hour meeting for ministers. "It was a memorable time of heart-searching and confession. We saw that until we (ministers) could shed tears of repentance and spiritual concern there was no hope of expecting our churches to experience the work of the Holy Spirit." He preached at both the Moody Memorial Church, and in Paul Rader's Chicago Gospel Tabernacle. "The Lord gave a great audience and many souls," he recalled.

Then on through winter snows to Iowa, to small places like Vinton and Ames and to larger places like Des Moines and Cedar Rapids. In Des Moines, Stephen shared a service with George Beverly Shea, a singer whose rich baritone was to be heard around the world as part of the Billy Graham Crusades. Stephen picked up the theme of Bev Shea's song that night "By Life or by Death," and used it as a springboard to urge the claims of Christ. At the invitation there was a surge of response and a high percentage of those who came forward were men.

Returning to Detroit, Stephen led a meeting where about two thousand young people packed the auditorium. Twenty-two came forward for salvation.

Then came the historic Wheaton Campaign (January 11-18, 1948). Wheaton is a bedroom community for Chicago and a mecca for religious organizations, numbers of which have their headquarters there. It has been familiarly dubbed as "the Holy City." Quite a number of Moody faculty and staff lived there. Numerous Bible-believing churches added to the general spiritual aroma of this well-to-do town. Stephen Olford was scheduled to speak during the day at chapel services at Wheaton College, a famous Christian college, and at the large and prestigious Wheaton Bible Church at night.

"The breakthrough started at the church," Stephen remembered. He preached on the Holy Spirit to a packed church on Sunday morning. Apprehensive at speaking in a college town, surrounded by well-taught theologians, he was anxious that his listeners understand that he was sound.

"Then came Sunday night. The crowd was somewhat depleted, but still substantial. My theme was the blood of Christ. I poured out my heart in what I felt was the essential gospel message and sensed unusual resistance. I can only describe it as hitting a tractor tire with a sledge-hammer! The harder I swung the hammer, the harder the words bounced back at me! I was disappointed and somewhat discouraged. I gave an invitation and I was never more shocked in my life. The devil just howled at me. There was indifference and absolute deadness. I pressed the invitation and no one responded.

"As I walked home with Dr. Joseph Macaulay, the pastor of the church, I invited him to pray with me for as long as he felt he could spare the time. My own heart was so burdened I wanted to pray through the night. As we laid hold of God it became very apparent that the Holy Spirit was leading me to change my whole strategy. So I stopped praying and looked into Joe Macaulay's face and said, 'Would I betray you if I ministered to believers rather than trying to preach to the unconverted? I don't believe there was an unsaved sinner in the audience this evening and I feel that what God wants to do here is a deep work in the lives of Christians!' Dr. Macaulay, who was a deeply spiritual and sensitive man, said, 'You do entirely as you feel God is leading you.' He left me as I continued to pray.

"Monday morning I spoke in the chapel session at Wheaton College; then came the evening service at the Bible Church. The church was two-thirds full. The message the Lord laid on my heart was 'Prepare ye the way of the Lord . . . And all flesh shall see the salvation of God' (Luke 3:4,6). As I preached on what preparing the way of the Lord entailed, in terms of spiritual issues in our lives, God broke in and I had to stop preaching. Every head was bowed, many were weeping, and I just sat down and waited as the minutes passed.

"Several prayed and broke down. The first man to walk the aisle was Peter Joshua, the brother of Seth Joshua, who was so mightily used in the 1904 Welsh Revival. He said, 'Mr. Olford, I want to say something. God has revealed to me the sin in my life. I have been preaching for years, but I am a hypocrite. I have been told by God to confess my sin.'

"That broke up the meeting. Dr. Macaulay stepped to the pulpit and said words like this: 'I rise to my feet to confess my sin to you, my people. I invited Stephen Olford to be our evangelist for an outreach to the lost. But

I have to state that we haven't prayed or prepared as we should have done. I doubt if we have even canvassed the area to invite the lost to attend these meetings. I also have to admit that in my own ministry I haven't had a passion for souls. I've been merely occupied in dotting my theological i's and crossing my theological t's to please the professors and the students who attend my church. My messages have not carried the burden and passion of an evangelist, and I feel I have failed my dear brother in asking him to do what is virtually impossible.'

"He had hardly finished that sentence when his wife came down the aisle and stood alongside him and simply said, 'I confess my sin also. I've encouraged him in his pursuit of popularity in this college community, rather than in seeking to reach the untold numbers who are out of Christ in this town.'

"With that a preacher in the audience rose to his feet and made a similar confession. That led to a time of unbelievable confessions throughout the entire congregation. We were there for hours! God had brought us all to the place of repentance, brokenness and readiness for cleansing and renewal. We went to bed very late that night.

"The revival carried over to the Wheaton College chapel hour the next morning. I did not even finish the message when God moved in and brought us all to our knees in repentance and confession. The acting president, Dr. Roger K. Voskyl, came to the podium and announced that all classes were canceled until further notice, and that professors and students were to form groups across the campus and engage in prayer and personal examination.

"The students asked me to cancel all further commitments in order to stay on at the college. They took up offerings to pay for all the publicity and costs, which had been incurred in connection with the meetings scheduled to take place on the West Coast. They phoned the various leaders in each city, pleading that I be released. They sent a petition to Dr. Voskyl saying, 'We have to go through with God. The revival must not stop!'

"Normally few people turned up in the college dining room for breakfast. However, the morning after I spoke on the importance of the quiet time hundreds rose up early in the morning to meet with God – and then turned up for breakfast – to the complete surprise of the dining room staff!

"Scores of students who responded during those memorable weeks subsequently left for the missionfield, or entered the pastorate at home. The five martyrs of Ecuador were among the number. Years later I learned from Elisabeth Elliot that her husband, Jim, immediately began keeping a journal of his quiet time as a means of self-discipline after hearing my message on this subject."

In his first entry (dated January 17) Jim wrote:

> I pray, Lord, that You will make these notations to be
> as nearly true to fact as is possible so that I may know
> my own heart and be able to definitely pray regarding
> my gross, though often unviewed, inconsistencies. I
> do this at the suggestion of Stephen Olford [a young
> British preacher] whose chapel message of yesterday
> morning convicted me that my quiet time with God is
> not what it should be. These remarks are to be written
> from fresh, daily thoughts given from God in
> meditation on His Word.[2]

Dr. Voskyl subsequently wrote: "Wheaton College was greatly blessed of the Lord in the ministry of Stephen Olford recently. He was mightily used in touching every heart on campus, whether faculty, staff and students in one way or another. There were quite a number who came to know the Lord for the first time. There were many more who were challenged to a consecration that, perhaps, they had never realized or understood before. At the end of the first week the students were deeply grateful for the release of Mr. Olford for another week. The messages on 'Reality' were heart-searching, heart-warming and very practical. The Holy Spirit was permitted to probe hearts and many things were made right with the Lord."

J. C. Macaulay added: "As I look back on the days you were in our midst as our special minister, and try to sum up my thoughts I can only use the exclamation of the psalmist: 'The Lord has done great things for us, and we are glad.' In many ways the 'great things' were 'terrible things in righteousness,' for the Word at your lips was a keen blade, skillfully wielded, and the Holy Spirit used you to search out the depths . . . So many in the church received specific and profound blessing that it is bound to affect the whole face of the church and lift the work to a higher level. I think I can truly say that I never saw such ready response on the part of our dear people to so high a challenge."

The 1948 Founder's Week Conference at Moody Bible Institute will long be remembered. Many were praying for these gatherings and God certainly heard. Dr. Maxwell Coder of Moody Press (and later Dean of Education) reported what happened on the Moody campus. He said: "A genuine work of the Holy Ghost was witnessed at the forty-second Annual Founder's Week Conference as the speakers poured out their hearts in searching messages from the Word of God. The large audiences were frequently bathed in tears. Heart-broken confessions of sin were heard. Prayer meetings were held at which Christian workers could scarcely speak, so deep was the probing of the Holy Spirit. Pastors, missionaries and other Christian workers, who have been longing for revival for years, expressed belief that God did a work during the conference, which will result in the kindling of revival fires all over the earth."

From Chicago, Stephen Olford went to Rochester, Minnesota for a thorough medical overhaul at the world-famous Mayo Clinic. The stress and strain of constant travel back and forth across the continent, overcrowded speaking schedules, the natural nervous exhaustion which results from preaching with abandon, passion and power to audiences great and small, day and night, and the spiritual burden for revival he carried everywhere in his heart, all made enormous demands upon his body. By now he was experiencing continual pain. He could no longer afford to ignore symptoms. He needed medical help.

Just the same he felt he still had a few more commitments he needed to honor. He went to Winnipeg, Manitoba for a follow-up meeting to Tom Rees's campaign. Then he took a long journey across half a continent to Providence, Rhode Island for meetings at Providence Bible Institute and elsewhere. The flight took four hours. Most of the way he had to take medication to alleviate the excruciating pain. It was a joy, however, for him to be met by his friends, the Carlton Booths, and the share the care and comfort of their home. The program ahead called for morning chapel hour sessions at the Bible Institute and also for evening evangelistic services.

"It is quite wrong," Stephen said, "if not impossible, to compare meetings in one place with meetings in another. Otherwise I would be tempted to say that the experience in Providence was the top rung of the ascending ladder of blessing." He gives just one diary entry by way of illustration. It records what happened on the Thursday of that week. "The days before," he said, "were wonderful and 'prepared the way.' The days after 'saw the salvation of God.' About 10:45 in the morning I began to speak. Suddenly—yes, just like that—conviction and a breaking down swept the audience in a manner that surpassed anything I have witnessed yet. Spurious confessions were instantly cut short by the Holy Spirit Himself. Men and women had to be real in order to open their mouths. The meeting lasted six hours, necessitating the cancellation of classes and meals. You can imagine what an impact this had on the evening rallies!"

Dr. Howard W. Ferrin, President of the Institute, said, "Testimonies are still being given to the spiritual quickening which came to many hearts and to the salvation that reached about every strata of society."

Stephen still had another eight weeks of meetings scheduled in the United States before returning home to Britain, but they all had to be canceled. He had a severe gall bladder condition which required surgery. The operation turned out to be a long one because the condition was far advanced and the surgeon had trouble removing the offending organ.

Indeed, the doctor told him afterwards, another week of strain would have caused serious complications. Throughout the entire ordeal Stephen saw God's protecting and providing hand.

The next big date was May 7, when Stephen Olford and Heather Brown sailed home on the *Queen Mary* to prepare for an even bigger day—June 30—their wedding day.

The year-long preaching tour had taken Stephen to over one hundred main cities in the United States and Canada. He had traveled well over 34,000 miles. He had held 1,096 meetings and had preached to some 132,000 people. He had recorded over a thousand conversions and countless consecrations. The figures took no account of people saved and brought into blessing by means of radio. Stephen Olford had caught a vision of what could be accomplished for God in a land where there were endless opportunities for radio and television evangelism and where creative outreaches were not stifled.

———

Almost twenty years later, in 1966, Stephen Olford was privileged to speak at the World Congress on Evangelism in Berlin, West Germany. A brainchild of Dr. Carl Henry, with the cooperation of Dr. Billy Graham and his association, this particular Congress was the precursor of similar events in Lausanne, Switzerland and Amsterdam, Holland. Stephen remembers: "I traveled from New York where I was then pastor of Calvary Baptist Church. For the return journey, I was graciously invited by Billy Graham to accompany him and his colleague, T. W. Wilson. We were to have flown from Berlin via Montreal and then head south to our home cities.

"We took off in rare form, but were told after fifteen minutes in the air that our landing gear had jammed! The captain then announced that we were changing course to land at Heathrow Airport, London. He explained that fuel would have to be jettisoned over the English Channel and that there should be no smoking and as little movement as possible. The situation was serious, but London had been alerted and fire trucks and all other emergency contingencies were in readiness. There was a quiver in his voice and a spirit of fear throughout the cabin. No food or beverage could be served, and everyone was to hold on! As the intercom clicked off, Billy Graham stood to his feet, and calmly said: 'Ladies and gentlemen, we are in the hands of God. Let no one panic. I am going to ask my fellow minister, Stephen Olford, to pray that God would undertake for us.' This was a tall order, but God gave liberty and clarity as I prayed for divine peace to fill all hearts through faith in Jesus Christ our Lord.

"The flight over the English Channel does not take very long (about an hour), but news of what was transpiring on that plane was already being announced on radio and TV programs in the U.S.A.! Indeed, Heather, who was at home with Jonathan and David, heard that Billy Graham, T. W. Wilson and Stephen Olford were on the plane.

"In the meantime, the chief engineer made every attempt to find out what, in fact, had happened to the landing gear—but without success.

"As we neared Heathrow, word from the control tower indicated that it appeared the landing gear was jammed in the mode for landing! So the captain, with extraordinary dexterity and bravery, prepared to land as we made the final approach. We could see foam on the runway, fire engines everywhere, the B.B.C., reporters and cameramen by the hundreds.

"Thank God we landed safely and nothing gave way as we taxied and turned around toward the terminal gate. The ordeal was over—except for a press conference and interviews galore!

"Knowing that news had already circled the globe, I phoned Heather to

Photo courtesy of the Billy Graham Center

*Dr. Carl Henry and Stephen Olford at a
pastors' conference in Novi Sad, Yugoslavia,
August 10-21, 1969.*

assure her that all was well, prayers had been answered, and that I would be catching the next possible plane straight to New York.

———

"One of the positive sequels to the Berlin Congress was a pastors' workshop in Novi Sad, Yugoslavia in 1969. Dr. Carl Henry and I were invited to minister to some two hundred brethren from countries behind the Iron Curtain. Heather had to mind the boys in New York, so was unable to join me; but Carl's wife, Helga, traveled with us.

"The schedule was extremely strenuous. In the ten days we were there we preached nearly thirty times—and all through an interpreter. There were delegates from Hungary, Poland, Romania, Yugoslavia, and the Eastern bloc. Looking into the taut faces of men who had been to prison for their faith we were humbled, challenged and enriched. It was a real joy for me to work with Carl Henry and we were completely one in the ministry. He covered the various doctrines and subjects from a theological perspective, while I treated the same themes from a pastoral and expository viewpoint. Expository preaching was little known over there and commentaries were rare. Through the generosity of our church I was able, on my return, to send expository tools to the English-speaking brethren. We were also able to dispense gifts to many of the delegates in great need and to pray with them individually before they returned to their countries. It was a moving experience and I thank God for the privilege of being a part of it.

"Two events took place during that visit to Yugoslavia that I will never forget. One afternoon Dr. Henry began his lecture with this simple statement: 'I want to speak on the subject of liberal trends in theology.' The words were hardly out of his interpreter's mouth when a dear old pastor stood to his feet and pleaded to be heard. In broken English he said, 'Dr. Henry, you have so far ministered richly to our hearts, but I must tell you— before you continue with your announced subject—that we are not interested in the trends of liberal theology! If you were to take a roll call of the pastors present, you would find that most of the brethren here have spent many years in prison because of their faith. Moreover, I can assure you that no one went to prison because of "liberal theology." Please give us something positive and profitable to take home with us!'

"At this point the atmosphere was electric. I was bowed in prayer for special wisdom to be given to my beloved brother, Carl. And, as always, he rose to the occasion. Setting aside his notes, he quickly and graciously acknowledged the pastor's point and then launched into his personal testimony. I had never heard him tell his story before, but as he finished, there wasn't a dry eye in the place. I had to speak after a brief intermission, and it was the toughest assignment I ever had to follow. In fact, I gave my own testimony. Carl's stock was always high in my estimation, but that afternoon it soared to the very heavens!

"The other memorable event was a picnic we had with the communist Minister of Religious Affairs. He invited us to his country cottage and laid on a meal for royalty. A whole pig was barbecued and served with vegetables, fruit and a variety of delectables. It was food 'fit for the gods!' Throughout this feast of good things, we were asked every question imaginable about our faith and its relevance to the rough and tumble of life. Needless to say, we preached the gospel and bore our witness. All this in communist Yugoslavia! The official eventually gave us a chance to rest on cots in one of his bedrooms. Carl and I lay there discussing this amazing turn of events. Suddenly it dawned on us that the room might be bugged! So we decided to quit talking and rest until we were called for tea and more to eat.

"God alone knows what our united testimony meant to the minister or his aids. Perhaps we will meet some of them in Glory, when all the secrets of men will be revealed."

——

In September 1968 Stephen Olford was invited to be the keynote speaker for the centennial meetings of the Baptist Union of New South Wales in Sydney, Australia. He gave an account of the trip in the November issue of his *Fellowship* newsletter. "I left New York on Monday, the sixteenth of September. On arrival in Australia, representatives of the Baptist Union of New South Wales, led by their president, gave me a warmhearted welcome. I was given a brief tour of the city and then taken to my motel room, overlooking Sydney's beautiful Hyde Park and harbor, where I met members of the press for an interview. That evening a dinner was given in my honor, at which time the Right Reverend Bishop Jack Dain, an old friend of mine, representing the Archbishop of Sydney, gave a welcome on behalf of Baptists and members of other denominations.

"The Centennial Assembly of the NSW Baptist Union officially opened on Thursday, September 19, with a communion service, held in Sydney's Central Baptist Church. The place was packed with delegates who had come from towns and cities all over the State. God spoke in power through His Word—so much so that a hush came upon that vast congregation as I preached on the implications of the Lord's Supper.

"The first major breakthrough in my tour came later at a youth rally in Sydney's Town Hall. Behind me a two-hundred-voice choir sang their way into the hearts of the three thousand young people who attended the meeting. Actually, there were three choirs, and after a program which featured all types of music, plus a pageant tracing Australian Baptist history I got up to preach on the role of youth. When I had finished, I made an appeal, to which young people all over the auditorium responded. It was a thrilling sight to see them make their way down from the balconies and the body of the hall to fill the space in front of the platform, and even a greater joy to counsel them in the things of the Lord!

"My first Sunday in Australia will long be remembered. In the morning I preached at a baptismal service, which was televised on the national network. The service was beautifully staged, and as a result of the message the producer was so impressed and so hungry to know more about spiritual matters that he telephoned me three times requesting an interview. The Lord had really spoken to his heart. That afternoon I addressed a men's rally, where I made a strong plea for reality in faith. When I asked all 'who meant business with God' to stay behind, almost the entire congregation of seven hundred men did so, many of them in tears. A number were also counseled for first-time decisions. In the evening I had the joy of preaching to a packed church at Gymea, a southern suburb of Sydney. There were chairs down the aisles, and again the service was broadcast.

"One day I had the opportunity of preaching to about two hundred ministers, where I stressed the need for spiritual anointing in their work. The fire of God fell upon that meeting, and there was such a hush that one pastor said later, 'I didn't want to leave that sanctuary. I only desired to wait in the presence of God.' I believe that this meeting was strategic for it determined the blessing for the rest of the meetings.

"Speaking of ministers, I had the privilege of speaking at a denominational ordination service where four candidates were set apart for the gospel ministry. I preached on the subject, 'Preach the Word,' and the Lord gave unusual boldness. I gave an appeal, unprecedented in ordination services, for expository preaching and utter reliance upon the Word of God. Practically all the ministers stood to their feet right in front of their own congregations.

"One morning I challenged 1500 women on the spirit-filled life—many of them pastors' wives and Baptist Union officials. Almost three-fourths of the number present responded when I gave the invitation. Following that service I walked to the heart of the city and preached to a crowd of about five hundred people at Hyde Park. The Australian Broadcasting Company carried the rally and televised it later that evening. It was thrilling to see people come from all directions in response to the message, and I considered the rally one of the highlights of my visit. That evening I spoke at a 'Work in the Homeland' meeting. At that service I outlined suggestions for the more vigorous prosecution of Baptist work in New South Wales.

Among suggestions made was that a tent or collapsible tabernacle for pioneering work in new towns be purchased. The following day a nurse made the first donation of five hundred dollars toward the project.

"A great missionary rally at the Town Hall concluded the centennial celebrations. I had been told that it was difficult to get young people to volunteer for overseas missionary work. The place was packed that night, and when I gave the invitation over one hundred young people came forward to indicate that they were willing to go overseas. Young couples stood to dedicate their children for missionary service, and at least one thousand stood to say that they had seen a new vision to pray and give. It was a powerful meeting!

"The three spiritual life rallies in Sydney climaxed a whole series of meetings connected with the one hundredth assembly of the NSW Baptist Union. God moved so mightily in every service that I had to reverse the invitation and ask people to leave who were not making a decision of one kind or another. The number who left decreased nightly. Out of all the meetings held in Australia nothing equaled those three evenings when God met us in revival blessing. One of the members of the committee said to me, 'I don't remember when the sense of God's presence seemed to be so in evidence.'

"While in Australia I also took meetings in such cities as Canberra, Newcastle, Orange, and Darwin where the Lord was pleased to do a real work in hearts. I was told that during the sixteen days I was in New South Wales I spoke nearly fifty times to more than twenty thousand persons. In addition to this I reached untold thousands by radio and TV. Space fails me in telling of all the blessings. Suffice it to say that as an outcome of these meetings in Australia a group of Baptists arranged to hold a prayer meeting for revival on the first Friday of each month. Tent evangelism has been launched in a way that has never been done before. There is a real hunger for literature on the deeper life and, above all, an entire denomination has been rocked for God and has been established as a force to be reckoned with in coming years.

"From Sydney I flew to Manila, in the Philippines, arriving just in time to address an evening church rally. Though physically tired from traveling and from days of strenuous ministry, the Lord wonderfully undertook and I preached for over an hour to an eager audience, many of who were regular listeners to our program 'The Calvary Church Hour.' The meeting had only been arranged a few days earlier, but so great was the faith of one pastor that he announced my coming to his congregation the Sunday previous, without knowing whether or not I was definitely available to speak. The next morning I met several Philippine Christians who took me to breakfast and showed me some of the Bible colleges in the area. I also had an opportunity to visit the studios of the Far Eastern Broadcasting Company and was able to see the great work that they are doing there.

"An invitation to visit Vietnam came three days before my departure for Australia, and was extended to me by the pastor of Saigon's International Protestant Church, the Reverend Gordon Cathey. After much prayer I felt that this was the leading of the Lord and I consented to come. Hurried arrangements for shots and visas followed. Unknown to me at the time, military regulations had changed since the February Tet offensive. On my arrival in Vietnam I was found to be lacking the proper visa for entry into the country, and so was promptly placed under house arrest. Handcuffs lay on the table, ready to be placed on my wrists, and I was told that I could very well be placed on the next Air France plane and sent to Europe, if clearance was not forthcoming. As it was, all consulates were closed, for it was Saturday afternoon, and it was only through the persistent efforts of Christian & Missionary Alliance missionaries, following a call to the British Embassy, that I was released and allowed through. I might add that back in the States my church was holding its monthly half night of prayer. Like Peter who was kept in prison (Acts 12), 'prayer was made without ceasing of the church unto God for [me]' and I believe that my release was a direct answer to those prayers.

"Right from the start my schedule was a heavy one, with six to eight engagements a day. I spoke at the Air Force Chapel, at the International Protestant Church, to American and Vietnamese war casualties in several hospitals, to chaplains and pastors. I met with top military leaders and government officials, who opened their hearts to me and provided me with a wonderful opportunity of telling why I had come. I had an interview with Gen. Creighton Abrams, a man of deep understanding and insight, tenderness and humanity, as well as a man of deep religious feelings. I was scheduled to have ten minutes with him but had forty instead. He asked me for every single copy I had of my booklet, 'God's Answer to Vietnam,' and urged me on in my burning desire to challenge God's people to pray urgently.

"I shall never be the same man again after my visit to Vietnam. What my eyes saw, my heart felt, and God did in me is indelibly stamped on my heart. My trip left me with some very clear impressions. The first is what I would call the horrors of the war. This was dramatically evident as I visited the third field hospital and a Vietnamese hospital, the latter containing four thousand war casualties. Just seeing these men with legs or arms blown off, eyes shot out, others paralyzed, made me sick at heart. However I was very impressed by the spirit of the men who were determined to see the war through. Their feeling was that to withdraw would be to pulverize the structure of the Christian church and to pave the way for the slaughter of Christians, who were already earmarked for liquidation. I saw the horror of moral corruption which always accompanies a war, and which has eaten into the life of the nation: little orphans, drug addiction, intrigue, black marketing. Then, of course, there was the destruction of the city itself and many areas around Saigon. I was given a flight in an open plane right into the war arena itself. I saw giant gaps where homes once stood, now completely devastated.

"I was deeply moved by the efforts of the church—particularly the Christian & Missionary Alliance, the oldest Protestant missionary agency in Vietnam. They were doing a colossal job in social concern: caring for orphans, providing wheelchairs, dispensing food and medical supplies, alongside of a steady gospel ministry (Evangelism-in-Depth program), designed to reach ten million souls. Everywhere I went it was evident to me that the church is very much at work in the midst of tragedy and suffering. I just couldn't help being overwhelmed by a sense of gratitude, pride and deep emotion as I looked into the faces of these men who were on the job—war or no war—to win men and women to Jesus Christ.

"One of the greatest things I saw was the revival going on among the soldiers. They were being converted all over the place. At one meeting, speaking as a dying man to dying men, the urgency of the gospel pressed itself upon my spirit, and when I gave the invitation fifty percent of the men came forward to make a decision for Christ. I shall never forget it. The chaplain in charge stood unashamed before his men, the tears trickling down his face and onto his khaki uniform. 'This is the greatest moment of my life,' he said, 'I am rededicating myself to God.'

"I came away more convinced than ever that we were not involved in a civil war, but rather engaged in spiritual warfare, against spiritual wickedness in high places, and that the only place it could be broken was at the level of prayer."

——

"Another 'spiritual safari' was a grueling six-week trip to New Zealand, Korea, Japan and the Philippines in the spring of 1984. Words fail to describe the full impact of the events that Heather and I experienced. We praise the Lord for protection in travel. There were some thirty-six take-offs and landings by plane. One bit of excitement occurred shortly after leaving the tarmac in Manila. We were airborne just about twenty feet when there was a terrific wrenching sound: a whole panel had blown off the underside of the plane! Fortunately, it did not affect our flight. For shorter distances, we were driven by car to places where we were to speak. God's protecting hand was on us in New Zealand and in Korea, where we narrowly avoided two collisions by inches!

"We thank God for good health throughout the trip. We weren't sick for one moment—truly amazing, considering the horrendous pace day in and day out. From the moment we stepped off the plane, we had to be ready for anything, whether we felt like it or looked like it. To most people, we had only been a name for 25-30 years; now they were meeting us for the first time. They went all out to make us feel at home and to maximize the time we were with them. We had to adjust to all kinds of food, to soft and hard beds, to chilly autumn nights in New Zealand, and blistering heat in Manila. When it came to driving, every country was different. In New Zealand, they drive on the left; in Tokyo, on the right; and in Korea and the Philippines they drive anywhere! Then there were the changes in currency. By the time we were accustomed to the New Zealand dollars, we had to exchange them for Korean wons or Japanese yens or the Philippine pesos.

"There were also the cultural aspects of our trip. The New Zealanders are mostly British in background and, therefore, conservative and reserved—that is, until their hearts were warmed and won. The fact that we were British was in our favor. We found Koreans to be very amiable and enthusiastic; the Japanese, gracious and polite. But behind Japan's technological advances we found a great spiritual vacuum, and our hearts were burdened for them in a new way.

"There was not much chance for sightseeing in New Zealand; there were too many press conferences, radio interviews, and extra meetings that occupied our time. Our main purpose throughout the itinerary was to preach the Word. We found churches, on the whole, to be quite small. The largest congregation in New Zealand numbers about seven hundred. All denominations and cults are represented, but we were saddened to see a great deal of division and confusion among Christians over secondary issues. The answer every time was the Word expounded and applied, and our confidence was strengthened as we witnessed its power to stir hearts, feed souls, and heal hurts.

"The original invitation to New Zealand was to speak at the Ngaruawahia Easter Convention in Auckland, but out of this came many more openings for ministry. We were in the major cities of Wellington and Christchurch, as well as lesser-known places. Everywhere we went we sensed a real hunger for anointed expository preaching. Radio stations HCJB and Rhema—very effective in New Zealand—had announced our coming, so we had capacity crowds. Some people traveled hundreds of miles to be at the meetings. The Easter Convention saw the largest turnout for many years. We shared the ministry with Dr. James Taylor III, grandson of the famed Hudson Taylor, and enjoyed precious fellowship with him and his wife. My Bible readings in Colossians were well received—particularly the message I delivered Easter Sunday morning on the home. When the invitation was given, the response was overwhelming. God met us in revival. Many wept in God's presence. This was followed by a communion service. We believe that one service will leave its mark on New Zealand for years to come.

"It was thrilling to meet many who had been converted through crusades we had conducted in years gone by or through radio (HCJB). One man said he was just a young Christian when he heard me speak in Minneapolis in the late forties and came into blessing; and for the past twenty-seven years he and his wife have been involved in church planting in Japan. Instances like this were repeated everywhere. Truly, when the Holy Spirit works, fruit remains.

"From New Zealand we flew via Sydney, Australia and Tokyo, Japan to Seoul, Korea—a journey of twenty-four hours, including layovers. Weary from our long journey, the hotel was a welcome haven. Nine million people live in Seoul—three times the size of all New Zealand. It has 3,500 churches, and one-third of the city's population attends church on a Sunday morning.

Dr. Olford with his interpreter,
John Masuda, at the Japan Keswick.

The Southern Baptists planned our meetings in Korea. The day after our arrival we drove some 35-50 miles to Billy Kim's church (he was the interpreter for Billy Graham in Korea). They have three to four services each Sunday morning, and I spoke at the third one.

"Three highlights characterized our six-day visit to Korea. First and foremost, was the Korean Christian Leadership Conference where we met with precious Korean pastors. One man, who had heard about the meetings through our FEBC broadcast, came 150 miles to be at the sessions. At first it was feared that these men might have difficulty in comprehending lectures, since many had never been to seminary, and half of them couldn't speak English. Scrapping what I had originally planned to bring, I worked up new messages and spoke as simply as I could. The men were so appreciative and could not praise the Lord enough for all they learned.

"This was followed by a retreat for missionaries, held at the U.S. 8th Army base in Seoul—a center used by various Christian groups. Again, God met with us in the preaching of the Word. There was one session where missionaries got right with the Lord and with one another. They confessed to bitterness and dryness of soul, to loneliness, and the temptation to quit missionary work altogether. It was a most moving time.

"The next day, I addressed sixteen hundred seminarians at the Asian Theological Seminary; and that night I spoke through an interpreter at the largest church in the world—the full Gospel Central Church of Seoul with a membership of over 350,000. Seven consecutive services are held each Sunday. I preached at midnight to a crowd of 15,000 gathered for their regular Friday night prayer service. Conducted in Korean, it alternated with music, singing, and bursts of praise and clapping. To hear 15,000 people pray in unison was unforgettable. I spoke on the release of Peter from prison in response to a church at prayer—people who knew how to storm the gates of Heaven (Acts 12). 'Do you believe that God can perform such miracles today?' and 15,000 people thundered a resounding 'yes' (in Korean, of course!). 'Do you believe that God can send revival to Korea, as He did in 1904-1905?' and again a cheer went up, like the roar at a football game. The power of God was so real in that place that we believed anything was possible. We left the church at 1 a.m. and they were still praying. How they turn out for prayer meetings puts us to shame in the West! God is truly working in Korea, and we could sense it the moment we entered any place of worship.

"A two-hour flight brought us to Japan, where we were met by Rev. John Masuda, who had been our interpreter on previous visits, and who had set up the preaching seminars. For a whole week we ministered at the Ochanomizu Student Christian Center in downtown Tokyo. Up to two hundred pastors, plus some missionaries who had come from long distances, attended the six seminars. How eager those young pastors were to learn! One half-blind missionary wrote furiously to capture every word. The lectures here were the most encouraging of any series we have done, and they were all videotaped.

"Perhaps the greatest thrill of our Tokyo visit was to speak at the thirty-fifth anniversary service of the OSC Center, founded by Miss Irene Webster-Smith. The spirit of that meeting was such that my interpreter and I got caught up in the spirit of evangelism and we were ready to go out on the street corners and preach to the thousands of young people passing by. Our Japanese brethren were visibly moved. From the service we rushed to catch the bullet train to Osaka, and on arrival we were whisked to a Christian center where some eighty pastors were waiting to hear a full hour's lecture. Following a quick break for supper I spoke at a rally of one thousand people. A second rally took place the following evening. Three to four hundred people responded between the two nights.

"It was election day when we arrived at the Manila airport, and the temperature was in the nineties. Fumes and smoke greeted us, while porters and street vendors swarmed around us, hawking their wares and services, while we attempted to locate a missing suitcase of clothes (it caught up with us days later). We were finally 'rescued' by Jun Vencer of the Philippine Council of Evangelical Churches. We were grateful to leave the heat of Manila and fly up to Baguio City, high up in the mountains, where the Navigators Conference was held. Here we met over eighty representatives from New Zealand, Australia, Korea, Japan, and Singapore. Each morning I delivered a Bible lecture on the subject of Christian leadership, while three afternoons were given over to interaction sessions, lasting two hours each. These provided some of the richest experiences we enjoyed. These men were not merely interested in chapter and verse, but the theology and methodology behind it. Just to minister to these men and their wives was a privilege. They took the Word of God seriously. As we were about to leave the conference, one Asian asked about the Institute for Biblical Preaching. 'Where is your Bible Institute located? Can I come? I want to learn.'

"Suffice it to say we came back with a new appreciation of worldwide missions. While we ministered to the masses, the exciting part was our involvement with individuals. To see the way the ministry was received was rewarding. All in all, I preached forty-eight times, not to speak of aftermeetings and 'mini conventions' in homes and at meal times. Heather's contribution was speaking, counseling and playing the piano. We saw the important role that 'Encounter' radio plays overseas, and we came back more convinced than ever of the distinctiveness and worthwhileness of our outreach."

——

Perhaps it is appropriate to close this chapter (which is only a sampling of Stephen Olford's many years of travel) with the type of report he would give his staff on his return. Whether in the pastorate or in itinerant ministry, he always followed the apostle's practice and procedure of gathering the church together and reporting on all that God had done in traveling and preaching (see Acts 14:27). Dr. Olford's homiletical secretary, Vicky Kuhl, jotted down his impressions in shorthand and later drafted an article entitled "Experiences of a Traveling Preacher." Here is her article:

> Shortly after 9:30 a.m. Stephen Olford walked through the front door of Encounter Ministries headquarters in Holmes Beach, Florida, greeted the receptionist warmly, and made his way to his office. Moments later, he gathered the staff together to share a report of his latest trip. After all, they were the ones who followed him with prayerful interest, so this was a responsibility he felt he owed them. As he talked animatedly, the mood is informal, the listening intent.
>
> "Thank you for your prayers," he began. "As you know, we flew from here to Virginia, where I spoke at the Trinity Baptist Church of Christiansburg. It was thrilling to see so many young people. That Sunday morning was a most terrific, fruitful meeting. Souls were saved and there was a real breakthrough. From there we went to Virginia Baptist Evangelism Conference in Falls Church, were I spoke four times on the man, the message, the method and the motive for evangelism, sharing the preaching of the Word with Vance Havner and Bertha Smith. On the final night I gave an invitation for people to come forward and kneel in prayer, asking God's Spirit to fill their lives. There was brokenness and blessing—especially among the preachers." His eyes moistened as he mentally recalled the scene.
>
> "Since then I have received several letters from pastors, telling what the conference meant to them. One wrote: 'Of all the sermons, the two on the message and the motive for evangelism drove me to my knees. I had to ask forgiveness for rebelling against God's guidance in the area of evangelism. We have

been involved in a program of evangelistic outreach in our church, but due to my own negligence it was about to die. Self had to be crucified. I thank God that Jesus is our message as well as our motive. Commitments have been made; God is blessing.' Another wrote: 'The Lord has really empowered me since the Evangelism Conference. I have been rising at 4:30 a.m. and spending several hours in prayer and the Word. . . . With the Lord's help I've led four men to Christ in the last week and shared with many more . . . [There has been] more power in witnessing and more results than I've had for a long time.'"

Dr. Olford continued: "Then it was off to Canada, where we held a Keswick Convention in the city of Halifax. No sooner had I arrived than I had to speak to a houseful of spiritually hungry people, whom my host had invited for the evening. The next morning I had to be up in time to speak at an eight o-clock breakfast. The Premier of the Maritime Provinces was there. Though a Catholic, he welcomed me 'in the name of the Lord Jesus Christ.' The Mayor was also on hand and later attended my meetings. The opening rally was held in the biggest church in Dartmouth, seating about seven hundred. The listening and sense of God's presence were real. Sunday afternoon I spoke at a youth rally and when I gave the invitation young people came forward eagerly. The attendance at the main rallies increased until two halls had to be used.

"While in Canada I had the privilege of giving the 'Dunlop Lectures' at Bethany Bible College in Sussex; and that night I spoke at another public rally—one of the biggest crowds we had. One busload came from seventy-five miles away through freezing weather. The first person to come forward and kneel at the front, when the invitation was given, was the president of the school.

"My final meeting was at a Wesleyan Methodist church. I spoke at the Sunday school hour and then at the morning service. I had hardly finished my message when God broke through. As the congregation sang the hymn, 'Have Thine Own Way,' people just moved from their seats to the front—some sobbing their hearts out. The pastor had tears in his eyes. 'This is the moment we've been waiting for,' he said, 'this is the beginning of a new day in my church.' Though physically spent, after such an output of abandoned preaching, I attended a luncheon that followed, where I tried to eat steak and answer theological questions at one and the same time. It was great!"

Few people, however, realized the adventures that often accompany Dr. Olford's itinerant work. For example, arriving at the international airport, where he had to change planes for Florida, he waited a half-hour for his luggage at the baggage claim area. It was nowhere to be seen. Neither were porters. A woman, waiting helplessly nearby with five suitcases, suggested that he might find his bags outside the terminal. Sure enough, he found one of them, and taking advantage of a huge pushcart, which happened to be standing there, he rolled it back into the terminal to the great delight of the woman, who in a gesture of appreciation and gratefulness promptly threw her arms around this knight in shining armor. An airport employee suggested that Dr. Olford might find the rest of his bags at the check-in counter for his next flight. So mustering all the energy he could find, he grabbed his bag and dashed across the airport. Arriving breathless at the ticket counter, he inquired about his luggage. The clerk pushed back the flaps to the motionless conveyor belt, revealing the two missing pieces which had jammed the carousel, causing it to stop. With a long pole, the clerk reached in, retrieved them and ordered him to open them up for inspection. Eyeing the clock, Dr. Olford remarked that he really should be getting on the plane. The clerk, puffing on his cigar, drawled, "Well, how do I know you don't have liquor in your bags? Where have you been all this time?" Pulling a sheet of paper from his pocket, Dr.

Olford replied, "Here's my itinerary, and here are my sermons," motioning to his briefcase. "I'm a preacher." The man waved him on and Dr. Olford literally had to run for the gate. The plane took off with just minutes to spare. All was well.

With the apostle Paul, Stephen Olford said: "I have traveled many weary miles. . . . I have faced grave danger. . . . I have lived with weariness and pain and sleepless nights. Often I have been hungry and thirsty and have gone without food; often I have shivered with cold. . . . [What popularity!]" (2 Corinthians 11:26-33, *Living Bible*).

Though, ultimately, the triumphs far outweigh the trials, one thing is sure: travel, for Stephen Olford, was never dull!

P.S. Shortly after this report was given Dr. Olford called from the airport and said that the loading ramp had gouged a hole in their plane, on the first leg of another overseas flight, necessitating a delay of two hours. A new adventure had just begun!

The last night of the 1950 Winnipeg-for-Christ crusade with over 4200 in attendance.

CHAPTER 7

The Evangelist

Do the work of an evangelist.
2 Timothy 4:5

In his memoirs, the renowned Bible scholar Professor F. F. Bruce tells how he set his sights on the world of scholarship and achieved all his goals. However one thing disappointed him: God never called him to be an evangelist.

But God did call Stephen Olford to be an evangelist. Sharing F. F. Bruce's remarks with the delegates at the first Lausanne Conference, when Stephen spoke to them on the gift of the evangelist, he declared, "I treasure the fact that God gave me the gift of the evangelist. It holds a very special place in my heart."

Over the years Stephen Olford conducted evangelistic crusades in numerous countries around the world. Some of them stand out as landmarks in his ministry. For instance, he remembered one of the first ones he ever conducted in London. He was responding to an invitation from Frederick Tatford, a leading elder, author and preacher in Plymouth Brethren circles. Mr. Tatford warned him ahead of time that he might encounter resistance from the elders of this assembly of believers because of the rigid views held by some of them. He urged him, however, not to hold back because of that.

The precrusade preparations were thorough, and much prayer went up to Heaven for an outpouring of the Spirit of God. The young evangelist set aside some days before the opening night to seek God's mind concerning the messages and to claim the anointing of His Spirit.

Stephen remembered: "We began with a youth rally on the opening night. The first innovation was the use of an organ and a piano! It was not customary for this local church to use such 'mechanical aids to worship' in their services. Some who came looked askance when they saw the musical instruments!

"The place was packed with young people and a spirit of excitement and expectancy prevailed. After the usual preliminaries I came to the pulpit and preached my heart out with a message aimed especially at young hearts and minds. God owned the preaching of His Word. When I gave the invitation scores of young people came forward confessing Christ as Savior and Lord. It was a beginning and we all rejoiced."

The next day was Sunday. It was the practice of the assembly of believers to gather every Sunday morning to remember the Lord at His table in the breaking of the bread. At such services no one individual took charge, no order of service was arranged. All was left to the leading of the Holy Spirit. Moreover, most people in the fellowship would subscribe to the teaching that required women to cover their heads on such occasions. This time, however, some of the diehards were in for a shock.

Stephen continued, "The service was invaded by scores of young converts who, as yet, did not know spiritually their right hands from their left. They were newborn babes in Christ, eager to follow up their commitment of the night before. As these new converts poured in and seated themselves some of the elders were outraged. The young were all informally dressed and, horror of horrors, not one of the women was wearing a hat."

The elders called a hurried meeting to discuss this flagrant breach of religious propriety. One of the leading elders was E. W. Rogers, a man well known in Plymouth Brethren circles as an able Bible teacher. He became the spokesman for the hard-liners. He demanded that all those present who were improperly attired, because of the lack of a head covering, be told to leave at once.

Mr. Tatford was scandalized. "No way!" he said. "These are but babes in Christ. They were invited to attend the service this morning. Later on they will learn what is expected of them. We cannot eject them now." A heated discussion followed but it was agreed to allow the newcomers to remain.

This discussion delayed the start of the service, but eventually things proceeded as usual. It was normal in those days during such gatherings that the service would proceed until such time as the Lord's supper was observed. Once the emblems had been passed time was allowed for any brother in the service to share a parting exhortation from the Scriptures. E. W. Rogers held his peace, waiting for this moment to come. As soon as the communion cup was returned to the table he rose to his feet and blasted away. He not only denounced the irregularity of the lack of head coverings, but attacked the crusade itself.

"Fortunately," Stephen said, "most of the young people had not the faintest idea what the man was talking about. Moreover, as soon as he sat down, Mr. Tatford arose, rebuked him for his conduct and called for a fresh vote of confidence in the evangelist, the crusade, and its results."

All this was quite a test for the young visiting preacher conducting one of his very first crusades. He must have felt like Paul when he preached in the synagogue. Stephen Olford, like myself, was raised in Plymouth Brethren circles so he fully understood what all the fuss was about and the religious shibboleths involved. He held his peace.

The crusade continued and God went on blessing His Word. The numbers grew night after night as keen soul-winners brought their unconverted friends. "Amazingly enough," continued Stephen, "E. W. Rogers continued to attend. He sat at the back, viewed it all, and kept quiet."

Then came the memorable night. Stephen spoke on the love of God and then gave the invitation. The first to come down the aisle was E. W. Rogers' son—the black sheep of the family! That was the final blow! Rogers buried his face in his hands and wept like a baby. His heart had been broken. He came up to Stephen later, shook his hand and apologized. They became the best of friends. The crusade continued and God gave a harvest of souls.

Reminiscing about crusades he conducted in Manchester, another English city, Stephen said, "I have led more crusades in the city of Manchester than in any other place in the world. I have held crusades, for example, in St. Ann's Church, an historic landmark in the city; every mile in all directions is measured from that church. When we had a crusade there we had to move right up into the balcony because the place was packed to capacity."

One of the first crusades he launched in Manchester was at the Houldsworth Hall, capable of seating well over a thousand people in the main auditorium and more in the tiered balcony above. Behind him was a wonderful committee of men who organized preparation meetings long before the crusade was to start.[1] Prayer meetings were started all over the city and were maintained throughout the crusade.

"Two highlights of that particular crusade have lingered in my memory," the evangelist recalled. "The first was a string of conversions which took place in one family. A lady came to the crusade and was wonderfully saved. Her life became so radiant she began to witness at home. Night after night she brought at least one member of her family, and before the crusade was over no less than seven people in that one family had come to faith in Jesus Christ. It was the talk of the town!

"Another highlight was rather unusual. It took place before the evening rally each night. Spontaneous open-air services were held along the main road that led to Houldsworth Hall. Young students especially who were on fire for God began to preach on street corners. People gathered. With testimonies and the simple presentation of the gospel, people were converted. What is more, the crowds followed these young people into Houldsworth Hall where they heard the gospel again. Many of them surrendered to Christ. On some occasions I shared in these open-air meetings. As a result of this creative approach to winning outsiders we had one of the highest proportion of unconverted people attending a crusade that I can remember.

In April, 1951 Waltur Laurence, an ex-Communist, slipped into the back of a hall in Manchester where Stephen Olford was conducting a month-long campaign. "Though I remember nothing of that first message," he said, "two nights later I was back to hear him speak in solemn terms on the most unpopular subject, Hell. God the Holy Spirit used this to convince me not only of its reality, but also that I thoroughly deserved condemnation. After some days of internal argument, distress of mind, and reading and rereading Mr. Olford's booklet, *Becoming a Child of God,* I was brought to confess my need of Christ and He came into my life."

Stephen Olford staged another Manchester crusade in the great boxing arena at King's Hall, Belle Vue Stadium (April 7, 1949), with about 6,500 people jamming the place. He preached from the boxing ring, rotating with almost every sentence so as to face each section of the crowd! Some two hundred professed faith in Christ.

Speaking of boxing rings, Stephen recalled the time he bought a ticket to a boxing match in Birmingham, England. He waited until the intermission and then slipped through the ropes, dashed for the center of the ring, seized the microphone, and announced: "Ladies and gentlemen, I want to tell you that a greater fight is going on in the Town Hall than you are witnessing here. I invite you to come." Before the astounded officials could intervene, Olford left as quickly as he had come. People came to the gathering and many were saved.

In addition to the prolonged crusades, which were so popular in those days, Stephen held one-night rallies all across England. These were well prepared and designed especially to reach young people.

One such rally was held at the Central Hall in Liverpool. Kenneth C. Greenwood, a schoolmaster, brought a group of young people from his school to the meeting. Stephen preached the Word of God and, as his custom was, gave the invitation to those interested to stay for the after-meeting. He always addressed those who came forward as a group before asking the counselors to talk to them individually.

Stephen remembered one young man who came up to him and asked for a personal interview. He was a giant, standing six feet, seven inches tall. "I led him to personal faith in Christ and then said to him: 'If God can use a little fellow like me, what can He do with a great fellow like you?'" That young man's name was Terry Waite. As a result of that meeting Terry later trained at London's Church Army College and went to Uganda as advisor to the local Archbishop. After three years he returned to England to work in spiritual and social ministries for the Church of England in Belfast and Bristol. Today, of course, the world knows Terry Waite as the Anglican envoy and hostage negotiator who went to Lebanon and was himself kidnapped and held hostage for nearly four years.

——

In 1950 Stephen held a crusade in the Canadian city of Winnipeg, Manitoba—a province bordering Hudson Bay to the north, and Minnesota and North Dakota to the south. At the time of this campaign, the population of this vast region was somewhat less than one million people, with half that population living in Winnipeg and its suburbs.

The previous year his friend and colleague, evangelist Tom Rees, had been in the city and God had remarkably blessed his ministry. He had suggested to the committee that they invite Stephen Olford to come the following year and build on the foundation that had been laid. The dates were set and Stephen was asked to come as the evangelist, his wife, Heather, as the pianist, and his friend, Dr. Carlton Booth, as the soloist.

Dr. Olford recollected: "God did a mighty work in the 'Christ for Winnipeg' crusade. The last two nights saw such crowds attending we had to double up on the evening meetings. Seldom had anything like this happened in my ministry before."

One story out of hundreds still remained fresh in Dr. Olford's mind, as he reflected on the Winnipeg crusade. "Just before the crusade," he said, "a young man named Edwin Mitchell arrived in Canada from England, determined to go into farming with his partner and make his fortune. A flood that inundated the area put a halt to his plans. The partners faced disaster. More than that, they fell out with each other. In fact they had a fistfight and Ed Mitchell lost his front teeth. He went away to think things over.

"He came back to Winnipeg and saw a banner spanning one of the main streets. It announced that a preacher from England was to conduct a crusade at the Civic Auditorium. Homesick and lonely, he decided to attend.

"Right from the beginning God dealt with Ed and early in the crusade he came forward to confess faith in Christ. Soon afterward he enrolled in a Bible school in Winnipeg, then went on for further theological training and was eventually ordained to the ministry."

What particularly thrilled Stephen Olford about this young man was the fact that he later became his associate at Calvary Baptist Church. "He proved to be both a man of God and a servant of God, a friend—one in whom I could confide, and a veritable pillar of strength on whom I could lean during those glorious but heavy years of ministry in the great metropolitan church. He was one of many who either went to the missionfield or who entered the ministry as a result of that crusade."

Now let us go behind the scenes of the Winnipeg Crusade to get a feel for the scope of this event. The Olfords arrived in the city by train in the middle of September. Enroute they bought a newspaper and were impressed to see three or four large advertisements promoting the crusade.

Thirteen broadcasts, twelve lunch-hour services, and three weeks of almost nightly services were arranged for Stephen. The committee had thoughtfully also planned several days of rest and preparation for the Olfords at Riding Mountain National Park before the grueling schedule began.

A week before the crusade got underway there were interviews with the press, radio broadcasts, and meetings with key committee members and workers. Finally, all was in readiness for the opening service on Sunday evening, October 1. "First nights are always worrying," Heather confided, "but this one, with the Lieutenant-Governor of Manitoba, the acting Premier, and the Mayor of Winnipeg all on the platform made it even more so."

But she need not have worried. Carlton Booth broke down all reserve on the part of the four thousand people in attendance as he led them in singing, "Tell Me the Old, Old Story!" About thirty people professed faith in Christ the very first night.

There were no Monday meetings throughout the crusade; it was a day off. Tuesday was work! work! work! Stephen had a broadcast in the morning followed by a noon service in Holy Trinity Anglican Church. Then came the evening crusade service. "We all feel too much is expected of Stephen," Heather wrote in her diary. "Once these broadcasts are over we hope he will have more time for rest and preparation."

By the end of the week attendance was increasing and eighty-nine people had professed salvation. The Olfords were strictly observing their rule: "No Visiting"; otherwise all their time would have been monopolized, had they responded to the countless well-meaning invitations to go here, there and everywhere. Just the same, Heather noted in her diary: "Stephen is very tired."

The auditorium was packed for the second Sunday night. Stephen preached on John 3:16. "How they listened!" was Heather's comment. She added that thirty-seven names were recorded at the conclusion. "We are not satisfied, but we do rejoice that souls are being saved every night."

The Mission was interrupted by Canadian Thanksgiving Day (October 9), and on Tuesday night the auditorium was not available because the famous jazz pianist, George Formby, had already booked it, so the service was moved to Young United Church. Stephen preached on the text: "Be sure your sin will find you out" (Numbers 32:23). The church was packed, but the atmosphere was notably different. There was hostility as well as conviction, Heather recalled. Only a dozen souls were saved.

The chairman of the crusade committee added his own observation (as reported in "The Life of Faith," October 18, 1950). He wrote: "Up to the present well over 160 persons have responded to the very challenging invitation. It is no secret that Mr. Olford makes it exceedingly difficult for any person to respond who has not had a genuine experience; and we find that those who come forward, for the most part, are absolutely clear as to the meaning of their decision, and require no help from the personal workers. The committee is saying that we have never heard such preaching in Winnipeg before."

Even at the hotel the Olfords found that the crusade was a general topic of conversation. The elevator boys, the newsstand girl, talked about the crusade. Even in Eaton's department store Heather was recognized by the saleslady as the evangelist's wife.

Wednesday saw Stephen Olford speaking at the noon-hour meeting and also at the university. In the auditorium, attendance had increased, but decisions were inexplicably down. Stephen "wouldn't be comforted," Heather commented. He felt there was a hindrance somewhere. Too many Christians were attending the crusade without bringing the unsaved. Yet, the next day—Thursday—many spoke of having been blessed the night before. It was noted, too, that only really live churches were cooperating in the crusade. The nominal church was either indifferent or actively hostile.

On Thursday night Stephen preached on the solemn subject of Hell and twenty-two people came to Christ. By the end of the second week it seemed as though messages on sin or judgment were getting the best results. An urgent call went out to all prayer partners as the last week of the crusade approached.

Sunday saw the auditorium packed again. Stephen Olford preached on the cross, but only fifteen were saved. He was depressed. He felt there should have been 150 at least. He had a cold coming on and did not sleep at night. After all, an evangelist is "a man of like passions as we are." Thankfully, Monday was the weekly day off.

The lunch-hour meetings continued. On Tuesday night Stephen preached against "churchianity" and some twenty-seven people came forward to receive Christ. To the Olford's surprise, their old friend Tom Rees showed up at the service. The next night he was persuaded to give his testimony.

By Thursday Stephen's tiredness was becoming chronic. The weeknight attendance had climbed to four thousand and although decisions remained modest, interest was growing. There was more prayer going on. One Baptist church held a day of prayer and fasting. Decisions for Christ were of a high caliber. A scientist confessed that he now believed in God and added that he would trust Christ. The superintendent of three large hospitals, a woman of about forty years of age, lay down the arms of rebellion and boldly confessed Christ.

At last the final day (Sunday) arrived. Both Stephen and Heather were completely worn out. It was 2:00 a.m. before they finally fell asleep and they slept through until noon.

"When we reached the auditorium," said Heather, "we saw the crowds gathering. By 8:45 it was packed and the doors were closed. They opened another hall and packed that. We were told that over two thousand were turned away. It was awesome to see crowds looking through the big doors and no room inside."

Stephen preached on the text: "What shall I do then with Jesus?" He preached with the anointing of the Spirit of God upon him. At the end he asked all the converts to come forward. It was an impressive sight to see three to four hundred people pour from all over the building, to be joined by the night's new converts. Stephen then went to the second hall and in the appeal there were many who came forward. "It was something none of us will ever forget," Heather wrote in her diary.

The crusade was over, but there was still work to be done. There was a final luncheon with the committee. All was sheer joy! Stephen emphasized the importance of follow-up and the urgent need to keep track of every convert.

The follow-up work began with four special meetings, held immediately after the close of the campaign in October and was conducted by Stephen himself. These were held in a central downtown church—Grace United—and were of exceptional value to the converts. The attendance for the four nights averaged between three hundred and five hundred people, and the messages given by Mr. Olford covered in a remarkable way the subjects of special interest and help to beginners in the Christian life. He was able to announce to the converts that the Winnipeg Bible Institute was starting a special evening school class for converts. At least one hundred people took application forms. The secretary of the Inter-Varsity Fellowship said that attendance at campus study groups had doubled since the crusade.

The next day Stephen Olford spoke to one hundred men at a gathering of the Winnipeg Christian Business Men's Committee and put the responsibility of follow-up in the months to come squarely on their shoulders. Then he preached on "A False Witness" and every man in the place broke down. The man who was asked to close the service in prayer choked up and was unable to get beyond the first sentence.

Back in his room, Stephen responded to an urgent request to go to the hotel lobby to speak with an Englishman from Durham. He went downstairs and there was Ed Mitchell, the young man who had come to tell the evangelist that he had been saved in one of the meetings and was heading for Bible school.

——

Some years later Stephen Olford was asked to conduct a citywide crusade in Norwich, England. "It was an unusual event," he said. "For one thing the Lord Mayor of the city was a Christian and had played a great part in the initial crusade preparations." The crusade itself was held in the largest auditorium in town.

The report, published after the crusade by the committee, makes interesting reading. Once Stephen Olford consented to conduct the crusade they felt they had "hooked a very big fish indeed." They discovered they had invited "a man who knew all about missions and who had suffered much at the hand of committees." They were impressed by his organizing abilities and by his absolute and unreserved dedication to God.

Under Stephen's guidance, prayer meetings were arranged all over the area. Bookstalls were set up in St. Andrew's Hall, offering a variety of literature to those just beginning the Christian life. Aggressive plans were made to publicize the crusade using all available means. The interest of the local and weekly press was secured. The slogan, "This Is

The Way" was adopted and displayed. Stephen insisted that four special meetings for Christians, to prepare them for what lay ahead, precede the campaign itself. Those meetings proved to be "searching, awakening, and disturbing."

The committee had a foretaste of what was to come when Stephen addressed a pre-crusade gathering arranged for members of the schools' Christian Unions and their school friends. The evangelist took advantage of the occasion to point out the way of salvation. No less than fifty-two young people, almost all in their middle teens from private schools and public high schools confessed Christ, including ten student school captains—leaders of their peers.

The campaign itself opened on the evening of Saturday, October 11, 1952 with a procession of witness. Three to four hundred people marched with sandwich boards and banners to St. Andrews Hall. One way or another it is doubtful if there was anyone in Norwich who did not know about the crusade. The first service was officially opened by Alderman W. E. Walker, J. P., the Lord Mayor of Norwich. He not only welcomed the young evangelist but gave his personal testimony.

The people came on foot, by bus and by car. Some were "fished" in off the streets. Lt. Gen. Sir William Dobbie of Malta (a national hero) attended one night. The Norwich Football Club announced one of the meetings over the loudspeakers at the football field to a Saturday crowd. Almost three hundred people of all ages came to faith in Christ.

Here is how the committee described Stephen Olford's preaching:

> His method is always to give an exposition of a verse or portion of Scripture. He uses but little anecdote and still less humor, but one is gripped from the first word until the last, and time seems to go in a flash. If one can withdraw one's attention from the speaker for a moment and observe the audience one notices that it is absolutely still. No one coughs, no one shuffles, and no one takes his eyes off the speaker. Stephen Olford's personal friends know that the effectiveness of these addresses, which flow from him so naturally as to seem almost extempore, has its source in hours of private prayer, careful study and intense preparation.

As to the invitation, the committee had a similar astute observation:

> This is the critical moment: the most solemn moment of the evening. Before praying, however, he

addresses himself to all to whom God has spoken during the sermon, suggesting that they say after him, in their hearts, a brief prayer which he repeats, and which involves surrender to Christ and acceptance of Him as Savior. He then deliberately breaks the tension by giving out a hymn which we all stand and sing. This is done so that no mere emotionalism shall move any to action that has not had its basis in a real spiritual experience. Meanwhile those who have already made the great decision are invited to come to the front during the singing to receive the right hand of fellowship. Before finally closing the main meeting, these are invited to stay for an instruction period to commence as soon as the main audience has left and the hall is quiet. All who are undecided, who do not perfectly understand, or who are in anyway interested are also cordially invited to remain.

"Two memorable happenings make that crusade very special to me," said Stephen. "The first is that half way through the crusade the Norwich soccer team was invited to attend. And almost to a man they turned up and were seated in a special section. On the same night, a Mr. David Sheppard, then studying at Cambridge University and already a famous cricketer, came to give his testimony. I recall praying with him in a little dressing room behind the platform, and telling him what passage of Scripture I intended to expound.

"As we prepared to ascend the platform I was called to answer an urgent telephone call. It was my mother speaking from Cardiff in South Wales. 'Stephen,' she said softly, 'your father is dying. The doctor says he may not last the night.' Needless to say I was shattered. 'What should I do?' I asked my mother, 'Shall I leave for Cardiff at once?' She said, 'No, Stephen, your dear father has asked me to give you this message. He said, "Tell the lad to preach the Word! Preach the Word! Preach the Word!"' Right there, holding the telephone receiver, I cried like a baby.

"With a heavy heart I mounted the platform and sat there, as the singing was going on, wondering how I could preach. But the Spirit of God came upon me. I picked up my Bible and went to the pulpit and told the congregation what had taken place. The atmosphere was tense.

"David Sheppard had given a wonderful testimony and prepared the hearts. He was an acknowledged sportsman and this had made a tremendous impact on the soccer players. Then I preached the Word, as my father had told me to do. To the best of my remembrance, there was a response both from the soccer team as well as a multitude of others. After the service the Lord Mayor came to me and graciously expressed his condolences. He added, 'All flags will be lowered in this city until you return in honor of your father.'"

The next morning Stephen left for his home in Cardiff, only to find on arrival that his beloved father had gone to be with the Lord he had loved and served so faithfully. Very deeply attached to his father, and feeling the bereavement most keenly, he remained only long enough to take part in the triumphant funeral and see his dear one laid to rest. Then he returned to Norwich on the Saturday to preach at the last two meetings of the campaign. Since those days he has met people all over the world who came to faith at that Norwich crusade.

Then followed the Duke Street years, when pastoral duties and family commitments kept the Olfords closer to home. Only in the second half of his ministry in Richmond did he yield to his evangelistic heartbeat and take occasional crusades, as time and his schedule allowed.

——

The first crusade he conducted, as minister of Calvary Baptist Church, New York City, took place in the beautiful Canadian city of Vancouver, British Columbia in the summer of 1961. Though surrounded by fir-clad mountains, its coasts washed by the warm Japanese current of the Pacific Ocean, it was a city that led the nation in liquor consumption and alcoholics. It also topped the country in drug trafficking. Evangelicals constituted not more than five percent of the three-quarters of a million population of the greater Vancouver area. The city was not noted for its united undertakings in evangelism. Only once before in more than forty years had the churches of various denominations joined together in such a venture. Yet this did not deter seventy to one hundred churches from joining hands to sound out the gospel for two weeks (including three weekends) in the Queen Elizabeth Theater, a new music hall in the city with superb facilities for such a venture.

During the weeks prior to the crusade, prayer was emphasized as the most important single factor in preparing for the meetings. From time to time, pastors would meet in the morning to pray and seek God's face. Two evenings before the crusade began there was a full night of prayer. The evangelist believed that where there is prayer there is power, and where there is power there is blessing.

Opening night saw the auditorium, seating 2,800 filled to capacity. Raymond McAfee (Calvary's Minister of Music at the time) led the congregational singing, directed the choir, and was the guest soloist. Heather Olford was pianist, and her sweet and gracious presence did much to foster the lovely spirit which characterized the campaign. The great redeeming truths of Scripture were proclaimed fearlessly—yet with a charming dignity—in the power of the Spirit. The combination of Word and music contributed to a profound and lasting impression upon all who attended. As always, the invitation was demanding and clear, the responses numerous and varied. At the end of the campaign over three hundred registered decisions were on file, each with its own wonderful story—among them a sea captain, a hopeless alcoholic, a professional engineer, a doctor, and a minister of the Dutch Reformed Church who had the responsibility of evangelizing fourteen thousand Dutch people in the Vancouver area. A high proportion of converts were young people and students.

Two years later, in the spring of 1963, Stephen Olford returned to England to conduct the "Croydon for Christ" crusade sponsored by National Young Life Campaign, churches of the area, and other Christian organizations. The effort was part of the civic celebrations marking one thousand years of the borough's existence. The civic recognition provided the borough with a brand new auditorium called Fairfield Halls, seating some three thousand people. The team could not have wished for better facilities, even though the auditorium proved too small before the crusade was over. Eventually folk who could not get into the main hall found themselves sitting in ancillary rooms, the coat room, and even the bar, to listen to the gospel over loud speakers. The manager of the Halls estimated that between 30,000-35,000 people attended the three-week crusade.

"The presence of God was manifest from the beginning, and we have seldom seen such evident brokenness and repentance on the part of seekers," reported Stephen at the time. "No less than 1,065 people were personally counseled, but that was only a token of the hundreds of men and women who came into blessing."

Associate evangelists, Frank Farley, Martin Higginbottom, and Don Summers (all British evangelists) visited youth clubs, schools, offices, and factories during the day—also the fire department and garbage collectors! In addition, the team reached out to civic and social groups, and paid a memorable visit to the House of Commons!

Three months after the crusade the impact left on Croydon could still be felt. At a Youth for Christ rally the speaker asked all those who had been saved at the crusade to stand up. The hall was absolutely packed with those who had found Christ at the crusade. Croydon's Spurgeon's Tabernacle reported some sixty people had been baptized and brought

Photo courtesy of the Billy Graham Center

Dr. Olford holds a three-week crusade in 1963
at Fairfield Halls, Croydon, Surrey, England.
Total attendance: 35,000.

into membership in that historic church. One local Brethren assembly tripled in size by the incoming of young and old who trusted Christ during the campaign.

——

Another crusade that carried warm memories took place in the fall of 1965 in Edinburgh, Scotland. At that time Dr. Alan Redpath was pastor of Charlotte Chapel in that city. It was he who initially invited Stephen Olford to come and conduct a three-week citywide effort in Usher Hall. At the time Stephen was still pastor of Calvary Baptist Church in New

York City. After much prayer and consultation on both sides of the Atlantic he accepted the invitation.

Preparations began. The Edinburgh committee represented an excellent group of people, chaired by Alan Redpath himself. The University, New College, churches throughout the city, and parachurch organizations were all recruited to make this a truly interdenominational effort.

Stephen remembered having a preliminary pastors' meeting the year before the crusade. "I delivered to those present my philosophy of mass evangelism. Following that meeting we had nearly two hours of discussion on the whole question of the need for such evangelism. It was tough going! My cause, however, was strengthened by the support of Dr. Skevington Wood, Principal of Cliff College who did a superb job of convincing many who were still wondering about the validity of mass evangelism. A start was made.

"Preparations were going ahead steadily when I received the tragic news that Alan Redpath had suffered a severe stroke and was entirely out of the whole thing. My first inclination was to cancel the crusade. When that news was communicated to Alan, who was still able to talk in a whisper, he responded: 'If Stephen doesn't come it will kill me.' So a new chairman was appointed—the Reverend Philip Hacking, vicar of an Anglican church in Edinburgh, and a young man full of enthusiasm. He did a superb job right to the end of the crusade.

"There were several things that made this crusade unusual. For one thing, I was able to raise, in the United States, all the money needed to pay for the fares, honoraria, and expense of the entire team. Traveling with us were Paul Liljestrand, Minister of Music at Calvary; William Hoyt, beloved teacher of voice at Columbia Bible College, who was our soloist; Richard Bennett, son in the faith and evangelist, who was responsible for outreach to students and young people; Martin Higginbottom, friend and evangelist, whose ministry was to factories, shops, and all kinds of places, including open-air meetings; and Vicky Kuhl, who handled daily office matters for the team. The fact that we were all coming to Edinburgh at no expense to the crusade made a tremendous impact on the committee and also on the city, since this was publicly announced.

"God worked in a most remarkable way. Mrs. Catherine Rose, whose task at the box office each night was to hand out counselor's badges and decision cards to incoming counselors, overheard some wonderful stories. For instance:

> There was a young man of twenty-five who was
> released from his second term of jail the day before

the crusade started. His family had disowned him. A local minister met him at the station on the day of his release from an English prison and took him home. He attended the first night of the crusade and was born again into the family of God.

A middle-aged man came right out for Christ. His wife had prayed for his conversion for nineteen years!

The crusade had an impact on many towns and villages around Edinburgh. There was a small village where no interest was shown at all and only the pleadings of a church elder to run a bus prevailed in the end. Eventually two buses came to the crusade and twenty were saved.

In another village a certain church was keen to run a bus but only four people said they wanted to go to the crusade. In faith the bus was booked and on the night specified forty turned up, thirty-eight of whom stood up in the Usher Hall to make a decision that night.

"Not only did we have overflow crowds in a nearby church, by means of closed-circuit television, but every night there were youth meetings in another part of the city where drug addicts and wayward young people were drawn by the music, the testimonies, and the plain preaching of the gospel. One Thursday night a young street fisher approached a very drunk man with an invitation to attend a late night special in Romano's café. 'I am not sure if I'll manage,' he said. 'You'll be welcome,' was the reply. These words sank home and some time later on arrival at the café (he was allowed in though with some misgivings) the gospel penetrated, despite his drunken condition, and faith was born. Friday was spent reading Billy Graham's book, *The Secret of Happiness,* and John's Gospel. On Saturday night in the Usher Hall he stood up boldly for the Lord Jesus Christ, a transformed man."

Stephen continued, "One night I gave my testimony. A Unitarian minister, who was present, published an article in the leading newspaper the next day challenging everything I said. This started a veritable debate between able members of the committee and this Unitarian minister. Instead of hurting the crusade, the publicity brought out even more people curious to hear what was going on.

"One very touching aspect of these meetings was the presence of Alan Redpath, who by now had partly recovered from his stroke. I can still see him, his left hand paralyzed, his face slightly distorted, his walk rather unsteady. He never missed a night of the crusade though it lasted almost a month! His own daughter, Caroline, came forward one night and subsequently started one of the most flourishing Christian Unions in her school.

"But I think the most striking event took place during the closing moments of one mighty evening rally, when God seemed to come down in a special way. When I gave the invitation a Scottish minister, dressed in clerical garb, came down the center aisle with twelve of his elders. He and all his men were gloriously saved that night. Back at the hotel we had a praise meeting.

"At the conclusion of the crusade I accepted an invitation to visit his church on the Sunday afternoon before our final rally at Usher Hall. Despite rainy conditions his church was packed. He wanted me to deliver a message to his people. I insisted that he give his testimony first and that some of his elders also share what God had done in their lives. By the time they were finished there was very little I had to say. There was hardly a dry eye in the congregation. A simple message and an invitation brought most of his people to the foot of the cross in repentance to yield their lives to the sovereignty of our glorious Lord.

"During the crusade itself the choir, led by Paul Liljestrand, sang so magnificently that people used to fill Usher Hall just to hear them practice for the evening rally. Several years later I visited Edinburgh and the choir was still intact and singing at all kinds of events.

"God used Bill Hoyt as he sang night by night, and my wife Heather as she played the piano and, indeed the whole team. I had the privilege of addressing the students at New College, and two men from America, who were there studying for the ministry, were saved. I also spoke at the University and many of those fine students came to the meetings and were subsequently brought to faith in Christ. The BBC heard of all that was going on and had us broadcast a half-hour program to the whole nation.

—　—

In 1973 Stephen Olford returned to Manchester for a mini crusade. A tent seating 5,000 people was erected at Platt Fields, and three thousand extra chairs were set up to handle the overflow crowds. The tent was packed night after night. During the eleven-day crusade some 35,000-40,000 people attended the meetings. A high percentage was young people. More than 1,200 confessed faith in Christ and thousands of Christians came into a new understanding of the lordship of Christ and the fullness of the Spirit in their lives. On the final Sunday afternoon Stephen spoke on the subject of marriage. Scores of couples came forward to get right with God and each other. Within a week of the crusade one pastor reported that a member of his church had already led three generations of his family to Christ.

——

Perhaps the most rewarding and abiding results of Stephen Olford's crusading ministry took place in the beautiful city of Messina, Sicily in September, 1974. Through a series of events he had come to know and love a man by the name of Mr. Anthony Rossi, a native of Messina, who had come to the United States as a boy, worked his way up to fame and fortune to become the king of the Tropicana orange juice business in Bradenton, Florida. During his rise to prominence he was saved and sold out to God. Indeed, his only purpose in making money was to use it for the furtherance of the gospel.[2]

His first burden, however, was for his large family in the city of Messina. So every September he would travel to Sicily to evangelize his relatives. Initially, he visited them one by one, distributing tracts and witnessing to the saving power of Christ. Many were converted and discipled. Then came the day when he had a supporting nucleus to launch a "crusade." Preparations were made and Stephen Olford was invited to be the evangelist for the nine-day effort.

One night Dr. Olford was preaching on John 14:6 when God poured out His Spirit and many souls responded. Among them was a family of four—father, mother, and two sons. Stephen counseled with each one (through an interpreter) and led them all to a saving faith in Christ. The father later became the first Gideon in Messina; the mother went on to be a worker in the church; and the younger of the boys went back to school to witness for his new Master. But it was the fourth member of the family—eighteen-year-old Gaetano Sottile—who captured Stephen's imagination. But let "Guy" tell his own story:

> Up until 1974 my life was without peace and satisfaction; but on the 23rd of September something great happened to me: Jesus Christ came into my life. I was raised in a Catholic family. God, for me, was a God of wrath, and I thought I had to please Him in order to gain eternal life. But how could I please Him without the power of Jesus in

me? That was impossible and, therefore, I forsook God and turned to the way of the world. One day my family and I went to a crusade meeting, organized by Mr. Anthony Rossi. The speaker was Dr. Stephen Olford and his text was John 14:6—'Jesus saith . . . I am the way, the truth, and the life.' I was seeking for a way and I heard that Jesus was the way. In a world of corruption I was seeking for truth and I heard that Jesus was the truth. I believed that religion was a part of my life, but I heard that life in Christ was the only life worth living. I felt terrible. My life up till then could be compared to the description of the earth in Genesis 1:2—'without form [waste] and void.' I wondered what I should do in order to get the love of Jesus Christ and learned that the gift of God was free; all I had to do was to accept it. Since Jesus Christ came into my life I have a joy and peace in my heart because I know that Christ lives in me. Now I can say that I have the power to please God and walk in His command-ments, because it is no longer Guy who lives, but Jesus in him.[3]

After Gaetano gave his life to Jesus he felt an inward desire to know more about Him. The Lord opened the way for him to come to the States to study at Columbia Bible College. He learned English and began to dream about reaching his own people with the gospel message. Knowing that only six percent of Italy's 57.4 million people are evangelicals, he yearned to give the rest an opportunity to have a personal relationship with a living Savior. In 1983 this vision evolved into what is now Italy For Christ, the first Italian evangelistic association. Stephen Olford offered to serve as an advisor on his board.

Guy began holding tent crusades in various places, including Naples, Rome, and Sicily. Wherever he went hundreds of souls came to know the Lord, including drug addicts, criminals, Mafia members, a nationally-known soccer player, and even the head of the Mormon church in Naples. The crime rate dropped so dramatically after the crusade in Naples that the city offered them property for a church. Today that church numbers over 240.

In November, 1991 Gaetano preached to thousands of people of Italian descent in Buenos Aires, Mardel Plata, and Rosario, Argentina during Billy Graham's crusade there. He appeared on radio and TV, was interviewed by the press and saw between 400-500 people make first-time decisions to receive Jesus Christ as their personal Savior. Prayer was aimed at the known houses of Mafia-run prostitution, as well as the eighteen centers of witchcraft scattered throughout the 'El Puerto' zone. Among the converts were chief spiritists, prostitutes, and a variety of criminals.[4]

As Stephen Olford has read and reflected on the exploits for God of so many of his sons and daughters in the faith, his sincere reaction has been, "I have no greater joy than to hear that my children walk in truth" (3 John 4).

———

It was stated at the beginning of this chapter, and it must be stated again: Stephen Olford was an evangelist. His convictions on this subject have been expressed on many occasions. But once more let us observe what he had to say on the subject of evangelism:

"To understand the true nature of the ministry of the evangelist, we need to think, first, of his gift, and then of his work. In other words, the New Testament reveals that there is such a thing as the evangelistic gift. The ascended Lord 'gave gifts unto men. . . . some, evangelists' (Ephesians 4:8,11). Now the gift of the evangelist is one of five enumerated in Paul's list. Many scholars maintain that the first two that are named are foundational and, therefore, restricted to the early apostles and prophets. Be that as it may, it cannot be denied that there were apostles after those technically known as 'the twelve,' among whom Paul includes himself. There was, for instance, Barnabas (Acts 4:36) who was called an apostle; also Epaphroditus who was so designated (Philippians 2:25). The word 'apostle' of course, means 'messenger' or 'sent one.' And I like to think that this gift is still represented by missionaries who go forth to the far-flung places of the earth as the sent ones or messengers of the local church.

"Then there are prophets. Without doubt, a certain element of the prophetic ministry ceased with the establishment of the early church. But let us not forget that the missionary church of Antioch had prophets (Acts 13:1), and that there must be a continuing prophetic ministry in the church if Paul's definition in 1 Corinthians 14:3 is to be taken seriously. There he says: 'But he who prophesies speaks edification and exhortation and comfort to men' (NKJV). As a preacher, then, a prophet's work is described as edification, exhortation and consolation. There is also a predictive element in this unique ministry of the prophet.

"Then we come to pastors and teachers. The pastor is a shepherd whose supreme task is to guide and guard the flock, whereas the teacher is envisaged in the New Testament as the instructor and expositor of established Christian doctrine. In contrast to the prophet, the teacher does not utter fresh revelations, but rather explains and applies truth already known.

"Now sandwiched between apostles and prophets, on the one hand, and pastors and teachers, on the other, is the evangelist. Before we go on to consider the function of the evangelist let me underscore the fact that the evangelist is a gift to the church from the risen Lord. He is so positioned, in the divine economy, as to hold together that which is fundamental and that which is developmental in the life of the church.

"Having established what we understand as the evangelistic gift, consider the evangelistic work. Writing to his son in the faith, Paul exhorted Timothy, 'do the work of an evangelist' (2 Timothy 4:5). The word *evangelist* is a noun taken from the verb 'to announce the good news' and is usually translated in our English Bibles as 'preaching the gospel.' In simple terms, the evangelist is the herald or an announcer of the good news of the gospel. In the words of Dr. William Temple, 'The task of the evangelist is so to present Christ to men and women, in the power of the Holy Spirit, that they shall come to put their trust in God through Him, and confessing Christ as Lord seek to serve Him in the fellowship of the church.'

"It is interesting to note that of the three mentions in the New Testament of the noun evangelist two of them describe the twofold aspect of the evangelist's task. The first is that of personal evangelism through the local church. Paul, as we have seen already, exhorted Timothy to 'do the work of an evangelist' in the church at Ephesus. Now whereas this undoubtedly included public preaching, the exhortation more probably had reference to his personal work among the unconverted contacts that attended the local assembly. The second New Testament reference is to Philip, who is described as 'the evangelist' (Acts 21:8). His ministry was, undoubtedly, a public one, and included what we term today as mass evangelism. Although he was capable of personally leading the Ethiopian eunuch to a saving knowledge of Christ, he is seen at his best throughout the Acts of the Apostles in citywide crusades. We are told, for instance, that 'Philip went down to the city of Samaria, and preached Christ unto them,' and such was the impact on the multitudes that Luke tells us 'there was great joy in that city' (Acts 8:5,8). Later we read that 'Philip . . . preached in all the cities, till he came to Caesarea' (Acts 8:40).

"So we see there is a place for mass evangelism in the total activity of the church. Our Lord preached to crowds during His own ministry; and we cannot but recall the effective preaching of Peter and of Paul to large congregations. Speaking of such mass evangelism, Dr. James S. Stewart has rightly said that 'there is clear evidence that there is still a place for this type of evangelism within the total strategy of the church's mission.'

"Before we leave this part of our subject, it might be well to observe that the New Testament makes it unmistakably clear that the evangelist's task is not primarily sociological or ecclesiastical, but rather evangelistic. We cannot read the Acts of the Apostles or the Epistles without observing that the sociological aspects of the church's witness was rather a matter of follow-up to evangelistic enterprise. Archbishop Temple confirms this when he said: 'Social witness is both a preparation for evangelism and a consequence of it.' In other words, it comes before and after, but it is not evangelism itself. Then it is important to note that when Paul writes to the Corinthians he says: 'Christ sent me not to baptize, but to preach the gospel' (1 Corinthians 1:17). This was not because Paul was uninterested in the ordinances and government of the local church; on the contrary, he writes more on these subjects than anyone else in the New Testament. Rather, he was making the point that his task as an evangelist was to preach the gospel. It is revealing to learn that in his evangelistic endeavors it was usually on his return journey that he strengthened the souls of the disciples, ordained elders and set up church government (Acts 14:22-23).

"So the task of the evangelist, whether in personal work or in public proclamation, is supremely that of declaring the message of the living Christ with a view to making disciples of all nations."

———

This is but a partial record of "all that Jesus began to do" through the crusade ministry of Stephen Olford. There were other crusades in Barking, Lurgan, Nelson, Derbe, Llandrindod Wells, and Pontypridd. The years have come and gone, but thousands still visualize the day when they said an eternal "yes" to the Son of God. In their mind's eye they see again the great crowds, hear the stirring choir, listen to the young evangelist, sense the intense listening, and recall how they moved out during the hymn of appeal, detaching themselves from the crowd and slowly making their way to grip the evangelist by the hand, often in tears, but all with a "Christ for me" determination written across their faces.

"The lasting effects of a city crusade are beyond computation," said Stephen Olford. "I am convinced that God is glorified by such efforts. It is also clear from experience that churches are strengthened, revived and united. Souls are saved, lives are transformed, and, to an extent not often realized, the life of the church is purified. Truly, a paean of praise has ascended to Heaven, over the years, from pastors, churches and converts. Their united chorus has been: 'The Lord hath done great things . . . whereof we are glad'" (Psalm 126:3).

Stephen Olford during his pastorate
at Calvary Baptist Church in New York.

CHAPTER 8

The Pastor

He gave some, ... evangelists; and some,
pastors and teachers.
Ephesians 4:11

Stephen Olford had his spiritual upbringing among the Plymouth Brethren. This movement, which rose to prominence in the 1800s, represented a Spirit-led revolt against the dead religious establishment of the day.

From its early beginnings an astonishing galaxy of able and godly men carried the movement forward. Their ranks included a large number of professional men and members of the British nobility. There were men like John Nelson Darby (related, incidentally, to Lord Nelson, Britain's most famous admiral), a man of sheer spiritual genius. Almost as a sideline, he translated the Bible out of the original languages into four modern European languages. There was the saintly George Mueller of whom it was said that in his lifetime "agnosticism did not dare to raise its head in Bristol" where he lived and ministered. There was Sir Robert Anderson, head of Britain's renowned Scotland Yard, a man with a keen intellect. There was William Kelly of whom Spurgeon said that he "had a mind made for the universe." There was Samuel P. Tregelles, one of the great authorities on the original Biblical text of his day, and many more who were of equal genius and ability.

The early Brethren rediscovered a number of key Bible truths. For instance, they went back to a literal, grammatical, cultural method of Bible interpretation and so rediscovered dispensationalism as an important key to understanding the Scriptures. They rescued the truth of the second coming of Christ from the debris of confusion, where it had been buried by prevailing, popular theology. They rediscovered the truth of the priesthood of all believers. They recognized the oneness of the body of Christ, the importance of the Lord's Supper, the key role of the local church in sending forth missionaries, and the necessity for missionaries and other fulltime workers to trust the Lord directly for their financial support and personal guidance.

The Brethren movement took rapid root in Britain and in a number of other countries. It produced an extraordinarily high percentage of missionaries. Stephen Olford's parents were Plymouth Brethren missionaries in Angola. Its teachers, many of them able and gifted men, were usually laymen rising to prominence from the pew rather than the pulpit. In its early days the movement made a tremendous impact on a world tired of a dead religious formalism. The early leaders of the movement revolted against denominationalism in all its forms and especially against clericalism. It adopted the use of scriptural universals to describe its people and its gatherings. They used terms such as *believers, Christians, saints, brethren,* and *disciples* to describe their status, and avoided denominational labels which they considered divisive and unscriptural. Their gatherings were called *assemblies.* The *church* was not the edifice down the street but the corporate body of believers themselves. Doubtless the movement would have had even greater influence had its leaders not entered into bitter squabbles among themselves over hair-splitting differences.

In spite of these tragic internal squabbles, such was the spiritual force of the movement that it became the predominant Christian group in countries like Italy, Egypt and Argentina. Its teachers produced libraries of useful commentaries. Men like Henry Morehouse impacted men like D. L. Moody. The books of Harry Ironside, later the beloved pastor of Moody Memorial Church, and of F. F. Bruce, the scholar and theologian (to name but two of their prominent authors), have found their way into the libraries of Bible students all over the world.

It was essentially the ecclesiology of the Plymouth Brethren, however, that put them at odds with the rest of the Christian world. In general, and for many years, they stood opposed to the pastoral system common to most churches. In the view of the Brethren, a local church should have a plurality of pastors. Human ordination was not necessary. The local assembly of believers should be governed by its qualified and spiritually gifted elders who should also be its shepherds or pastors. The pulpit should not be dominated, in their view, by only one man; it should be open to anyone in the fellowship with the necessary spiritual gifts. Each member of the local church should be encouraged to discover, develop, and exercise his spiritual gift. If these include the gift of evangelism or teaching, the pulpit should be available for him to use that gift for the evangelization of the lost and the edification of the saved.

The Brethren are conservative in their theology, evangelical, Bible-believing, missionary-minded Christians. They are frequently found active in parachurch organizations. They appreciate good preaching. They are usually supportive of evangelistic crusades and missionary outreach. They tend to be suspicious of denominationalism and some are exclusive in their fellowship.

When the Olford family settled in Newport, South Wales, they belonged to the fellowship of a relatively large Brethren assembly and lived in a missionary home owned and maintained by this group.

The assembly ran a Sunday school that numbered over a thousand members—a considerable achievement for any British church in those days. The membership was split down the middle along theological lines. One group stood for "the old paths" and a narrow exclusivism. The other group was open in its fellowship and willing to cooperate with believers in the denominations. The Olfords gravitated automatically toward the open group. Indeed, Stephen in particular soon found himself in the bad graces of the so-called "exclusives."

The more conservative members were opposed to the Olfords' identification with the Soldiers' and Airmens' Christian Association—an organization that ministered to large numbers of wartime military personnel in town. They considered such an affiliation to be sectarian. Indeed, the leaders of this faction would have liked to bind Stephen Olford with the cords of their own narrow views, just as the elders of Judah wanted to bind Samson—but they were just as unsuccessful.

One result of the growing controversy was that a number of families left the assembly to form a new and more open fellowship across town, the Nant Coch Church. The leaders of the new church welcomed the Olfords and soon Stephen was busy in their midst. This new gathering of believers soon began to make an impact on the city. A downtown high school was rented for Sunday evening services. These services were timed to coincide with the ending of the majority of Sunday evening services, so that many from various denominations came. John Capper, a well-known businessman and a close friend and confidant of Stephen Olford, usually led the services. The program was lively, the speakers frequently came from area churches, and the emphasis was on evangelism. All this was quite revolutionary. Stephen Olford functioned for some time in a semi-official capacity as "pastor" of this new and outward-looking Brethren assembly. It was a step that made Stephen Olford's acceptance of a more conventional pastorate, in due course, that much easier.

Duke Street Baptist Church

Stephen's first call to the pastorate came from the Duke Street Baptist Church in Richmond, Surrey, a London suburb. It was a church that already had a long and illustrious history. Richmond is a very old town, once the home of kings. The church itself, situated in the center of town, was a picturesque Gothic structure known as "the Octagon." It stood in narrow Duke Street for eighty years. Eventually it was replaced by a more modern building.

The church was founded in 1870, the year Charles Darwin died and at a time when William Gladstone and Benjamin Disraeli vied with each other to be Prime Minister of Victorian England. The first attempts to build this church, which had the blessing of C. H. Spurgeon, made little headway. Then came young F. B. Meyer, fresh from college and filled with the Holy Spirit. He put the church on a firm footing and went on to an illustrious career as preacher, philanthropist, and author. The lantern-like building was built in 1881.

The church had its ups and downs. At one time it found itself without a pastor, struggling with debt and threatened with closure. The tide turned in 1940 when Alan Redpath, who had given up a promising secular career to go into the Lord's work, accepted an invitation to become the church's pastor. He was to transform that humdrum suburban church into one of the fastest-growing churches in the country.

One revolutionary move he made was to get the church out of the crowded and inadequate sanctuary on Sunday nights and into the nearby 1200-seat Richmond Theater. He soon had it packed, Sunday after Sunday, and it became a vibrant center of evangelism.

Then came Alan Redpath's call to the pulpit of the famous Moody Memorial Church in Chicago. Immediately the question arose as to who would be God's man to take his place at Duke Street? It would have to be someone with the gift of the evangelist, capable of filling the theater. It would have to be a pastor, someone able to shepherd a congregation still hurting from a split. Alan Redpath knew exactly who it should be—Stephen Olford.

God already had been preparing Stephen's own heart for a significant change in his ministry. For years he had been engaged largely in itinerant evangelism throughout the British Isles. He described it jokingly as "an exciting, but exhausting sequence of separations, suitcases, and sermons!" In the summer of 1952 his son Jonathan was born and with his strong sense

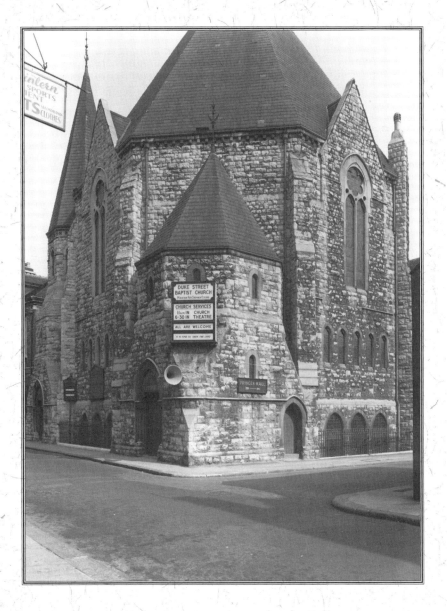

*Duke Street Baptist Church,
Richmond, Surrey, England.*

of family responsibility, Stephen began to weigh increasingly the desirability of being at home, now that he was both a husband and father. However, he and Heather were determined not to rush ahead of God.

For three months they prayed for definite guidance. They had made up their minds, however, (to use their own words) "that no human persuasion, material provision, or personal ambition should affect our understanding of the Lord's will." Thus it was that when the invitation came from Duke Street in June 1953 they recognized the call of God and were ready to go.

The service of ordination and induction took place in October with Geoffrey King, pastor of the East London Tabernacle, bringing the charge to the pastor. Appropriately enough, he spoke on Stephen, the great servant of the Lord mentioned in Acts 6—a man full of faith and the Holy Spirit, full of wisdom, full of grace, and power. Leith Samuel gave the charge to the church, taking as his text: "Behold, I have set before thee an open door, and no man can shut it (Revelation 3:8). With holy joy, Stephen Olford preached his first Sunday morning sermon from Hebrews 12:1-2 on "Running the Race" and the need for looking unto Jesus.

He was a worthy successor to the dynamic and anointed Alan Redpath. His congregation soon discovered that their new pastor knew exactly what he was doing and where he was going. Indeed, he set before himself seven major objectives as he assumed the pastorate of the church.

First and foremost, he aimed for the restoration of the unity of the church. Prior to his coming to Duke Street, the church had suffered a major split. A young brother, recently returned from overseas had sown the seeds of dissension by propagating false doctrine—especially among the young people of the church. This led to scores of people leaving the church. The division was aggravated by the fact that in some cases it brought about separation between husband and wife, and often between friend and friend. Stephen Olford came to a church that needed to be in love. He brought a series of messages on the subject of uniting love as revealed in 1 Corinthians 13.

Next he set about establishing a New Testament eldership for the church, based on his conviction that in every local church there should be elders as well as deacons (1 Timothy 3; Philippians 1:1). The deacons should be responsible for handling temporal things and the elders for taking care of spiritual matters. Elders should be under-shepherds of the local church. The presiding minister had an obligation to train his elders and to feed and lead the flock (Acts 20:28). Accordingly, he established up to twelve elders over twelve groups in the Richmond neighborhood. Each group met monthly to discuss the Scriptures, pray together, keep themselves informed about the church's missionaries, and to explore the possibilities of evangelism in their respective neighborhoods. This ministry of undershepherding helped to bring the church family closer together in love.

To further encourage love and good works (Hebrews 10:24), the new pastor introduced a prayer calendar to the fellowship at Duke Street. It was an innovative idea that "took off" from the word *go!* The entire membership was divided into the days of a normal month in alphabetical order. The church was then exhorted to pray on the first day of the month for the group in which his or her name was listed and proceed in cyclical fashion. Assuming that this was done morning and evening, it would follow that everyone in membership was prayed for twice every day. No one could conscientiously engage in such intercessory ministry without seeking out and sharing with the people they had prayed for. At the end of the list of names were special people who were always remembered. They were the missionaries who had been sent forth from Duke Street. The impact of such intelligent and intense prayer had a tremendous effect. People really began to love one another. Prayer meetings were a must, and the spiritual climate for the preaching of God's Word was evident to all who had "their senses exercised to discern both good and evil" (Hebrews 5:14).

His third goal was the evangelization of Richmond. To this end he launched a course on personal soul-winning and was gratified when young and old alike enthusiastically took part in it. Various kinds of evangelistic outreaches were a regular part of the program, but the services in the theater became the chief means of reaching people. It was conservatively estimated that 1,006 genuine, first-time conversions resulted from this evangelistic outreach during the six years Stephen Olford was at Duke Street. A careful survey was able to account for all these people—where they were, what they were doing, and how they were active in the Lord's work.

His fourth goal was to mobilize a Young People's Christian Fellowship. During the first years of his ministry in the church he made sure he attended its weekly meetings. By doing this he was able to meet, know, love, and teach these potential soul-winners and future mission-aries. He divided the group up into five sections, each representing one of the five continents. "I can still remember some of the thrilling missionary rallies and programs we had," he said. "I can still smell the curry and rice of the Chinese night!" The Young People's Christian Fellowship grew beyond his ambitious expectations and from its ranks came many who went to the missionfield.

As a fifth goal he formulated a missionary policy for the church and, in so doing, proved himself to be just as efficient an organizer as he was an effective preacher. The Duke Street church did not only adopt the policy, it served as a model for other churches.

The sixth objective was to expand the church's evangelistic ministry. At least once a year, with the full cooperation of the boards and membership of the church, he conducted a crusade in some strategic city or area of the British Isles. It was a thrilling experience to be commissioned for the task by the church and then return and share with them all that God had done. Sometimes members of the boards of elders and deacons would travel to be part of the closing hours of such a crusade. This was not only an encouragement to Stephen Olford's own heart, and a tremendous testimony to the churches supporting the crusade, but a thrilling experience for the brethren from Duke Street.

His final goal was to build a new sanctuary. The Richmond Theater was a great place to stage evangelistic meetings but it certainly did not serve the general needs of a local church. It was not long after his arrival that he and the members of the church began to pray and plan for a new sanctuary. In time an architect was hired and plans began to move forward. The completion of this goal was not achieved until after Stephen Olford left for New York, but at least the church had begun moving in this direction.

It was as a preacher, however, that Stephen Olford made his biggest mark at Duke Street. His preaching was marked by exposition, exhortation, and expectation, supported by example. He filled both the theater and the church. He preached for souls, urging lost people to come to Christ. He preached to saints, proclaiming the life-transforming truth of an indwelling Christ. He preached for surrender, calling Christians to lay their all on the altar, to lift up their eyes and look on the fields, to give themselves to the work of the Lord.

Evangelist! Pastor! Teacher! Administrator! Such was Stephen Olford when at the helm of a church. His master passion, however, was for lost souls. He yearned over the lost! He besieged heaven for the lost! He reached out to the lost.

Nowhere did this come out more clearly, perhaps, than in the way he threw his personal support, and the support of his church, behind the 1954 Billy Graham Harringay Crusade in London. He and Billy Graham were close friends. God had used Stephen Olford, years before, to lead Billy Graham into the fullness of the Spirit. Now Billy Graham had leaped to international fame as an evangelist. His "Hour of Decision" program was carried on radio stations all across the United States and Canada. His crusades captured the attention of the media. What he did and said was news. He was the friend of presidents, the honored guest of royalty, and the confidant of many in high places. He was lionized and applauded.

It is singularly characteristic of Stephen Olford that he was absolutely free from professional jealousy. He rejoiced in all of Billy Graham's successes. He flung himself wholeheartedly into the Harringay Crusade effort. It never occurred to him not to support Billy all the way. C. H. Spurgeon once said:

> It takes more grace than I can tell
> To play the second fiddle well.

In the scriptures this humility is exemplified in the willingness of Barnabas to forget himself and support and promote his gifted friend Saul. Nobody manifests this gracious spirit more than Stephen Olford. He and Billy Graham were one. They loved and served the same Lord, they shared a passion for souls, they were both filled and anointed by the same Holy Spirit.

Stephen saw the Harringay Crusade as a glorious opportunity to capitalize on a growing citywide, nation-wide interest in the gospel of Christ. Again, his organizational genius taught him how to mobilize his church and maximize the possibilities of winning souls to Christ.

He said: "We saw our church treble in its membership, largely through the Billy Graham Crusade at Harringay. I introduced a program that we called 'Operation Andrew,' which Billy Graham now uses all over the world. It was born right in our church. We organized about twenty-four big buses that went out from our church every night. Each bus had a team of seven (three women and four men) who could counsel and handle any situation that arose in their bus. We had reserved seats at Harringay.

"Every single night I preceded the buses back to the church to be on hand when the buses returned. We also had hostesses waiting at the church with tea and coffee and other refreshments. The buses would empty and the people would come in. I would greet them and say: 'It's been wonderful to be your hosts tonight, and to take you to hear Billy Graham. If you have made a commitment to Jesus Christ I want to tell you what we plan to do at the end of the crusade.' Each person was given a syllabus. Many were saved as a result of these efforts and our own follow-up work."

One such referral was nineteen-year-old Arthur Abraham, who had come to England the year before to attend college. An Armenian born in India, attending Acton Technical College, he worked as an apprentice part-time in Wembley. One day he passed a poster that advertised Billy Graham's Harringay Crusade. He went, found Christ, and became a Christian believer. He was told to find a church and grow spiritually.

While visiting a cousin who worked at a Barclays Bank in downtown Richmond, he ended up on Duke Street in front of a Baptist church. By his own admission he "was scared, shy and confused," but he made up his mind to attend this church the next Sunday. Arthur gives the following testimony:

> Then I met Pastor Stephen Olford and heard him

preach. For a few Sundays in a row I sat in the back pews and listened spellbound as he expounded from the Word of God. As a young babe in Christ, I learned about the love of God and His Son, Jesus. I remember eagerly awaiting the evening service at the theater. I vividly remember how he blessed me and made the truths from the Holy Bible come alive. I grew in the knowledge of Jesus Christ. I can recount many glorious experiences. I remember him teaching the congregation the chorus:

> Give me oil in my lamp, keep me burning,
> Give me oil in my lamp, I pray
> Give me oil in my lamp, keep me burning,
> Keep me burning till the break of day.

I remember he had guest preachers like Grady Wilson. I remember Carlton Booth coming to sing that beautiful hymn, "The Stranger of Galilee." I remember the open-air services led by Mr. John Baldock down by the River Thames.

After three or four months I walked up to Stephen Olford and introduced myself. Shortly thereafter, the Moody Chorale came to London on tour and he suggested I apply to Moody Bible Institute and go study the Bible in the U.S.A.

In the fall of 1955 I went to Chicago and enrolled at Moody. I recall how Mr. Olford visited the Institute and addressed the student body on love, courtship and marriage, and that Sunday spoke at a Bible church outside of Chicago. I was thrilled to see and hear him speak again—as always under the anointing of the Holy Spirit. Afterwards I talked for a few minutes with him. As usual, he encouraged me to "fight the good fight" and then he was gone.

It has been almost thirty-nine years since Chicago, but the name of Stephen Olford will live with me forever. In all my recollection no one . . . made such a profound and lasting impression on me as he did—

especially in my early days as a Christian. I remember him as a warm, gracious, humble, and kind man. I recall, after the services at Duke Street, when I shook his hand and looked at him, the joy of the Lord showed in his face. On my way home I would praise the Lord for him and his sermon. The same Jesus he showed me how to rely on back in the early '50s is still with me now (Hebrews 13:8). I adopted him as my pastor long ago and still feel he is my pastor.

Those years at Duke Street Baptist Church were both memorable and momentous. Time and space do not permit me to record the many "extras" that were packed into that relatively short period. Stephen recalled with evident pleasure "the joys of family life." Although Jonathan and David were very young, as much time as possible was spent in fun things like picnics at Windsor Castle or on the banks of the River Thames; the yearly horse show a mere block or two from the manse; the visits to London city and sites; and the famous Kew (botanical) Gardens. Stephen also enjoyed weekly golf matches with Mr. A. Lindsay Glegg (outstanding engineer, elder statesman, and effective preacher) and Dr. W. E. Sangster (the illustrious Methodist preacher and pastor of Westminster Central Hall, London). Stephen remarked, "I learned more about sermons than I did about scores! I also welcomed an occasional day at Lord's Cricket Ground, where England fought it out with Australia, West Indies or some other cricket-oriented country."

But just as precious and profitable were the events that took place at the church. Said Stephen: "Our missionary conferences were very special. To this day, Heather (in particular) and I still pray and keep in touch by letter with many of the missionaries who went out to serve during our tenure at Duke Street. Then there were the fellowship times we hosted on the lawn behind our manse. It was a beautiful setting where refreshments were enjoyed, testimonies shared, and the Word expounded. We were a closely-knit family of believers, and Heather and I will be forever grateful for the encouragement and enrichment we derived from the elders, deacons, and members of that beloved church.

"Of course, we were part of the London life as well. Nothing of importance happened in the Christian world that was not reflected in the evangelical life of London. So a good deal of time was spent attending events that deepened our spiritual experience as servants of the Lord. We thank God for the years in Richmond, and especially at Duke Street."

By 1959 Stephen Olford's ministry at the church was drawing to a close. He had received an invitation to go to New York to pastor the great

Calvary Baptist Church. The closing months of his ministry at Duke Street were times of continued blessing. On the first Sunday in 1959 Stephen announced that he would be leaving London. He gave the church a stirring word from God: "As your days, so shall your strength be" (Deuteronomy 33:25).

At first, the church did not want to release its pastor. It caused pain both for the Olfords and the members of Duke Street. But an ingenious solution was suggested and implemented by the Olfords' dear friends, Dr. J. Eric Richardson and his wife, May. Dr. Richardson addressed the church at a specially called meeting where he explained that it would be improper to challenge God's call to Stephen and Heather Olford. Instead of viewing the situation negatively, why not consider the invitation to the United States as a "missionary call"? This was taken seriously, and at an appropriate gathering in the Richmond Theater the Olfords were duly "valedicted" for "the work whereunto [God had] called them" in New York City. This was a most meaningful experience for both Heather and Stephen. They retained their membership at Duke Street, and the church subsequently was given a piano from Calvary Baptist Church to honor and preserve the link between the two churches.

Public farewell services for the Olfords began as early as April 4 with a rally in the Free Trade Hall, Manchester, sponsored by the Christian Business Men's Committee. Probably there were more "babes in Christ" in Manchester over the years than in any other city, due to several citywide campaigns, four mammoth rallies, as well as other gatherings. On May 23 another public farewell service was held at Westminster Chapel. Stephen Olford's long-time friend, Mr. A. Lindsay Glegg, presided over the service; the London Emmanuel Choir sang Frances Ridley Havergal's great consecration hymn, which immortalized the words, "Take my life, and let it be / Consecrated, Lord, to Thee." Rev. A. T. Houghton, Rev. George Duncan, and Dr. J. E. Richardson were the speakers. Miss Joyce Silcox, Heather's close friend, represented Tom and Jean Rees and the entire staff of Hildenborough Hall. Once again she sang the words that first challenged Stephen to dedicate his life fully to the Lord—words that were the focal point of their wedding service and of their whole lives:

> Only one life to offer—
> Jesus, my Lord and King;
> Only one tongue to praise Thee,
> And of Thy mercy sing (forever);
> Only one heart's devotion—
> Savior, O, may it be

Consecrated alone to thy matchless glory,
Yielded fully to Thee.

Avis B. Christiansen

Stephen picked up the theme in his remarks and, as always, called for a verdict. As a crowning joy, a number of young people came forward to give their lives to the Lord for fulltime service.

Duke Street Baptist Church had their opportunity to say goodbye near the end of June. The church family farewell took place in Princes Hall, and the public jammed the Richmond Theater the following evening to wish the Olfords Godspeed. Each of these occasions brought "a tear in one eye and a twinkle in another"; yet the weekend was one of triumph and victory. With the blessing of the church and the Christian world behind them the Olfords took their leave of England and set their faces westward.

Calvary Baptist Church

In 1957 Billy Graham held his great crusade in Madison Square Garden in New York City. He invited Stephen to come over from England for the first three weeks to speak at ministers' workshops and conduct follow-up classes for the converts of the crusade. While he was in New York, Mr. Olford was asked to speak at the famous Calvary Baptist Church on West 57th Street in midtown Manhattan. About a year later he received a call to become its senior pastor.

He hesitated for a long time. It would mean uprooting his family. Added to that, Calvary Baptist Church had enormous problems typical of most inner city churches. He later declared to a group of pastors, "You name it, we had it!" Still, through his mother, he had American roots. Also Calvary Baptist Church was on the radio, and that was a big plus in his mind. Indeed, it was reputed to be the oldest broadcasting church in America.

New York itself was a monumental challenge. It had a population of almost 8 million people. It was home to people of seventy-five different language groups. It was a city of gleaming skyscrapers of stone and glass and bronze. It was also a city of squalid tenements, many of which were devoid of even the barest conveniences of heat, hot water or sanitation.

It took over a year of voluminous correspondence, phone calls, deep soul searching, and waiting on God before the final decision was made. He wrote to the church listing reasons why he thought he would be unacceptable. After numerous letters he wrote again, listing conditions he would require to be met. Patiently, prayerfully, the deacons and the church weighed the issues. They were getting a clearer picture of the man they were inviting. A thousand American pastors would have been eager to send their portfolios and credentials and jump at the chance to

Calvary Baptist Church
on West 57th Street in Manhattan.

pastor so prestigious a church, but not Stephen Olford. He was concerned that as many potential misunderstandings as possible be eliminated, that agreements be put in writing, and above all, that God's will be done. The deacons and members prayerfully considered the matters raised and reconfirmed their call. It was during their Christmas vacation in 1958 that the Olfords finally received assurance from the Lord that this was His call.

In September of 1959 Stephen Olford was installed as pastor of Calvary Baptist Church. Alan Redpath, who was then minister of Moody Memorial Church in Chicago, gave the charge to the pastor and Billy Graham gave the charge to the people. It was a joy for Stephen to be flanked by these dear friends as he commenced a new and exciting chapter in his life.

If the people of Calvary Baptist Church had any doubts as to the kind of minister they had called to their pulpit these were soon dispelled. The very first Sunday Stephen Olford issued a clarion call for consecration; the response was immediate, as people streamed forward to make commitments. Souls were saved that Sunday, setting a pattern for the next fourteen years.

Once installed as Calvary's new pastor, he summoned the church to a meeting to hear what he envisioned for the years ahead. It was an impressive session. With almost his first breath he had a story to tell of a recent conversion. A young doctor—an outstanding man who had won all the top honors in medical school—had been challenged by the gospel message just the Sunday before. He had gone home to think things through. Then, that very afternoon, he had phoned Mr. Olford to say he wanted to trust Christ. "He came to my study, and after a few hours of conversation had yielded to the claims of Christ." Stephen saw this man's conversion as "the earnest" of what lay ahead for him and that strategic Manhattan church.

Though he had not been in New York City very long, already Stephen had a burden that kept him awake at night. "I am aware," he said, "that there is very little by way of a sound witness at the heart of this great city. O, God! How are we going to break through? How are we going to move from our possessiveness and from self-interest to see this vast, teeming city of lost men and women, who are out of Christ?" It was the kind of heart-cry heard in olden times from God's great prophets. He called on the assembled gathering to get under the burden of the great, lost city and as a church move into action in prayer, ministry, and fellowship with God-given leadership.

He set before the church a threefold plan. There was *the ministerial plan*—the plan that he, as their pastor, set for himself, his preaching ministry, and the music of the church.

He informed his people that his method of preaching was going to be

Photo courtesy of the Billy Graham Center

*Stephen Olford kneels for the prayer of commissioning
at his installation service, Calvary Baptist Church.*

expository in nature in the anointing of the Holy Spirit. This would demand hours of prayer and sermon preparation. "Nothing can be hurried in this area," he told them. "Preaching," he affirmed, "calls for the incarnation of the Word as well as the presentation of the Word. It calls for concentration, observation, meditation, and stillness of soul. His morning quiet time, Bible study, and sermon preparation were part of the overall plan. From 9:30 a.m. until noon, he told his people, he would be virtually unavailable—except for absolutely unavoidable interruptions and emergencies.

He was determined that in every service music and message should be happily married. Music was not to be a performance but a ministry. Doxology was to complement theology. He wanted music that was going to be worshipful and meaningful. He let it be known that he would stand for "no crosscurrents of short-circuiting of God's power by the choir." Plain speaking indeed!

He recognized that in a large midtown church such as Calvary there would be innumerable requests for personal counseling. Therefore he envisaged a pastoral session on Tuesday evenings from 5:00 to 7:00 where he could meet with folks desiring spiritual help or where he could conduct interviews, as the occasion demanded.

He was burdened about the literature ministry—the writing of tracts, books, and booklets. Already evangelical publishers were knocking on his door for appointments, asking for manuscripts from his pen. Then, too, there was the voluminous correspondence that demanded his attention. Even before he had left Britain's shores to accept the call to Calvary he had received hundreds of letters—some congratulatory; others inviting him for crusades and conferences; still others from evangelical leaders asking him to sit on this council and that council. Most of them he declined. He could see that the workload was going to be daunting, requiring some pastoral plan of action.

More than anything else—more than the preaching, the counseling, the writing, and the planning—he wanted to be a man of God, to exercise a living ministry. "We can't manufacture that," he stated, "we can't work that up. It's a life to be lived." His greatest fear was the barrenness of a busy life. He asked the members to shield and guard him in that respect so that, in turn, he could give himself to them, and through them to a desperate world outside.

He found it hard to find men of his own spiritual convictions—mentors with whom he could pray and discuss mutual interests. But observing that Christian leaders, preachers, and missionaries passed through the city every week he made it a practice to meet with some of them—men of giant intellect and spiritual maturity—to pray and grapple over the great issues of the day.

Next came *the general plan.* Monday was to be his day off; he felt he owed that much to his wife and children. Before the day was out, however, he had written out a list of assignments to be cared for throughout the week. As they were accomplished he checked them off. Discipline was the key word.

By Tuesday, for instance, he had selected his Sunday subjects, had dictated the morning sermon and had a one-page synopsis of the message prepared for the Sunday bulletin. Moreover, in concert with his minister of music, the hymns and anthems had been chosen, and anything else affecting the order of worship. Tuesday afternoon, following lunch and a round of prayer with the entire staff, he met with members of his pastoral staff to go over the weekly agenda. Evenings would be taken up with the pastoral session, followed by meetings with various committees.

Wednesday was given over to the midweek Bible study hour and prayer meeting. The day was spent in dictation of the sermon and preparation of the heart. Occasionally, when Stephen was in the midst of a special series, he would prepare an accompanying sermon outline for his people. In the evening the service itself would include singing, special music, an announcement from the bookstore, and then forty to fifty minutes of Bible teaching. From time to time he would introduce a Christian leader or missionary who happened to be passing through New York and ask them to bring "a word of greeting." Usually a half-hour of corporate prayer followed. None of this breaking off into little groups. Pentecost came when "all [were] with one accord in one place" (Acts 2:1). Inevitably, he would ask one of the church officers to lead in prayer, followed by anyone who felt so led. A four-page prayer sheet listing specific requests gave fuel for further intercession. Usually Stephen finished up, lifting his congregation higher and higher to the very throne room of Heaven, so that as people left they sensed they had been in the presence of God Himself.

Thursday was taken up with sermon preparation for Sunday night. Later in his ministry he used the afternoon hours for the taping of the "Encounter" radio programs. In the evening there was choir rehearsal. While this was a special workout and absolutely necessary, he otherwise encouraged members to keep this night free. He felt it was not healthy for a church to be strained to its limits by endless meetings. "Let's live normal home lives too," he requested.

Friday, he noted, was youth recreation night, and he was all for the young people enjoying a bit of sanctified fun under good supervision. He expressed the hope that occasionally he might be able to free up time to join them. Such was the impact of his fourteen-year ministry that over a thousand young people yielded themselves for fulltime service, answering

Photo courtesy of the Billy Graham Center

Platform participants at installation service
at Calvary Baptist Church, September 10, 1959.
Dr. Howard Ferrin, Rev. Alan Redpath, Dr. Billy Graham,
Rev. Stephen Olford, Rev. Richard Hamilton, Elton Irwin, Sr., David Wright.

God's call during regular church services, Christian life conventions, or annual missionary conferences. Over one hundred of these pursued formal training in Bible schools, Christian colleges, and theological seminaries. Many found their niche in the Lord's work as pastors, missionaries, teachers, or fulltime workers. Eight young men were ordained by Dr. Olford in Calvary's sanctuary.

Then there was the importance he attached to Sunday. The pulpit was always the focal point of Stephen Olford's ministry at Calvary. In the ensuing fourteen years he would average over three hundred sermons a year. Sunday mornings saw the church sanctuary and wings packed to capacity. He would dedicate the Sunday morning service to worship. He paid tribute to the radio outreach of the Sunday morning service. He was sure that people could be saved listening to the kind of message he would bring week by week. The emphasis would be on feeding God's people.

Sunday evenings, when many Manhattan churches were closed, Calvary Baptist Church always had an excellent crowd. The service was devoted to all-out evangelism. Pastor Olford estimated that as many as ninety-eight percent of the people currently attending were saved. He reminded them that it was pointless to preach the gospel to Christians. He challenged his people to catch the vision of bringing the lost to the weekly Sunday night "continuing crusade."

The last Sunday evening service of each month was to be a "celebration of witness," reserved for baptisms and a call to open confession. Candidates for baptism would come to the microphone, one by one, and give a brief testimony as to how they met Christ, what He meant to them, and why they were being baptized. When the last one had come up out of the water Stephen Olford would invite those who had trusted Christ the preceding month and desired to obey God in the act of baptism to come forward. He also asked those who had been saved in the service to come forward as an act of witness. These would then remain in the sanctuary for an instruction meeting. "That safeguards against all the high pressure methods that turn some people off."

Stephen made sure he kept his finger on what was happening. For instance, he took charge of the counseling, which he saw as a critical part of each service. As people came forward he made sure they were properly received, matched up with a counselor, and followed up. He streamlined the counseling procedures at the end of any given service. Trained men and women were expected to pay close attention to the message so that they could follow up its theme when sitting down with an inquirer. He issued instructions on how counselors should evaluate and respond to the needs of the individual. He even outlined how to record and report decisions.

In the early weeks following his installation Stephen Olford taught an eight-week discipleship course on the basic principles of New Testament Christianity with a strong emphasis on application. The subjects covered Christian certainty, daily devotions, believer's baptism, church fellowship, consecrated living, systematic giving, dedicated serving and a lecture on the covenant of membership. At each class outlines were handed out with room for additional notes. Though topical in nature, each study was based on an appropriate Scripture reading. These notes, provided by Stephen, could be amplified, illustrated, discussed and applied. This course was compulsory for all members as well as prospective church members. It not only put their understanding of the Christian life on a sound footing, it helped to revitalize the spiritual lives of older believers too. By the time the individual had completed the course he would pretty much know what was expected of him.

Turning his attention to the leadership of the church (1 Timothy 3:1-13; Philippians 1:1-2; Titus 1:5-9), Stephen outlined a plan to meet with the church's trustees and deacons for a period of five or six weeks in order to minister to them from his heart. Later, he expected to draw from both bodies a group of men he would ordain as elders and appoint as deacons. The elders would be the leaders of the church, while the deacons would be responsible for practical matters: finance, church property, the Hotel Salisbury, the bookstore, radio, and later TV.

Realizing that the bigger the church, the harder it is for all to get to know one another, it was decided to divide the church fellowship into regional groups with an elder over each group. Once a month they would meet in a suitable home for a time of prayer, sharing, and light refreshments. He envisioned possibly twelve groups (one for each month). In the course of a year he would get to meet a different group each month, thereby getting to know every member of the church. This "Shepherd Plan" was ultimately implemented in 1967. The program did much to develop spiritual leadership, as under-shepherds were trained and given areas of service and spheres of responsibility.

At other times he and Heather held receptions at the church so as to personally meet with groups of members on an informal basis, according to alphabetical order. It sparked a new initiative among church members and led to a dynamic program of social as well as spiritual concern and action.

Then he turned his attention to committees. He planned to streamline them and maximize their structures, leaving them to conduct their business honestly and honorably. He didn't want to consume endless hours at committee meetings that could be better spent in prayer and the study of God's Word.

Next, he worked on the church's missionary program. All outgoing missionaries would spend up to six months, at the church's expense, in a staff internship program. This would enable folk to get to know them personally so that when they departed for the field the exposure would culminate in a meaningful commissioning service from the pulpit, "when we would lay our hands on them and pray for them. By this sacred symbolism the missionaries would know they were going out with the backing of the church fellowship (Acts 13:1-4)."

Stephen Olford personally challenged the church's Mission Board. There was to be no mere perfunctory, routine prayer, "Lord, bless our missionaries." Rather there was to be in-depth focus on total missionary needs through weekly reports and missionary conferences. "When they are up against a hostile tribe; when they don't know how to break through satanic opposition, we at home are going to be praying for them. We are going to get a new evangelistic burden through missionary praying!" And on their return he wanted them to have an honorable homecoming. He wanted them to appear on the platform to tell of their work. He wanted members to love the missionaries and give them welcome! An evident testimony to Stephen Olford's commitment to missions is found in the budget of Calvary Baptist Church during his pastorate. No less than three-fifths of the budget was designed for home and foreign missions, including radio and television ministries.

During his ministry at Calvary scores of people offered themselves for overseas service as missionaries and were accepted by recognized mission boards. Others joined the ranks of home missions and various Christian service organizations throughout the greater New York area. These were added to the missionary family of Calvary Baptist Church. In 1969, under Stephen's leadership, Calvary Baptist Church began to support national workers who were engaged in sound gospel ministries in their own native lands.

Finally, Stephen Olford focused on what he called *the special plan.* He announced his intention of launching an "Each One Reach One" campaign. Those with cars were encouraged to bring their neighbors. The telephone could be turned into an instrument for evangelism. He anticipated a team of young people going out in pairs from the church twenty minutes before the evening service to take up their positions at strategic locations in the area to invite passersby to come to the service in the hope of being brought to Christ.

He projected open-air meetings. He wanted an open-air mobile unit, complete with a raised platform and public address system, staffed by people gifted to sing and preach. He, himself was prepared to be part of the program at times.

Open-air preaching was subsequently inaugurated in cooperation with Open-Air Campaigners. Interested young men and women received training in open-air work and fanned out to all parts of the city. Stephen Olford, following the example of our Lord, the apostle Paul, John Wesley, George Whitefield, General William Booth and a host of other evangelists, believed in the advantages of open-air preaching. After briefing Calvary's members as to the method of procedure in singing, preaching, tract distribution, and personal counseling, they went to Columbus Circle just outside Central Park, where hundreds of people would be sitting, walking, jogging and, hopefully, listening! The city gave permission to use loud speakers. The choir and instrumentalists rendered familiar gospel songs. In no time a crowd formed. There were brief testimonies. Then Stephen preached the gospel. When the invitation was given scores of people came to receive literature, and Calvary's soul-winners went into action. Afterwards he invited them to come out of the sweltering summer heat and hear him preach in an air-conditioned sanctuary just a few blocks away. He was like the Pied Piper. They followed him down Central Park South and along Seventh Avenue to the church, and many came to Christ.

Another avenue of evangelism the church adopted was the Friendship Meal where a good restaurant was the site of a free evangelistic banquet. The ticket of admission was an unconverted person. In a warm, convivial atmosphere the stage was set for the presentation of the gospel. Many who would have never considered coming to church heard the gospel and responded to it at these banquets.

Then he wanted to inaugurate an annual convention for the deepening of spiritual life, such as was held in 1875 at Carnegie Hall with Spirit-anointed men like W. Griffith Thomas, A. J. Gordon, R.A. Torrey and F. B. Meyer. The Lord answered Stephen's prayer, and in 1960, only six months after assuming the pastorate at Calvary Baptist Church, he started what was called the Christian Life Convention. Interdenominational in scope, its motto was "All one in Christ Jesus."

The Convention was patterned after the famed Keswick Convention in England with a specific truth for every day of the week. Monday exposed human failure; Tuesday emphasized God's provision for holy living; Wednesday focused on the Lordship of Christ; Thursday dealt with the fullness of the Holy Spirit; and Friday, on service for God at home and abroad. Speakers like Alan Redpath, William Culbertson, Paul S. Rees, G. Allen Fleece, L. E. Maxwell, Major Ian Thomas, and Stuart Briscoe were invited to share in what became a week of renewal for the churches of metropolitan New York. Hundreds of young people responded to the closing call to share Christ anywhere, at any time, and at any cost.

Stephen Olford also helped to pioneer similar conventions throughout the United States and overseas. The fact that he had been a popular speaker at Keswicks throughout the United Kingdom helped to fire his interest in promoting "normal" Christian living around the world.

By the time he was finished the people of Calvary Baptist Church in New York City knew that they had installed more than a pastor. They had on their hands an evangelist, a soul-winner, a teacher, a missionary, an organizer, a pragmatic visionary, a motivator, and a man of God.

He also helped the church capitalize on the fact that the congregation owned and operated the 17-story, 320-room Hotel Salisbury on West 57th Street, next door to the church. Completely renovated, its charm, elegance, and Christian warmth combined to make any stay there a pleasant and memorable experience. All was designed to pave the way for receptiveness to the gospel.

In each room there was an attractive red Bible supplied by the New York Bible Society. These were not hidden in a drawer but put on the dresser, opened at Psalm 23. Sunday services from the church were carried into each room by means of closed-circuit television. A card on top of the set advertised the times and the services in the church. On another channel continuous sacred music was aired. Also available to guests was information about available tapes by Dr. Olford on appropriate subjects and a direct phone line to the church.

Later in his ministry, Stephen felt a great need for a more comprehensive New York School of the Bible for the training of laymen, with special consideration for the needs of minority groups. The Bible school became a reality in September 1971. The aggregate enrollment for the three terms of the first year was 685 students. The faculty included members of the church's pastoral staff as well as experts in youth work, children's work, open-air campaigns, Jewish evangelism, and counseling. Stephen Olford's friend, Dr. Joseph C. Macaulay, the school's first dean, led the school to new heights of scholarship and spirituality.

The principle of "storehouse tithing" was also adopted as church policy, even though it was generally practiced long before this. This principle of giving had always been one of Stephen's convictions. Before anyone could be considered for election to any of the church's boards or committees, he or she had to subscribe to and practice this kind of tithing.

Throughout all this multifaceted activity Heather Olford not only ran the house and mothered the boys, she chaired women's meetings and was the pianist at Sunday (and sometimes Wednesday) evening services. Her place at the piano was symbolic of Stephen's conviction that the ministry of music should complement the preaching from the pulpit.

Stephen wrote the verses for a number of hymns and choruses and Paul Liljestrand, the Minister of Music, composed the music. A choir covenant was drawn up, and all who aspired to sing were required to sign it. The covenant set a high standard for commitment to Christian living and singing.

In 1972 an electronic computerized Allen organ was installed in the church. The old one badly needed to be replaced. It was inefficient and finally was damaged beyond repair by a flash flood. The new organ cost $75,000 and gave new impetus to the music ministry of the church.

Of all the ministries, however, that made up the sum total of Stephen's pastorate at Calvary Baptist Church, none loomed larger in his thinking than radio and television. He saw their enormous potential and cherished the opportunity of harnessing mass media to reach the city, the nation, and the world.

Calvary Baptist Church had been on the air since 1923. It was a leader and a pioneer in church broadcasting. Before Stephen Olford left the church, there were three programs going out weekly. There was "The Calvary Church Hour" which beamed the Sunday morning service. "We belted the world with our one-hour broadcast, ministering to millions, including nationals and missionaries. Everyone heard an hour of worship with forty-five minutes devoted to expository preaching." This program expanded into dozens of new markets. Beginning in 1960 the evangelistic Sunday evening service also took to the airwaves. Then "Encounter" radio was launched in May 1964 to treble the scope of Calvary's outreach. Along with this came an ever-expanding tape ministry that emerged in response to an increasing volume of requests for Dr. Olford's messages. They were used in individual and group Bible studies and many found their way to jails and missionfields overseas.

Stephen stands awaiting the taping of an "Encounter" television program. The primary station that aired the program was WPIX, Channel 11, in New York City (1960-1975).

The "Encounter" television program began out of sheer necessity. "I almost got shot," he said, "by going to an apartment building as a pastor and saying, 'I'm a minister. Here is my card. I should like to visit the people in this apartment.' The guard said, 'Out! And reached for his gun. He wouldn't believe me!

"Then I began an investigation. I discovered that security in all the high-rise apartment buildings was the same. People paid a high price for their privacy. They reserved the right to be protected from people who might interfere with them.

"I thought, *Very well then! We won't be beaten!* We started a mailing ministry. We sent specially designed leaflets to the addresses of those apartments. We only succeeded in annoying people. They wrote back terrible letters demanding that we remove their names from our mailing lists.

"Then we tried the telephone. We went through the phone book. We put together a team and trained our members to call people in those apartments. We soon received the same kind of feedback, which made us stop that endeavor too.

"At last I decided that television was the answer. I had never done any television work in my life. I decided, however, right from the start, not to go on television to amuse people. So I came up with a tailor-made thirty-minute program that was launched in October 1960 and ran for fifteen years. The format was interesting, varied, well produced, hard-hitting, and effective. For two years the television program was aired each Sunday afternoon over WPIX-TV, Channel 11. Afterward it was moved to a nighttime hour, which proved to be a fruitful change.

"Soon the phones were ringing. Some callers were seeking salvation and were pointed to Christ then and there. Others requested interviews and appointments were made. Some had problems and sought counseling. Some simply wanted to express thanks and appreciation for blessings received. Some responded by mail, opening the door for follow-up letters, literature and counseling sessions.

"We printed a survey card. At the top it said: Television Survey. The card invited people to give their comments regarding the time, and whether the program appealed to them or not." The viewer was asked, "What do you expect in a religious program?" Stephen examined the cards when they came in. Most viewers responded, "We want the Bible explained. We want more preaching."

The television program was an immediate success. It proved to be the answer to penetrating high-rise apartments.

——

Stephen Olford said that the fourteen years he spent at Calvary Baptist Church were the greatest years of his life. He sums up events in broad outline as "trials in the ministry, triumphs in the ministry, and thanksgivings in the ministry."

"*Trials in the ministry* included everything and more that a pastor normally experiences in a local church. But remember we were in New York City! Every day presented the unexpected. Quite apart from the pastoral problems were happenings like these:

• "Before we installed a permanent clock on the pulpit with countdown signals for accurate radio restrictions, I used a regular stopwatch. Every time I failed to pick it up at the conclusion of the service it was *gone!*

• "One Sunday, after the morning service, the congregation was invited to stay for our 'Encounter' TV program which was aired at 12:30. A good percentage of the people remained to watch and listen. I followed with an invitation, to which a number of people responded. While all this was going on, two men dressed like movers entered the sanctuary and with brilliant dexterity unplugged the huge TV set and walked out with it. I mean it was *gone!* Everyone seemed to be alert, but no one gathered what was happening!

• "On another Lord's day, someone with inside information picked the formidable locks of the choir room and rifled every ladies' handbag and every man's jacket! A considerable amount of money was *gone.* Fortunately we were well insured.

• "A guest singer parked his car across from the church so as to get away quickly after the service, only to find everything (including two suitcases) and the four wheels of his car *gone!*

• "David, our younger son was given a new bicycle by a dear friend. With two of his pals he went for a spin in Central Park. However he had no sooner turned a corner when some lads jumped him and the bicycle was *gone!*

• "Perhaps our most frightening experience happened in the early hours one night. At the time, we were living in an apartment building on New York's East Side. There was a man in our church who claimed to know and love the Savior. He came into membership long before I became pastor. Whenever I spoke to him, he appeared awkward and aggressive. He always displayed a tie clip shaped like a gun. He was married to a very beautiful lady and mother of a little boy. On several occasions the lady came to me in great distress, crying that her marriage was on the rocks and her life threatened. I made an appointment with the man and tried to find out the facts to solve the problems. He refused to divulge anything, but warned me that if I ever reported him to the police, he would shoot me.

Photo courtesy of the New York Times

*Relaxing in his study in the
14th floor "parsonage" at the Hotel Salisbury.*

"Weeks went by and the problems in the home worsened. Then I had a phone call from the wife to say that her life was in danger; she was targeted to be shot that night. I took counsel with my elders and we decided to tell the police and made provision for the woman's safety. We gave the police the necessary information and warned them that this man was dangerous.

"Later that night (2 a.m.) I had a personal call in my apartment (my number was unlisted). A voice said: 'I have just shot and killed two policemen and I am on my way to shoot you.' (Incidentally, the man was a window washer on some of New York's highest skyscrapers.) Of course, I phoned the police at once, only to learn that they knew already that two of their men were dead. They circled our apartment building and set up radio communications with me and stationed one armed officer in our living room. Mercifully, our two youngsters slept through the whole deal.

"The man, however, was carrying out his threat. He was on his way to shoot his wife when he encountered the two policemen and shot them dead, took their guns and proceeded to his home. He told his wife what he had done, then made her kneel down and read Psalm 51! (Obviously he was attempting to transfer his own guilt by making this sacrilegious demand.) He then said, 'Read quickly, I'm on my way to shoot the pastor.' In the meantime, the police had caught up with him and surrounded his house. He could hear the sirens and could see the flashing lights outside. Realizing that he was outmanned and out-gunned, he turned his pistol to his head and shot himself. The poor wife was still on her knees as he dropped dead. I could hear everything by police radio—even the report of the pistol. What a relief as the police exclaimed: 'It's all over, you are safe Rev. Olford!'

"Many times, during the fourteen years at Calvary, I had to have plainclothes detectives in my congregation. Hate mail from radio—and especially TV audiences—compelled me to take these precautions. But God had called us to New York City, and until our work was done we were immortal!

"But then there were the *triumphs in the ministry.* This would take a book to record—and the some! Early in my ministry, I instituted a half-night of prayer. It was always on Fridays—to link up with the universal Revival Prayer Fellowship held in London, England on the first Friday of the month within its own time zone. We met in the choir room because the entrance was through the Hotel Salisbury. This was not a stated meeting of the church nor was it restricted to our membership. As far as I can remember, this prayer meeting was never canceled throughout my entire ministry at Calvary. Even when I was away someone else would lead it. To me, this was the secret of the blessing we experienced at home or abroad. We started at

7:00 p.m. and prayed until midnight. People came when they could, and left when they had to.

"Without rigidly conforming to any pattern, we followed certain guidelines so as to maintain a progressive thrust in our prayer time:

7:00-8:00	Prayer for brokenness and cleansing
8:00-9:00	Prayer for personal and general revival and our nation
9:00-10:00	Prayer for church needs and activities
10:00-11:00	Personal prayer requests and testimonies
11:00-12:00	Worship and praise

"These nights of prayer were followed by times of refreshing from the presence of the Lord. Sometimes a breath of revival swept over the church. Christians got right with God and with one another. Occasionally God moved in power during a series of evangelistic messages. Two instances especially stand out. We prayed earnestly in our half-night of prayer that God would pour out His blessing on a series of expository sermons on the Decalogue (the Ten Commandments). The Puritans used to say that you cannot take people to mount Calvary until you have taken them to mount Sinai! Well, that is just what happened. In the fourteen years at Calvary I never remember such conviction, repentance and readiness to embrace the gospel. Hundreds of souls were saved!

"On another occasion, we went to prayer for the more than one million Jews in New York. We felt that we were not reaching them. So I advertised in the New York Times that I was going to preach for a number of weeks on 'The Gospel According to Moses' (evangelistic messages taken from the Pentateuch). Once again, God answered prayer and we saw more Jews come to the meetings and declare their faith in Christ than during any other period in my years at Calvary. I could multiply these triumphs of grace, but I have chosen these examples to show that 'as soon as Zion travailed, she brought forth her children' (Isaiah 66:8). Only when we travail in prayer are children brought to faith in Christ.

Among the triumphs in the ministry were the people who came into blessing. Let me tell the story of three of them.

Joan Gibbons was born in London, and educated in England and France. In due course, she married an American pianist, Carroll Gibbons, who went to England and distinguished himself in various fields of music. He was well known to B.B.C. audiences. But Joan herself was also an entertainer. During the Second World War she sang across England for the troops and became very popular. The Gibbons had wealth, fame, lovely homes, and many servants, but no real happiness or fulfillment. In fact, Carroll Gibbons became an alcoholic and made life miserable for Joan. Eventually Joan divorced him, and in 1946 came to America to fill a position with an English firm that manufactured earth-moving equipment. After a while she left that job to become a professional model. Joan was a beautiful woman. Her face and form could be seen in various magazines and journals, but Joan was not satisfied.

One day she saw a movie advertisement for *The Inn of the Sixth Happiness*. It was the story of an amazing woman, Gladys Aylward, who was turned down by missionary societies because of her lack of training and poor health. But Gladys Aylward had her heart set on China—and especially the unwanted orphans of that country. So in total faith in God and no support from the United Kingdom, she set out to do what she believed was her life's work. She succeeded. In fact, she became world famous; hence the film which was now playing in New York. Joan Gibbons went to see it and was profoundly moved.

Not long after this she happened to cross the street from her apartment building on Manhattan's East Side—something she rarely did. As she passed a small Evangelical Free Church that was tucked in one of the buildings there, she saw on the outside bulletin board that Gladys Aylward was going to appear personally. Joan made a mental note to attend. The sanctuary was packed, but Joan got in and sat spellbound as Miss Aylward told her story. At the close of the service, Joan pushed her way through the crowd and asked to speak to Miss Aylward. "I want to do something for God," Joan said. Sensing that Joan needed careful counseling, Miss Aylward told her that she had just learned that in a short time an English pastor was to be installed at Calvary Baptist Church on West 57th Street. She wisely advised Joan to wait and seek his help. So Joan left unsatisfied, but curious. Next day she phoned the church and secured all the information she needed about the coming of Stephen Olford and his family to the church.

Then came the installation services. While these lasted a week, it was the induction service that stirred Joan Gibbon's heart. As he knelt for the prayer of commissioning God came down upon the proceedings with an awesome sense of His presence and blessing. Joan often spoke to her pastor, Stephen Olford, about that specific moment in the church and in her life.

Of course, Joan started to attend the church and listen to the new preacher as he expounded the Word of God, and on the eighth of November 1959—only a few weeks after that installation service—Joan met the Savior in a living, transforming encounter. From the moment of her conversion, she grew by leaps and bounds in the Christian life.

She became involved in many aspects of church especially as the makeup artist for the "Encounter" TV taping sessions.

Joan Gibbons was determined to master the Word of God and prepare herself to return to England to witness to the society people with whom she had shared life in the fast lane in her unregenerate days. Stephen Olford bears witness to Joan's astonishing determination to be "[equipped] unto every good work," (2 Timothy 2:21). For two years she made the Wednesday Bible Study Hour her first priority. She took copious notes, asked numerous questions, and fleshed out the truths she learned by witnessing at every possible opportunity.

She was a joy to have in the weekly prayer meetings, following the Bible Study. If there was a pause in the flow of prayer, Joan would jump up and, in polished English, pray in a most refreshing Spirit-anointed manner. Stephen recalled how on some occasions she indirectly rebuked the elders, deacons, and members by crying out to the Lord and saying, "O God, while my fellow believers are trying to find words to pray, I must share my burden for those who are lost." Then she would recite names of people with whom she worked that she longed to see saved. She was a spiritual tonic to the whole church.

After some two years she felt it was time to leave for her home country. The parting was hard and there were many tears, but her vision was clear and her burden was heavy. She went back and God gave her an effective witness. She spoke in churches, cathedrals—and especially in the homes of the rich and famous. She introduced hundreds of souls to the Savior—many of whom were compatriots in sin during the war years. Eventually she was invited to be a witnessing member of the Movement for World Evangelization in the United Kingdom. Here her ministry was extended to an even wider Christian public.

One final story must be told about Joan. She was deeply concerned about her immediate relatives who lived in Nassau in the Bahamas, so she went to stay with them for a time. One night a masked burglar awakened her in her upstairs bedroom who was looking for money, jewelry, etc. He said to her, "Don't make any noise." She answered, "I have no intention of making a noise. All that concerns me is what you are going to say to the Lord when you have to face Him—and you will have to face Him." She added, "I'm not afraid to meet Him. Are you?" It turned out the burglar had at one time made a profession of faith, but was not living the life. Her words and testimony to him were so powerful that the would-be robber ended up sitting on the floor beside her bed while Joan told him about the Savior. So convicted was he by her words that he handed back the money he had stolen, which was about fifty dollars. He told her, "I can't take money from a Christian!" He got up to leave, and she gave him ten dollars and told him to keep it and not steal anymore. Then she wished him goodnight. She never heard from him again. Off and on she prayed for him, as the Lord brought him to mind.

One of the unique aspects of the ministry in New York City was the open door to internationals. During the weekly roll call and the visitors' reception, following the Sunday morning service, the number rarely dropped below the forty mark in representative countries. Sometimes it was well above that figure. It often made Stephen think of the day of Pentecost when "men from every nation under heaven" heard Peter's sermon! Thank God, like Peter, the pastor also witnessed many conversions. One of these was a young lady from Japan by the name of Asae Ukiya. She was an art student from Tokyo. She was the daughter of a noblewoman who was a confirmed Buddhist. While studying in New York, Asae was befriended by one of Calvary's members who was a keen soul-winner. Little by little, Asae was exposed to the gospel and the work of the Spirit.

In due course, she came to Calvary and sat under the preaching of the Word of God. As she listened, like Lydia in the New Testament, "the Lord opened her heart to heed the things spoken" (Acts 16:14, NKJV). Later she was baptized and became part of the Calvary family.

After two years she returned to Tokyo and began to share her faith—especially with her Buddhist mother. At first there was great resistance, but Asae continued to pray, as did others. One day their house caught fire and burned. God spoke to Mrs. Ukiya through this incident and she was saved.

Eventually the house was rebuilt, and with her artistic gifts Asae transformed a large upper room into a chapel with stained-glass windows depicting the ninefold fruit of the Spirit. She installed an excellent public address system and a white electronic organ. Services were held, and when there wasn't a guest speaker several young men took turns reading and translating excerpts of Dr. Olford's book, *Heart-Cry for Revival*. On Wednesday nights she played Stephen Olford's cassette tapes on Proverbs and translated the messages. Souls were saved and edified. Most of the attendees were young people.

Stephen added, "Then came the day when Heather and I visited Japan and were welcomed to the Ukiyas' spacious home in a wealthy Tokyo suburb. What a joy it was to see Asae again and meet her delightful mother! She looked like a queen—petite and beautiful. Heather and I were treated to a delicious meal laid out so artistically that it seemed a shame to touch a morsel. Right in the center of the spread were five loaves and two fish.

"After the meal, we were joined by young people who sang choruses and then listened to a message I had specially prepared for the occasion. It was a precious experience for all of us.

"Since then we have returned again and again to this home and have ministered God's Word. Now that chapel and part of the home have become the headquarters for Overseas Missionary Fellowship in Japan. This is the kind of story that makes the ministry so worthwhile."

Quite a different story is reflected in a letter Stephen received dated March 1980. It read:

> Dear Dr. Olford,
>
> It is with great joy that God has given me the opportunity to send this love gift for your ministry over radio ($100.00).
>
> You are my father in the faith. It was in 1968 that God's Word, from your lips over a Newark, N.J. radio station brought me to saving faith in our blessed Lord Jesus Christ. I was a member of Calvary for a year, through the encouragement of Dennis Miller [Minister to Students]. I was in the fast-food business in New Jersey, which enabled me to set up the snack bar at the Billy Graham Coffee House during his crusade there in New York. Under your ministry at Calvary, God laid his hand upon me for the preaching ministry, and at age 30 (in 1969) led me to California for Bible training and seminary.
>
> He has seen fit to [involve] me in two churches in northern California. He enabled me to heal a split church and disciple six men, one of whom, at age 45, is leaving law enforcement to study for the ministry. God used you in my life; now me in this man's life. The 2 Timothy 2:2 process in action! I am now waiting upon our Lord for His next place of ministry.
>
> I am eternally grateful to our sovereign Lord and your faithfulness to His calling upon your life. You have been and will remain my preaching model.
>
> Joyfully in Jesus.
> Gene D. Vreeland
>
> P.S. I'm the big, big fellow you called up to the platform at Calvary when I came forward to publicly confess my salvation through your radio ministry. You looked up at me (I'm 6'6" and 300 pounds) and said to the congregation, "I'm sure glad this man's

saved. I wouldn't want to meet him unsaved in a
dark alley!"

Stephen continued by saying, "I must also say a word here of thanksgivings in the ministry. I thank my God upon every remembrance of the
leaders, members, pastors and staff. It would be impossible to name them
all, but they all enriched Heather's life and mine. We learned so much of
Christ in the progressive outshining of glory we saw in their faces and lives.

"My wife and I will ever give thanks for the pastoral staff that stood
by us during the trials and triumphs of those years at Calvary: the
Reverend Ed Mitchell, who was my faithful and godly associate; Bob
Straton, whose tenor voice and gentle spirit blessed me every time we
shared the platform or stood before the TV cameras; Dennis Miller, whose
work among the young people—and especially students—was second to
none; Dr. J. C. Macaulay, dean of the New York School of the Bible, whose
saintliness and mature wisdom helped me through many a crisis; Paul
Liljestrand, our minister of music who could make music out of any
instrument or individual; and Colin Jackson, a man of God who became
one of the first members of my Board of Directors for Encounter
Ministries, Inc. Then there were all the wives as well—true partners in the
Lord. Special mention must be made of Mr. George Johnston and his wife,
Viola. I would have never made it through fourteen hears of ministry
without this fellow worker in the gospel. He was our Executive
Administrator and took over all the organizational aspects of the church—
especially during the renovation years, when both hotel and church were
given a good face-lift. Two of my leaders who undergirded me throughout
the fourteen years were Mr. Elton (Tex) Irwin, and Mr. Louis Schenkweiler.
Tex was a giant in stature (he fought as a boxer at Madison Square
Garden!) and in spirituality. It was he who negotiated all the arrangements
for our coming to Calvary. Louis Schenkweiler was chairman of our
deacon board and carried in his coat pocket a coded filing system. There
was no information I needed that he could not supply regarding church
matters. He was also a man of God.

"Then there were the secretaries and other members of our staff. Our
Tuesday lunch times were fun, food, and fellowship! That is where we
learned to know and respect one another in the Lord. Two of those
secretaries followed Heather and me from New York to Florida, to
Wheaton, Illinois and on to Memphis, Tennessee." In 1994, Stephen sat
down and spoke further of the contribution of these two ladies to his
ministry: "There is Victoria Kuhl, my homiletical secretary, who has been
with me for over thirty years. She knows more about my heartbeat and
heart burden than anyone on staff. She has typed every sermon or book

that I have written and can recall any subject or sermon that I need and present it to me at the drop of a hat. Nothing can spell loyalty and efficiency in Christ better than her ministry throughout the years. Her companion, and my personal secretary, is Elinor Carmen, who has also been with me for thirty years. Her spirituality and sensitivity have more than qualified her to be my confidential member of staff in all matters of correspondence, public relations, and complicated travel." In 2002, Vicki after a brief illness, went home to be with the Lord. Ellie currently resides in Florida with family.

"I must mention one other name that Heather, Jonathan, David and I will cherish until we see her in Glory. Her name is Mrs. Adelaide Dobson. She was a Jamaican who proudly possessed a British passport. From the word *go* she adopted the Olford family as her own. Hardly a Sunday went by, while we were at Calvary, when she did not turn up with a three- or four-course dinner for the entire family! She always insisted in serving us, cleaning up, and then sending us to rest, before the evening service. Christ radiated through her life and everybody knew it. Her spirit of sacrifice and service will ever be an example to Heather and me—but especially to Jonathan and David who accepted her as their second mother. Yes, there was great cause for thanksgiving during those exciting times at Calvary.

"Every Sunday was a surprise. In the congregation would be some famous actor or actress. Agnes Moorehead, of screen, stage and vaudeville fame, always sat in the front row of the balcony and considered Calvary as her church. There was concert pianist Van Cliburn (who was a member of Calvary); the royal Ballet of London; and United Nations ambassadors. On one occasion, President-elect Richard Nixon, in company with Billy Graham, attended a morning worship service. There were hundreds of other illustrious names. It was awesome and yet exciting to minister God's holy Word to people of this caliber week by week! Those were great and wonderful days, and I thank God for them."

———

But then disaster struck. Stephen Olford fell a victim of paroxysmal tachycardia. "I went to Mayo," he said, "and was told the reason I had it was because I had suffered vicariously with the broken lives of New York City. Most of these tachycardia episodes occurred at night and for a while they seemed to grow in intensity and duration. Now and then mild attacks occurred while preaching. The condition mandated a leave of absence." In February 1971 Stephen announced to the church that he would have to have a complete rest. The leave of absence lasted for eight months.

In the fall he was able to come back on a reduced schedule. Until

Christmas he was only preaching on Sundays; the rest of the week he gave to study and some writing. Two days each week were spent in the country for rest and relaxation.

What a welcome back he received! In spite of a torrential rainstorm and flooded roads, the church was absolutely packed the Sunday morning he returned. Strange to say, the text he had chosen was: "I will pour water upon him that is thirsty, and floods upon the dry ground" (Isaiah 44:3). God gave great liberty. Stephen could hardly believe he was back in his pulpit doing expository preaching again. The impact on the church was tremendous. Scores of people came into a new experience of consecration.

The official welcome home service, held in the afternoon, saw a full church despite continuing bad weather. Dr. J. C. Macaulay, now on the ministerial staff, led in prayer. There was hardly a dry eye in the place. In the

Photo courtesy of the Billy Graham Center

Stephen Olford chats with Republican presidential candidate,
Richard M. Nixon, and Evangelist Billy Graham
after the Sunday morning service, October 20, 1968.

reception that followed the Olfords shook hands (and gave hugs) with close to a thousand people. "We have never experienced such an outpouring of affection," Stephen said.

Even though he was back in the pulpit, he had to take a hard look at his schedule. He drastically cut from his calendar work that could be done just as well by others. The handwriting was now on the wall. On November 29, 1972 he submitted his resignation to become effective a month later. However he agreed to remain for an additional six months to help the church through its transition period. He took advantage of the occasion to state some of his future goals and to underline some of the problem areas he detected in the church he was leaving.

"As you all know," he said, "the gift that God has given me is supremely that of the evangelist. This is a gift that cannot be tied down or hemmed in for very long. For nearly fourteen years now I have sought to exercise it within the confines of this local church, but I have had an increasing burden to use the rich experience of these years to serve the total church through mass communication and leadership training. Needless to say, the extent to which God can use me will depend on physical strength and doors of opportunity in days to come. I might add here that never before have invitations been so numerous, insistent, and strategic; therefore I cannot ignore this Macedonian call."

Stephen Olford's resignation stunned the church. He was implored to reconsider. The church offered to come to some working arrangements whereby he could remain senior pastor with a mandate from the church to support his wider ministry with the church's support and blessing. It was a generous offer; but acutely aware of the Lord's leading in his own life and with strong feelings of what would be best for the church in the long run, he stood by his resignation. He pleaded that acceptance of his resignation be unanimous.

On January 10, 1973 a special meeting of the church was called and the joint boards regretfully urged the church to accept their beloved pastor's resignation. The boards of elders and deacons formally loosed Stephen Olford from the pastoral responsibilities of the church, saying: "We set him apart, along with his devoted wife, to the work to which the Holy Spirit has called them, and send them forth with the assurance of our prayerful and practical support." Then in February a recommendation from the joint boards was adopted, bestowing on Dr. Olford the honorary title of Minister Emeritus "in recognition of his meritorious service during the past fourteen years."

In July, the Olfords said their goodbyes and moved to Florida bringing several legacies with them from Calvary Baptist Church. There was Encounter Ministries, Inc., which assumed a new dimension of significance. Also there was Vicky Kuhl and Ellie Carman, Dr. Olford's two secretaries who came along to ensure a smooth transition to the future of Encounter.

In a farewell letter to his fellow members of Calvary Baptist Church, Stephen thanked them again for their love, prayerful interest, fellowship, and generosity. He solicited their prayers for the new ventures ahead. He reaffirmed his love for them all. He put things in focus with the words of an old hymn:

> Though sundred far, by faith [we] meet
> Around one common mercyseat.
>
> Hugh Stowell

Photo courtesy of the Billy Graham Center

*Taping his weekly half-hour "Encounter" radio
program in the studio at Calvary Baptist Church.*

CHAPTER 9

The Communicator

Their sound went into all the earth,
and their words unto the ends of the world.
Romans 10:18

S tephen Olford had always been fascinated by the power and potential
of radio and television as a means to reach the masses at home and
abroad with the gospel. In Britain that was not possible because the
British Broadcasting Corporation was a state-owned monopoly. It dutifully
allotted time for religious broadcasting but shied away from Christian
broadcasting as it is know in America.

On his first trip to the United States, Stephen had his eyes opened. Here
was a land of opportunity indeed! Any enterprising church, organization, or
individual could get on the air. Opportunities to broadcast his message
came his way almost at once on his very first trip to the States. He was
thrilled! The desire to make use of the media was planted in his heart.

When he was invited to become pastor of Calvary Baptist Church in
New York City one of the deciding factors in accepting the call was the fact
that this particular church had one of the longest histories of broadcasting
of any church in the United States. In 1959, the church had only one local
radio station carrying its morning service (WABC) and one foreign outlet
(HCJB). Stephen Olford soon expanded that. "The Calvary Church Hour"
was carried to England and Europe via TWR (Monaco) and Radio Manx; to
the south Pacific via HCJB in Ecuador, by ELWA in Liberia, West Africa, and

PJA-6 in the Netherlands Antilles; and across the United States on a variety of stations.

The idea of going on television was first conceived in Stephen's mind long before leaving England. During his first summer in the States (1960) plans were formulated for such a venture and actual taping began that fall. First, however, important decisions had to be made. Who would pay the bills? What would the program be like? Who would share in the actual production of the telecasts themselves? After much prayer a start was made. That start was both inspired and implemented by Mr. Fred Dienert, president of Walter F. Bennett & Company in Philadelphia, whose agency handled all aspects of the media ministry for the Billy Graham Evangelistic Association. Fred knew his business, and with his team of experts piloted Stephen through the currents and crosscurrents of radio/TV production and promotion.

Initially taping sessions were conducted in a makeshift garage in Rutherford, New Jersey (Sports Network). The new program had several handicaps. It had an inexperienced TV host, few props—just a pulpit and a piano—and a few technicians.

Stephen recalled some of those first rehearsals. There was Paul Liljestrand at the piano preparing to accompany the soloist, Fred Von Stange supervising the focusing of the cameras, and Marvin Detweiler putting the makeup on the preacher. Then the program was rolling: first with the musical theme and then Stephen Olford sitting in an easy chair against the backdrop of bookcases and a window scene of New York's skyline. On the set he used no notes, no script, just a cue card when interviewing a guest. He kept his eye on the camera lens so that he could make continuous eye contact with the viewer. The sermon consisted of fifteen minutes of straight talk, preaching, hard-hitting points, and a sincere and uncompromising appeal. Though all was rough and ready in those early days, over the years the program became polished and was well produced in modern studios, using the latest technology and a team of professionals, including Mr. Robert Straton, a dear friend and member of the pastoral team at Calvary.

The first "Encounter" program was aired on Sunday, October 9, 1960 at 12:30 p.m. At its conclusion counselors manned telephones for calls from concerned people who had been touched by the truth of the gospel. Letters poured in from Christians who were joining in prayer for this venture and from individuals who had experienced life-transforming encounters with Christ, including a fashion model, a high school teacher, a geologist, and a drug addict, to name but a few.

For two years the telecast continued at the 12:30 p.m. slot on Sundays over WPIX, Channel 11, a secular station with a powerful signal. A survey estimated that about forty-nine percent of television sets in the vast New

York metropolitan area were turned to WPIX on Sunday afternoons. So a decision was made, even though costs soared, to move the program to Sunday at 3:00 p.m. At once the mail showed more viewers, and the phone calls increased in both number and interest. Eventually the program was moved to 11:30 p.m. each Sunday. This attracted yet another viewer audience—people looking for a temporary escape from the harsh realities of life in an interesting late show.

The format settled down to a two-part program. The first part consisted of a guest interview, followed by a fifteen-minute message delivered by Stephen. He talked to an invisible audience of hundreds of thousands as easily as if they were seated before him. Usually he had a three-point outline, often punctuated with relevant questions addressed to his listeners. Many viewers testified it was just as if he were speaking directly and personally to them.

Over the years Stephen interviewed a glittering galaxy of guests. This included such celebrities as Bobby Richardson of the New York Yankees; Congressman John B. Conlan of Arizona; Madeline Manning Jackson, an Olympic runner; Dr. Robert Jervis, a nuclear scientist; Dr. Ernest Wilson, former heavyweight boxer and jazz player with Louis Armstrong's band; and Lt. Comdr. Steve Harris, whose ship, the *Pueblo,* was captured in North Korean waters in 1968.

Another time Dr. Olford interviewed Winston Hill, an offensive tackle for the New York Jets who stood six feet tall and weighed about three hundred pounds. The camera crew made the most of that by having them stand side by side. Stephen said he felt like David standing next to Goliath and mentioned this to Winston. Instantly the football heavyweight came back with the quip, "Just as long as you don't hit me in the head with a stone!"

And so they came, an endless stream of interesting people whose appearance on the show helped ensure a captive audience. There were others—Jo Schenkweiler, a woman who was director of a home for unwed mothers; Allan Hartley, a cartoonist of the famous *Archie Comics;* and Dr. Quentin Hyder, a renowned New York psychologist, noted not only for his skill in analyzing psychological problems, but for his ability in finding Biblical answers to them.

The programs usually opened in song by some well-known guest artist. Dr. Olford kept a watchful eye and a firm hand on the type of music he allowed on the program. Usually he sat at a wide V-shaped desk for the interview portion of the program. Sometimes, for variety, he answered questions submitted to him by viewers. The program always ended with a soul-searching message. Often Dr. Olford would pick up a statement made by his guest in the course of the interview and use it as a springboard for his message.

The first known convert of "Encounter" was a hotel clerk who "heard the program and followed it up with a visit to Calvary Baptist Church, where he was introduced to Jesus Christ."

If the first known convert was a hotel clerk, one of the most remarkable stories concerned a Roman Catholic nun—Sister Carmel. She was in charge of about five hundred sisters who taught and influenced hundreds of children in parochial schools. Sister Carmel appeared in her white habit at one of the evening services at Calvary Baptist Church. In fact, on occasion, she brought several of her colleagues with her. At the conclusion of the usual "instruction meeting," she came up to Dr. Olford and, with a directness he never forgot, looked him straight in the eye and affirmed, "I have been born again!" She then went on to explain how she had watched "Encounter" for a number of weeks, carefully listening to the simple gospel appeal. Then one night she heard Dr. Olford expound John 3 on the new birth. Before that program was over she knelt at her TV set and surrendered to Jesus Christ. She was radiant. She began to share her faith everywhere, including a number of Protestant churches.

When she learned that Stephen Olford was leaving the pastorate of Calvary Baptist Church, she asked a favor of him. During a special visit and a lengthy discussion of spiritual things, she asked if he would come and address the five hundred sisters who were under her care. Dr. Olford accepted the invitation and the arrangements were made. Stephen told the rest of the story:

"I arrived at the chapel with Heather, my wife. Sister Carmel took us to a little prayer room where she went through the order of worship and pointed out that she had included my favorite devotional hymn on the program, 'May the Mind of Christ, My Savior.' She requested that the invitation be left to her to handle. 'No one will escape the challenge,' she promised. Then we knelt in prayer with several of her senior sisters. After that we proceeded to the chapel and she led the service. When it came time for me to speak she astonished me. With dignity and sincerity she announced, 'and now it is my unique privilege and joy to present to you— not Dr. Olford, not the Reverend Stephen Olford—but my pastor! I have asked him to speak on the message that brought me to a living relationship to Christ from John, Chapter 3. He will speak on "the New Birth."' With that she took her seat and whispered as I passed her, 'take all the time you need.' As she told me later, scores of these dear women were gloriously saved. If our TV program in New York City was ordained of God for this one event alone it was more than worthwhile."

Conversions even took place right on the "Encounter" set between taping sessions. It was not unusual for members of the crew—a floorman, a cameraman—to knock on the door of Dr. Olford's dressing room between programs. Thinking there might have been a mechanical breakdown that needed rectifying, he was relieved to discover a spiritually hungry heart who simply wanted to meet Jesus. Such was the case of a young technician who was intrigued by Dr. Olford's message and the vibrant testimony of Rick Carreno, one-time drug addict and former member of the "Hell's Angels" motorcycle gang. Rick had made a guest appearance on the program. Dr. Olford introduced this man to Rick and through his witness he was led to the Lord. Another staff member, a young Jewess, asked questions and sought information about Jesus Christ, who was so foreign to her.

At the peak of its broadcasting, "Encounter" was heard twice a week in the greater New York area—Sundays at midnight and again on Thursday mornings at 9:30. The evangelistic thrust provided a unique opportunity each week to reach a potential of 21.6 million people in the New York City metropolitan area. Aimed primarily at the nonchurchgoing public, "Encounter" penetrated urban high rises and established itself as the prime gospel witness in New York; then proliferated itself to key cities across North America, plus five cable TV channels. In addition, as opportunity afforded, the "Encounter" television program was aired overseas in places as far away as Lagos, Nigeria and Manila, Philippines.

Stephen's basic philosophy for producing his "Encounter" television programs was very practical. As one of his staff members, David L. Carlson, pointed out at a workshop session of the thirty-first annual convention of the National Religious Broadcasters in January 1974, Stephen Olford had a threefold aim.

First he aimed at *simplicity*. The average listener was likely to be unsaved, unchurched and theologically unsophisticated. He would not be able to handle a doctrinal dissertation, even assuming he had sufficient interest to sit through one. So, right down to the basic format itself, Stephen aimed at simplicity.

Then he aimed at *sincerity*. Stephen realized from the outset that any attempt to hide behind an artificial front would be detected at once. In any case, Dr. Olford is far too honest and genuine a man to do or even give the appearance of any such thing. Hypocrisy, pretense, phoniness and sham would quickly result in the program being turned off. Even the camera crew had to fall in line. Dr. Olford refused to be stage-managed. The camera shots had to show him in unrehearsed, eye-to-eye contact with the camera and, therefore, with the viewer.

Finally, he aimed at *spontaneity*. He shied away from anything that would box him in. He wanted nothing to be stilted, artificial or formal. Variety and versatility were to be the heart and soul of the program. He refused to be poured into someone else's mold.

By the time the telecasts were being produced in the modern studio facilities of CFTO in Canada, his tenure at Calvary Baptist Church was coming to an end. He was forced to face the fact that overwork, tension and a crowded schedule had caught up with him. His condition known as paroxysmal tachycardia eventually precipitated, first, a leave of absence from his beloved church, and then a move away from New York altogether. He had one severe attack in June 1970, when he was in the middle of a taping session. The symptoms were persistent and ominous: trembling, weakness, constant nausea, and difficulty in breathing, all threatening unconsciousness. Even so, at the height of it, Stephen wrote in his diary: "Poor Heather is just beside herself. Will have to completely rethink the future . . . I still think I have 35 years . . . must concentrate on what we are really going to do . . . probably radio and television."

Stephen Olford finally came to the point where he had to leave Calvary Baptist Church. The doctor bluntly told him New York would kill him. He moved to Holmes Beach on the west coast of Florida and took Encounter Ministries with him. For awhile the telecasts continued, but eventually the enormous costs involved in producing 13-15 programs in three to four days—not to mention the astronomical costs of buying air time—forced their discontinuance. It was a sad day when Stephen Olford had to phase out his beloved "Encounter" TV program. His only consolation was the substantiated evidence that through the more than 400 produced programs men and women had come to a personal knowledge of Christ as Savior and Lord, and were now integrated in churches across New York City and beyond. A good number became active members of Calvary Baptist Church.

One such man was Wayland Stephens. He will never forget that day back in 1961 when "by sheer accident" he happened to flip the channels and came across "Encounter." He had heard the gospel all his life and thought that he was a Christian, yet as he listened and watched the program "it was at once apparent that this man, Stephen Olford, had hold of a dimension of life about which I knew absolutely nothing." He continued to view the program in succeeding weeks and sought the counsel of Pastor Olford and his associates, who graciously pointed him to the source of their joy and radiance—the living Christ Himself. His life was revolutionized and he subsequently went into the ministry. In fact, Stephen had the joy of preaching at his ordination and installation as pastor.

One night, at the end of a service at Calvary Baptist Church, a well-spoken and highly educated young woman came forward. She had waited through a long service, and after-meeting and a counseling session. She said, "I don't want to waste your time. I have come to tell you that some weeks ago, after listening to your television program, I knelt on my kitchen floor and received life in Christ. I don't need counseling. I am having my daily quiet time and am linked with a church. I have only come to tell you my good news." With that she opened her handbag and gave a sum of money. "This is a token of my love and gratitude for your ministry," she said. She then left and called for a cab. Later it was learned that she had traveled between twenty to thirty miles by cab just to give this testimony.

Another man, J. M. O'Malley said that business prosperity, a fine suburban home, leisure time, and a happy marriage did not bring him peace. For a year before his encounter with Christ he had been searching for something. He had read and pored over every book in the Lutheran Church library near where he lived. He had ransacked the religious section of the public library. All he knew was that he and his wife were not right with God.

Late one evening in 1964 he and his wife were half asleep when the "Encounter" program came on. At the end of the program Romans 10:9-10 was flashed on the television screen: "If thou shalt confess with thy mouth the Lord Jesus, and shalt believe in thine heart that God hath raised him from the dead, thou shalt be saved. For with the heart man believeth unto righteousness; and with the mouth confession is made unto salvation." The man and his wife were suddenly wide awake. "That's it!" was his wife's excited comment. They could be saved through the Lord Jesus Christ! They rejoiced together at the startling revelation.

O'Malley remembered, "Dr. Olford's message the next week was from Psalm 40:1-4. What assurance came as we heard our first message as Christians! Week after week we could not wait for God's Word!" J. M. O'Malley went into training for the ministry. Imagine his delight when, about to receive a doctorate from Luther Rice Seminary, he noticed that the name above his, in the alphabetical listing, was that of Stephen Olford!

There were times during the fifteen years when enemies of the cross assailed "Encounter". Indeed, the management of WPIX-TV was often under pressure to cancel the program. But God protected this strategic outreach until His time had come.

Then something happened. Stephen Olford was invited to the central offices of WPIX and given a lavish reception with all the directors present. After appropriate words were mutually exchanged, Stephen was asked to proceed to one of the studios. He recalled how his heart pounded. He recounted: "This was not a Christian setting, nor was I to be interviewed by anyone. After makeup, I learned that no one other than Mr. Richard Hughes, the well-known critic and analyst from WPIX was to 'take me on.' I sent up a fervent and fast prayer and took my seat before the cameras. Facing the little red light, Mr. Hughes began (and I paraphrase): 'I'm Richard Hughes, and my normal role is to analyze and criticize; but this appearance is for something far more pleasant. I am here to bid farewell to the host of "Encounter," Dr. Stephen Olford, who has held his own on this station for fifteen years. I have to confess that when I first saw and heard him I was his greatest critic; now I am his greatest convert! I just could not imagine a man with an English accent and an open Bible lasting for more than a few weeks on this station. It seemed to me to be totally out of character, but he has made it and has a phenomenal following.'

"Then turning to me he put out his hand and warmly congratulated me, and began to ask me questions that were positive, profitable and personally rewarding. I could not have crafted or formulated words any better in the quiet of my study. As the floormen gave the signal to wind down, Mr. Hughes beckoned a young lady to come forward. She was carrying a plaque. Taking it from her hand, he turned to me again and read the inscription with slow and deliberate articulation:

To

DR. STEPHEN F. OLFORD

IN

RECOGNITION OF

15 DYNAMIC YEARS

OF

REACHING THRU TELEVISION

'ENCOUNTER'

1960-1975

WPIX-New York City

"I was overwhelmed, but managed to compose myself and respond as appropriately as the occasion demanded. That plaque hangs in our Center to this very day. This was an honor conferred on me by the managers of a secular station!"

While "Encounter" TV closed a chapter in communication, "Encounter" radio continued to grow. Then came a crucial decision that Stephen had to make. He was burdened about reaching overseas listeners. Two interesting experiences led to this crossroads in his radio ministry.

The first took place at the International Conference for Itinerant Evangelists in Amsterdam, Holland, July 12-21, 1983. Dr. Olford had delivered a keynote address on "the Evangelists' Gift and Ministry." His appearance on the podium had exposed him to many overseas nationals who, heretofore, had heard his voice over ELWA (Eternal Love Winning Africa), the S.I.M. radio station from Liberia, West Africa.

One night he was sitting in the audience waiting for the service to start when a tall African, dressed in a bishop's habit, took his place immediately behind him. Turning around, Stephen extended his hand and greeted him with the words, "The Lord bless you, my brother. My name is

Stephen Olford."With that the bishop's eyes lit up and jumping to his feet he exclaimed, "You Stephen Olford? You Stephen Olford?" And before Stephen could reply the bishop picked him up in his arms and started to dance an African jig! The service was already in progress, but our African brother was too enraptured to notice. He danced away until Stephen could calm him down.

"Come with me," said the bishop, and literally carried Dr. Olford to a side room and sat him down. Then opening his satchel, he pulled out a wad of notes and asked, "Do you recognize anything familiar about these notes?" Dr. Olford examined them for a moment and then grinned with pleasure. "They are notes of sermons I have preached over radio ELWA!" "Yes," exclaimed the bishop, "I seldom miss your broadcasts. While I listen, I take copious notes which I then write out in full. I preach the sermons myself and then share them with all my pastors across the Cameroons. So your ministry reaches hundreds of congregations in our country; and now to think I have met my mentor at last!" As Stephen Olford put it, "That testimony not only moved me to tears, but confirmed to me the need to continue radio overseas as long as support at home made this possible."

The second experience was a little different, but no less exciting. In 1979 Stephen and Heather were in Liberia for the twenty-fifth anniversary of ELWA. The event was celebrated with special meetings at the mission compound, plus lectures on expository preaching at three seminaries for national pastors. One morning, Dr. and Mrs. Olford were invited to the executive mansion of His Excellency, Dr. William R. Tolbert. Dr. Olford knew that the president of Liberia was a regular listener to "The Calvary Church Hour" and later the "Encounter" half-hour program. After a delightful conversation over a cup of tea, the president asked the press and TV crew to come into his stateroom where he presented Stephen Olford with a gold medallion minted to commemorate his own presidency of the Organization of Africa Unity for 1979. He explained that this was a token of his appreciation for what Dr. Olford had done for his nation. He declared, "There is only one thing that will save our country and that is the preaching of the Word of God." He went on to tell Dr. and Mrs. Olford that he was mandating the teaching of the Bible in all the schools. Then he turned to the mission-aries, who accompanied the Olfords to the executive mansion, and requested that Dr. Olford should be allowed to change his schedule in order to preach in Tolbert's newly refurbished two thousand-seat Centennial Pavilion in downtown Monrovia.

Stephen remembered the gasp that left the lips of the missionaries. How would this be publicized in such short order? How could counselors be trained? Would anybody come? However, a presidential mandate was nothing to be refused. So they left the president's stateroom and hurried back to the ELWA compound to plan their strategy. Stephen was confident that if ELWA's technicians could hook up the equipment to broadcast from the auditorium there would be no problem in drawing a crowd. For years Olford's voice had been heard across Liberia, Nigeria, and as far away as Cape Town, South Africa.

The first night some two hundred people were mustered to attend the evening rally. But at the service Stephen or "Tivi," walked to the microphone and quoted John 3:16 in the Chokwe language: "Mumu chócho Zambi wazangile akwahashi, achize wechele Mwanenyi wasemewa umuwika, hanga mweswawo mafuliela kuli Iye, kechikatoka, alioze akapwe ni mwono wa miaka yeswe." He then announced, "Your president has invited me to speak each evening for the rest of this week in this beautiful auditorium. I invite you to attend the services and meet my wife Heather and me. You have been my unseen audience for many years, but now I want to see you face to face!"

The results were beyond all expectation. The next night the auditorium was packed, some coming by car, others by bicycle, and still others on foot. By the end of the week there was standing room only. The gospel was preached each night and hundreds responded to the call of Christ. Every missionary, national pastor, and lay leader was busy counseling.

Once again, Dr. Olford was convinced of the power of radio for overseas ministry—not only for nationals, but also for "starved" missionaries in lonely places who were planting churches, translating Scriptures or doing medical work. As far as he was concerned, radio must go on. He was convinced that radio around the world was not only a necessity, but an investment. This was missionary work in its most extensive dimension, but little could be expected in terms of financial returns. Stephen Olford would have to trust God and look to his constituency to give specifically to this aspect of Encounter's ministry. So it was that Encounter Ministries retrenched in order to move forward. The world increasingly became Stephen's parish.

On June 1, 1970 the media side of the ministry was legally constituted under the name of Encounter Ministries, Inc. It was a wise move. The new corporation became the umbrella organization for his worldwide radio ministry, his preaching, his tapes and books, and later for the Institute for Biblical Preaching.

The response to Dr. Olford's global strategy was overwhelming. His mailbag and files bulge with stories that bear witness to the correctness of his far-reaching decisions.

One listener from Trinidad said that he was left, as a child, in the care of a Hindu grandmother. Nevertheless he was raised a Roman Catholic and

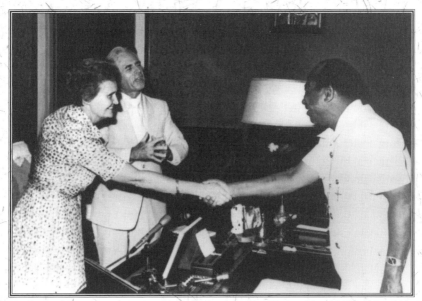

Photo courtesy of the Billy Graham Center

Dr. and Mrs. Olford with the President of Liberia,
His Excellency, Dr. William R. Tolbert, November, 1979.

attended a Roman Catholic school. As a young man, however, he rebelled and joined a gang.

He came to know Christ through the ministry of an American family and was thereafter cold-shouldered by his Hindu grandmother and Muslim in-laws. He began attending church. His Muslim wife became a Christian. He went to Bible school and then into Christian work. "A classmate," he said, "introduced me to the ministry of Dr. Stephen Olford and encouraged me to listen to his radio broadcast as it came over a South American station." Later this man, Anthony Kawalsingh went into the pastorate. He wrote, "I have been greatly challenged, helped, and influenced by the ministry of Dr. Olford. His writings and his sermons are a great source of inspiration in my life."

An English student raised as a Catholic, moved to Italy with his family at the age of sixteen. There he was quickly disillusioned about religion, so he embraced atheism, became a Marxist and a Communist militant. Three years later he faced the fact that Communism, too, was nothing but an elaborate hoax. He sank into a deep depression and considered suicide. When he went to Italy he hungered for English language broadcasts. That was how he eventually found Trans World Radio and discovered "Encounter." His first reaction was a mixture of derision (because he considered himself an atheist) and fear (because his concept of God was that of "a strict, demanding old man, quick to punish the slightest wrongs"). Listening to Stephen Olford he learned that God loved him so much He had given His Son to die for his salvation—a God who would forgive; a God who would change lives and change his. As a result, Gianantonio Rozzini decided to accept Christ as his Lord and Savior. He gave up his political activities in order to "concentrate instead on loving God and people."

A man in Ghana wrote, "I am a lawyer by profession. I am so impressed by the preaching of Dr. Stephen Olford that I am planning to leave the profession and become an evangelist." He asked for help in the form of cassettes and literature. "I never miss your program," he added. "Even when I travel and find I will not be at home by 7:00 a.m. on Sunday (Ghana time) I take my small radio along. God bless your program and all of you."

Samson Ogbonna, a Nigerian, tells how he was raised in a home where his mother was a nominal Christian who made her children go to church each Sunday. His father was an idolater who would take his boy with him when he went to sacrifice chickens to his god. The boy grew up in a time of civil war. He had a traumatic experience when, walking down a jungle trail, the friend he was with stepped on a hidden mine and was seriously injured. Even as he stooped to help his friend he opened his heart to Christ. Later he moved to the United Republic of Cameroon. He knew he should join a church but was disgusted because, in the nearby church he attended, the elders were preaching while drunk. He decided never to go to church again. Then "one bright Sunday morning," he said, "I turned to station ELWA and heard some wonderful preaching by Stephen Olford. I wept beside my radio as the Holy Spirit of God convicted me of my sins." He became a regular listener to "Encounter." He cleaned up his life. All doubts about his salvation vanished. He added, "Each week when Dr. Olford starts to preach, my knees are on the ground as I pray that God will use the message for His glory."

A man from Latin America wrote; "In August 1973, while making my way up our largest river to hold classes, I met a group of Americans on board ship. One young fellow had a cassette recorder and was playing an 'Encounter' tape. Since one of my hobbies is listening to public speakers in order to evaluate their effectiveness in communicating, I was immediately attracted to Dr. Olford's preaching." This man was a teacher by profession. He specialized in remedial English and linguistics. He listened with interest to the style, diction, and accent of the speaker on the tape, making his usual mental notes as he listened. He showed such interest that, as he left the boat, the American gave him the tape. "At home," he continued, "I played the tape seventeen times, analyzing oratorical and linguistic techniques, all the while managing to ignore the content. One day I decided to listen seriously to the message, which was from John 3, on how Nicodemus encountered the living Christ. While Dr. Olford spoke I realized that I was hearing, for the first time in my life, a sane, intelligent, and relevant presentation of the gospel. At the conclusion of the tape I prayed inviting Christ in to my heart.

"What a change Christ has brought into my life!" he continued, "what joy, peace, and purpose He has given me. Immediately I shared the good news with my family, fellow workers, and friends. My wife, and eldest son, and later my eldest daughter accepted Christ.

"Since receiving Christ I have begun to study the Word of God and pray systematically. The Lord has enabled me to witness extensively. Thus I hold Sunday schools, do a bit of preaching when the occasion demands, and organize groups of believers. I hold services in an old wooden building near a river, since there are no churches there. The response has been good. I began having Bible studies and many made professions of faith. In May 1975, forty-five people were baptized by immersion. Since then the number of believers has increased to 120. In October of last year thirty other persons were baptized. We praise God for His blessings. We have organized ourselves into a church and meet three times a week. We have ten Sunday schools and twelve preaching stations where we hold open-air services. 'Encounter' has been a very useful tool to bring us all to Christ."

From the Caribbean, Dr. Olford received a well-expressed letter from R. Theodore L. V. Browne, an attorney-at-law in Kingstown, St. Vincent. He wrote: "It was a most refreshing experience to hear your voice once more on a radio station in the Commonwealth of Dominica in the West Indies. Your powerful, incisive, and penetrating expositions of God's Word have always affected my heart and head. I thank God for bestowing upon you such mighty gifts. May He continue to anoint and inspire you as you seek to open up oases in the arid hearts of men. Since I was a schoolboy—at which time you were the pastor of Calvary Baptist Church—your stirring messages stimulated my mind, disturbed my conscience, and redirected my life. Indeed, your messages have had a devastating effect in my natural life in that they destroyed my limited and lowly concepts of God, radically heightened my aspirations in life, and dramatically extended my mental horizons. Through our Lord Jesus Christ, my life is characterized by a quality hitherto unknown." He went on to ask for information about the work.

In 1991 the Baptist governor of the Bay Islands, off the coastal areas of Honduras, Guatemala, and Belize—Dr. Glen R. Solomon—was concerned with the physical and spiritual well-being of his people. He had heard many excellent reports about "Encounter" radio and felt that "in a world of drugs and alcohol (of which his islands were not exempt) the program could play a significant role in presenting Christ as the answer to their needs." Arrangements were made, tapes were shipped, and "Encounter" began airing twice a week on Station HRGS (Heaven's Redemption Gives Salvation) out of Tampa, Florida.

Another man who wrote to Encounter was Nishi Sharma. He never saw a Bible or met a born-again Christian until he was twenty-nine. He was born and raised in India in a Hindu family. From childhood he learned to memorize and recite Hindu texts. When he was a teenager he began to question Hinduism. The Hindu doctrine of reincarnation, with its relentless fatalism, always frightened him. He became disillusioned about God and by His seeming silence. At university he became interested in mysticism through the writings of a Tibetan lama. He began to practice astral travel and became involved in the occult. In 1969 he went to work for the Ministry of Education in Nigeria. Material success, however, brought him no closer to happiness. He said, "Spiritual loneliness and the serious effects of astral traveling and other similar experiences led me to attempt suicide. But in those last moments, when I realized that the end of my life was very near, I made a last cry to the Creator, whom I didn't know, to save me." God answered his prayer. From then on he read all kinds of religious books, hoping to find out something about God, but it was all in vain. God seemed as silent and remote as ever. Then it happened!

"One day," he said, "I was tuning my radio to find some nice music at the beginning of a lazy Sunday morning and suddenly I heard someone talking about God. I stopped and listened to the man who was speaking in such a way as if he had really met God in his life. There was something compelling about him. Later it was announced that the message was delivered by Dr. Stephen Olford from Calvary Baptist Church, New York."

For seven months he listened to the program every Sunday morning. "One morning," he continued, "while listening to Dr. Olford's message, I was convinced that only Christ could give me fulfillment in life, and I asked Him to be my Savior." He found out afterwards that some Christians he had known had been praying for him. He went to England for training and then went back to India as a missionary to work with Far East Broadcasting Corporation, making Christ known by radio to his own people.

Some years ago Stephen was in Soweto, South Africa. He was speaking at a giant rally in a big YMCA facility. After waiting through the preliminaries for three hours he was finally able to take the platform. The Holy Spirit came down in power and blessing. "Afterwards," he recalled, "I was standing there talking to people when I heard a voice say: 'I can hear him! I can hear him!' Looking around, I saw a blind man tapping the ground with his cane and making his way right to me. As he tapped on the floor he said, 'You are Stephen Olford.' I said, 'I am.' He said, 'I never miss you any Sunday.' I said, 'All right, what did I preach on last Sunday?' I paid the price for that question! I stood there for twenty minutes while he told me. The man had never seen me and will never see me. But he knew me."

It is said of the great American revivalist Charles Finney that his very presence was enough to produce in people an agonizing conviction of sin. On one occasion he simply walked through a factory and people fell alongside their machines into the aisles, crying out to God for mercy.

It can be equally said of Stephen Olford that his presence produced in people a desire to be like him, just as he was like his Lord. It was not just his radiant face and magnetic personality. It was not simply his spirituality and authority. It was not simply the fact that he gave his complete attention to the person to whom he was speaking. It was not only the remarkable success that crowned his efforts as evangelist, soul-winner, pastor, and teacher. It was not the fact that he was such a gifted communicator. It was simply that he practiced what he preached. The life of the indwelling Christ he proclaimed was the life he lived.

Many years ago there lived in the land of Israel a certain woman of Shunem. We do not know her name. The Holy Spirit, however, gives her a rare title. He says that she was "a great woman." She was intrigued by a man who came and went and to whom, from time to time, she extended the hospitality of her home. One day she said to her husband, "Look now, I know that this is a holy man of God, who passes by us regularly" (2 Kings 4:9, NKJV). The man was Elisha. He was a man who lived in the power of a double anointing of the Holy Spirit. What the Shunammite said of the Old Testament prophet could be said of this present-day prophet, and for the same reason. He was a holy man of God; hence the power of his ministry.

Photo by Todd Hampten Lillard, ©1993

The Stephen Olford Center for Biblical Preaching,
Memphis, Tennessee.

CHAPTER 10

The Teacher-Preacher

*The things that thou hast heard ...
among many witnesses,
the same commit thou to faithful men,
who shall be able to teach others also.*
2 Timothy 2:2

Stephen Olford was a superlative teacher. When I was a boy of twelve or thirteen years of age I heard him deliver a gospel message on John 14:6:"Jesus saith unto him, I am the way, the truth, and the life; no man cometh unto the Father, but by me." I can still remember the outline, though it was over sixty years ago that I heard it.

"In this text," Stephen declared, "Jesus answers the three greatest questions of the human heart: How can I be saved? Jesus said, 'I am the way'; How can I be sure? Jesus said, 'I am the truth'; How can I be satisfied? Jesus said, 'I am the life.'"

The three existing universal gifts given by the Holy Spirit to the church are that of the evangelist, the pastor, and the teacher (Ephesians 4:11). Stephen Olford was one of those rare individuals who excelled in all three.

It is rare, for instance, to find a man who is both an evangelist and a teacher. Many evangelists I have heard seem to be very shallow in their understanding of the great doctrines of the Word of God. This was not true of Stephen Olford. His teaching never lost sight of the great heart-need of saint and sinner alike. It never satisfies itself in appealing solely to the intellect. By the same token, his preaching was teaching set on fire. In other words, when Stephen the evangelist stepped into the pulpit he was still a teacher. When Stephen the teacher stepped behind the lectern he was still an evangelist.

The teacher has to deal with the mind. His task is to impart to the student knowledge, understanding, and wisdom. A simple illustration will show the difference between the three.

A little girl is watching her mother do the ironing. She is fascinated as the iron darts here and there across the fabric eating up crinkles and creases and always hungry for more. The little girl longs to get her hands on that iron. Ironing looks like fun! Presently the telephone rings and Mother is called away. She says to her little girl, "Don't touch that iron. It's hot." She now has *knowledge*—the iron is hot.

No sooner is Mother's back turned, however, than the littler girl's desire to do some ironing herself completely masters her. She reaches out to take hold of the iron but touches the metal instead of the handle. She receives a nasty burn. She now has *understanding*—the iron is hot.

A week later Mother is ironing again and, once more the little girl is watching, just as fascinated as before by the process. Once again there is an interruption, and as the mother leaves the room she says to her little girl, "Don't touch that iron; it's hot." The little girl looks longingly at the iron. The temptation to try a little ironing is as strong as ever. Her hand steals out toward the iron. Then she remembers her burn, puts her hand behind her back, and walks away. Now she has *wisdom*—the iron is hot.

The first function of the teacher is to impart knowledge. The student has to learn all the relevant facts. Then he has to learn how to recognize the principles he has been taught when he comes across them in various situations or forms. He has to have an understanding of the principles and precepts he has been taught. Finally, he has to relate those facts to life. When he does that he displays wisdom.

This learning process is well illustrated in the story of Philip and the Ethiopian (Acts 8). Philip was a teacher-evangelist. At the Holy Spirit's urging, Philip made his contact with the Ethiopian. It was at once evident that the man had access to all the facts before him on the open page. He was reading the words of Isaiah 53, and he had knowledge about the sufferings of the One of whom the prophet had written. The facts dealt with great and mighty truths. The eunuch had evidently been turning this new knowledge over in his mind.

But he was completely devoid of understanding. Philip suspected this. "Do you understand what you are reading?" he asked. The Ethiopian readily admitted his limitations. "How can I?" the Ethiopian said in response to Philip's question. "Of whom does the prophet say this? He asked, "of himself or of some other man?" Philip at once pointed the man to Christ.

Not long afterward, the chariot came within sight of an oasis. "See, here is water. What hinders me from being baptized?" Exhibiting wisdom, he was eager to apply the truth he had learned in a practical way to his life.

The teacher, then, must be a communicator. He must inform, motivate, test, challenge, and inspire. Essentially all education is designed to change behavior. Since this is so, it is imperative that the Christian teacher embodies in his own life and ministry the precepts, principles, and practices he seeks to impart to others. It is this that set Stephen Olford's teaching on fire. He not only conveyed truth in a particularly clear, pungent, and authoritative way, but his life adorned his teaching. He embodied and exemplified the truths he taught.

It all began many years ago. Stephen recalled that following his theological training in London, England he had an irrepressible urge to teach. He just wanted to share with others what God had taught him and accomplished in him—especially while he was at the Missionary Training Colony in Upper Norwood, London. On his return to Newport in South Wales, he was greatly disturbed by the status quo of his home church. The young men including his two brothers, Paul and John—were spiritually starved. So after much prayer and preparation he started a Bible class for men only. Little by little the class outgrew the living room of his parent's home. At the same time the "girl friends" complained that they were not being catered for. So Stephen's mother started a class for the girls. Eventually, the two classes were brought together and met in a spacious upper room over a tool shop in downtown Newport. The group was called The Young People's Christian Fellowship.

As the war years went by, this Y.P.C.F. became a spiritual force to be reckoned with in the religious life of the town. These young people were the initiators and inspiration for spiritual life conventions, two or three citywide crusades, and open-air meetings in the Welsh valleys. They were also the supporting force behind a center for servicemen and women each day of the week and a special after-church evangelistic rally on Sunday evenings in a rented school auditorium.

Even more important than the outreach of this group were the teaching sessions every Friday when Dr. Olford systematically taught God's Word. In essence, it was a Bible school. To this very day, there are men and women who are living tributes and testimonies to the grounding they received in the Word: Bill Parry—a ministering brother in his own right; Dan Maynard who distinguished himself in business and in the work of Gideons International as president and chaplain; Stephen's brothers, Paul and John, who have successfully combined professional and preaching ministries; Doreen Greer (now Mrs. Arthur Schneider) who was the backbone of the Y.P.C.F. and an able Bible teacher. I, myself, was an early member of the Y.P.C.F. I was just entering the teenage years at the time, and Stephen Olford fired my imagination. His teaching laid a solid foundation in my mind and memory and contributed to my own subsequent ministry.

This taste for teaching carried over to Stephen Olford's first pastorate. As soon as he accepted the call to Duke Street Baptist Church in Richmond, Surrey (1953-1959), he made sure that his midweek service would be more than a brief devotional followed by a prayer meeting. It was once again a Bible school. He expounded the Word on Sunday mornings, and preached the gospel Sunday nights; but teaching was reserved for his midweek Bible school—with question and answer periods, homework, and even test papers!

More was to come when he assumed the charge at Calvary Baptist Church in New York City. In the early weeks and months of his ministry he taught a course on church membership at the Wednesday night Bible studies, which became the basis for his Discipleship Class talks. This was followed by his ten-week course, "Successful Soul-Winning." Over the years he lectured on prophecy, the person and work of the Holy Spirit, the deep truths of the tabernacle, and conducted in-depth studies on such books as Acts and Romans.

During the winter term of 1960 he also taught at the New York Evening School of the Bible that met on Fridays at Calvary under the auspices of Providence-Barrington Bible College (Rhode Island). But then the ministry placed greater demands on his time. The first Christian Life Convention was started. Publishers wanted him to write books. Overseas ministry beckoned. The "Encounter" telecast was born. There were faculty changes too, and as a result the New York Evening School of the Bible was discontinued.

However, Stephen's dream of having an evening school never died. In the fall of 1971 it resumed, this time on Monday nights. Dr. Olford invited his dear friend, Dr. Joseph C. Macaulay, to be dean of the school. Dr. Macaulay previously taught at Moody Bible Institute, Chicago and was president of the London College of Bible and Missions, London, Ontario. He had also pastored several churches, including Wheaton Bible Church in Illinois. Joe Macaulay expanded the curriculum to include courses in Bible, systematic theology, Christian education, preaching, missions, Christian writing, and a host of other offerings. Enrollment grew to the hundreds. Graduation was always a great event at Calvary Baptist Church. Diplomas carried credit for further studies in academic schools. To the glory of God, the New York School of the Bible is still going on.

The illness that precipitated Stephen Olford's resignation from active ministry at Calvary led to the subsequent move to Holmes Beach, Florida. In the years that followed he gave himself to intensive study of the whole subject of expository preaching. In fact, he completed a doctoral degree with the research and writing he did for that study. The purpose however, was not for academics but for action. The vision and burden to restore anointed expository preaching to the pulpits of our land evolved from a vision to a veritable passion. The only question that remained was how to translate passion into action.

In 1976, and again in 1978, Dr. Billy Melvin, Executive Director of the National Association of Evangelicals—an organization that represented thirty-six thousand churches and sixty-six denominations—invited Stephen to conduct seminars on expository preaching across the land. Almost every leading seminary was visited with one-day institutes. Pastors, seminarians, and lay leaders came in droves to listen and participate in these learning events. Perhaps the most enriched learner was Stephen Olford himself. He learned that there is a great gulf between content and communication. Anyone can learn the principles of hermeneutics and exegesis and yet be ignorant or inept at transposing such knowledge into practical homiletics. A pastor can possess the best exegetical commentaries available today and yet be a hopeless failure as an expository preacher. There is a difference between teaching and training when it comes to communication.

These preaching tours ultimately led Dr. Melvin and his Executive Committee to invite Encounter Ministries to join forces with N.A.E., thus broadening E.M.I.'s platform and strengthening its witness. In 1979 the Olfords moved their operation to Wheaton, Illinois. Two valuable years followed.

In Wheaton in 1980 Dr. Olford produced the first of seven volumes of sermon outline resources now known as the *Expository Preaching Outlines*, designed to assist pastors in the ministry. The volumes are not "canned" sermons, but are designed to take a pastor, with limited training and a meager library, through seven years of pulpit preaching. They are crafted to help a preacher produce and develop his own expository sermons. The volumes were an instant success and continue to help men in the ministry at home and abroad.

Over a period of time this only served to fuel Stephen's desire to have a permanent center somewhere in the United States where he could effectively train men in the art of expository preaching. To seek the mind of the Lord the Olfords took a six-month sabbatical in the summer of 1984. There were several options open to them, but one by one these possibilities were ruled out after due consideration and prayerful investigation.

Then came an invitation from Dr. James Latimer, pastor of Central Church in Memphis, Tennessee. This offer was to come to Memphis and house the center in the church facilities until neutral ground could be found for building or buying property to serve the designed purpose. Stephen had ministered in Memphis at a Mid-South Keswick Bible

Conference, but otherwise knew very little about the size or suitability of the city. But after a thorough evaluation of the demographics, it became apparent that Memphis was a strategic venue for a center for Biblical preaching. He discovered it was the fifteenth largest city in America, beautifully located on the Mississippi River. It was a good distribution center, had an international airport, and was not cluttered with the busyness of cities like New York, Dallas, or even Atlanta. Located in the "Bible Belt," Memphis boasted of hundreds of churches. The fact that Tennessee was surrounded by eight states that touched its borders made Memphis an ideal site from which to reach more preachers per square mile than anywhere else in the world.

So the decision was made to move again—office staff and all—and for the first three years Stephen and his team worked out of Central Church. The pastor and his staff "showed us unusual kindness" for which Stephen will be forever grateful.

After much house hunting, a beautiful and suitable property was found—located on a forty-two-acre wooded estate in southeast Memphis. God miraculously overruled the financial negotiations so that the Olfords were able to take possession by selling half of the land to lower capital expenditure. The faithful Board of Directors was squarely behind the entire enterprise with prayers, gifts, and moral support.

On June 4, 1988, the property was dedicated and named The Stephen Olford Center for Biblical Preaching. As such, it became the international headquarters of Encounter Ministries, Inc. and houses the Institute for Biblical Preaching. Friends from near and far attended the ceremonies, and Dr. Charles Stanley of First Baptist Church, Atlanta delivered the dedicatory address, which turned out to be a moving testimony to what Stephen Olford's ministry had meant to him personally. Also taking part were Dr. Adrian Rogers, pastor of Bellevue Baptist Church, Memphis, and Dr. James Latimer who gave a brief history of the call to Memphis. A greeting was also read from Dr. Billy Graham. The whole service was a meaningful event. In 1999, Encounter Ministries, Inc. changed its name to Olford Ministries International.

Since the dedication of the property numerous Biblical preaching institutes and workshops have been held yearly at the Center. The desire of the Institute as explained in the Olford Ministries International brochure is "to provide biblical instruction and practical training to encourage and equip preachers and teachers to 'rightly divide' the Word of truth." After many years of pastoral and global ministry, Dr. Olford believed that "the ultimate answer to the problems of every age is the anointed expository preaching of God's inerrant Word. Such preaching must be restored to the contemporary pulpit."

Photo by Joe Gleason

Participants in the dedication of the Stephen Olford
Center for Biblical Preaching.
Dr. David Olford, Dr. W.F. Andrews, J. Herbert Fisher,
Dr. James Latimer, Dr. Adrian Rogers, Dr. Charles Stanley,
Dr. Stephen Olford, Sir J. Eric Richardson, Dr. Ted Rendall.

One pastor who attended an Institute was astonished by the personalized attention given to him by Stephen Olford. "I never thought," he said, "that I would meet a man of his caliber who would take the time to minister to me personally. I am grateful for this ministry." Another pastor said, "One week here with Stephen and David Olford is equivalent to two years in the ministry. I didn't know how much I didn't know about preaching until I came here, and now I am going back with double vigor to incorporate what I have learned."

High on the Institute agenda is sermon preparation and presentation. The heart of Stephen's ability to communicate the great truths of the Bible was expository preaching, which he defined as "the Spirit-empowered explanation and proclamation of the text of God's Word with due regard to the historical, contextual, grammatical, and doctrinal significance of the given passage, with the specific object of invoking a Christ-transforming response." This can apply to a text or passage of Scripture or can relate to a topic, a series of sermons, or a whole book of the Bible to be preached over a period of weeks or months. In his thinking, preaching will never go out of date. "There is," he said, "in preaching, a quality which is eternal (see 1 Corinthians 1:11-25). Nothing must be allowed to take the place of preaching."

Dr. Olford deplored the popular misconception that envisions a running commentary, rambling on from verse to verse, as expository preaching. All too often someone who is too lazy or too unskilled to produce a proper homiletic plan or outline employs that kind of preaching.

The expositor, with the open Bible passage before him, must ask himself: What does this passage say to my heart? What does it say to my church? The answers that emerge from this survey will suggest doctrinal, devotional, ethical, and expositional patterns. In preparing his expository sermons Dr. Olford first settled on the choice of a subject. He then constructed the skeletal framework of the sermon: its introduction, exposition, application and conclusion. The body of the sermon would normally be expressed in three main headings, each supported by two or three subheadings. All these were carefully crafted to relate to the main theme or subject and follow a logical sequence.

The hallmark of an Olford expository sermon is the outline, which is invariably alliterated. The outline that emerges from a study of the Biblical text is plain and unadorned. Importance is placed on tying the points of the sermon together by means of alliteration or other literary devices that aid the hearer's memory. Such artistry must employ all words with the same letter, word ending, or number of syllables. The words should be familiar and accurately convey the truth of the Biblical text. They must relate to the main theme or subject and carry perfect sequence. This cannot be overemphasized. "Without this structural and sequential treatment of the text there will be confusion both in the pulpit and in the pew." The preacher, seeking to alliterate his major points and his sub-points, must never force the alliteration. He must never sacrifice the sense for the sake of the sound. Nothing could be worse. It demeans the sermon. It irritates and annoys the listener. It defeats the whole purpose of alliteration, which is to add art to science and enhance the points with a pleasing and harmonious phonetic appeal.

Dr. Olford explained: "I use alliteration for my many headings and very often for my subheadings. This is to aid my memory, as well as help the listeners retain the essence of what I have said. Very often in actual delivery I might break the sequence of alliteration so as to foil listeners who are merely looking for an outline."

The outline is just the first step in building an expository sermon. The process of putting meat on the bones of the outline calls for thought and research. There must be a careful examination of the text, along with meditation, reference to commentaries, textbooks, and resource material in one's files. There must also be a constant quest for illustrations.

Dr. Olford urged his listeners to "use commentaries, Hebrew and Greek lexicons, read other sermons, particularly the Puritans, C. H. Spurgeon, and the edited sermons in *The Biblical Illustrator.* The main purpose in such reading is that ideas beget ideas. I expand my vocabulary, and sometimes gather suggestions for outlines, but refuse to use other people's sermons or copy their style."

Then comes the actual composition of the message. "When possible," said Dr. Olford, "I like to write out or dictate the sermon in full, giving special attention to the introduction and the conclusion. The introduction should be designed to arrest attention, remove prejudice, and place the subject in perspective. The conclusion should always demand a verdict."

The final step in the process is the delivery of the sermon. Dr. Olford said, "I never preach a sermon that doesn't live to me. I use three tests when it doesn't live in my heart prior to its being preached (usually a day or so before). The first test is physical: Am I tired and in need of rest? The second test is moral: Do I have sin in my life? Is there any break in my fellowship with God? The third test is spiritual: Have I obeyed the truth myself or am I asking people to do things I refuse to do?"

He continued: "There has to be a spirit of expectancy even though I always go into the pulpit in fear and trembling!" He confided: "The reaction of the audience is not what matters, for as Paul said: 'We can do nothing against the truth, but for the truth.' It is the glory of God that must be my supreme passion."

He also had sound advice on the preacher's appearance, mannerisms, tone of voice, and authority in the pulpit. Simplicity and sincerity, Dr. Olford said are the cardinal rules. "If a man is transparent in the pulpit, people will take anything from him."

Those who have heard Stephen Olford teach or preach have often been impressed by his eloquence and spontaneity in the pulpit. He rarely uses notes. He seems to be preaching extemporaneously. He explained this: "The fact that I may use a lot of my material verbatim can be attributed to the Spirit of remembrance who has been promised to every preacher who claims the divine anointing."

"God never promised to bless my sermons or my stories," said Dr. Olford, "but He has promised to bless His Word. I have come to see that the most fruitful and abiding work follows expository preaching. No matter if I'm talking to a group of children, teenagers, students, graduates, in a church or an evangelistic crusade, I always preach an expository message. I'm committed to expository preaching." He preached through Bible books. He said: "It lifts an entire burden from me because I don't have to wonder what I'm going to preach on next week. I know if last week was chapter 1:16, I start with chapter 1:17. Moreover, expository preaching has a way of speaking to issues one might normally evade if the desire is to be popular with one's congregation. If the expositor is going to be honest, however, he cannot dodge an issue. He can't go through the Epistle to the Romans, for instance, without touching on such issues as civil rights, government, surrender, the holy life, Jews in prophecy, honesty, business—everything!"

Stephen spoke with authority, like his Lord and Master. His outlines were crystal clear, relevant, and to the point. His exposition of the Biblical text was penetrating and accurate. His expository sermons appealed to the intellect, the emotions, and to the will. His conclusions challenged the conscience and demanded a response to the Word of God. He preached with the anointing of the Holy Spirit. He was never frivolous, rarely told a joke as part of his message. He often shared illustrations from his early life, and invariably took his listeners to various parts of the Bible to back up his message. He frequently exegeted a Hebrew or Greek word or phrase. He started slowly but the fire built as he progressed. He was unfailingly courteous to his congregation and to others who shared the platform with him. While he was surprisingly short in stature, such was his personal magnitude and divine unction that his stature was rarely noticed. In the pulpit he stood ten feet tall! When he spoke he towered "head and shoulders above all the people."

At this point it is only appropriate to record that a fair proportion of Stephen Olford's teaching ministry was associated with conventions for the deepening of the spiritual life (know the United States as The Victorious Life Movement). Such teaching took him literally around the world. In Great Britain, he spoke at "Keswicks" in England, Wales, Scotland, and Ireland. Again and again he shared the convention platform with godly men like Northcote Deck, Lionel Fletcher, Montague Goodman, Stuart Holden, E. L. Langston, Herbert Lockyer, G. Campbell Morgan, W. Graham Scroggie, and in more recent years, E. M. Blaiklock, George Duncan, David Jackman, Alan Redpath, John Stott, and Ian Thomas. In America, he stood shoulder to shoulder with giants like William Culbertson, Paul S. Rees, and A. W. Tozer.

While he was at Calvary Baptist Church he started fourteen Keswick Conventions in the United States and the Caribbean. For five consecutive years during this period Stephen co-directed the Ben Lippen

Summer Conference and then became its director. For three weeks during July and August, the whole family traveled to Asheville, North Carolina to help lead and speak at a conference that was founded by Dr. Robert McQuilkin and inherited by Dr. G. Allen Fleece. Dr. Fleece and Dr. Olford made a perfect team. Dr. Fleece was the teacher par excellence! His walk with God, his profound insights into "the deep things of God," and his ability to make the complicated simple were evident to all who heard him. The Olfords cherished their friendship with Allen and Isabel Fleece, and thoroughly enjoyed ministering together. Only eternity will reveal the full results of transformed lives and the worldwide impact of those years at Ben Lippen. As Stephen and Heather traveled overseas they met scores of missionaries who heard and heeded the call of God to serve "anywhere, at any time, and at any cost" at Ben Lippen. In fact, that is where both Jonathan and David responded to the Lord for fulltime Christian service.

Perhaps one of his greatest joys in convention ministry was to speak at the one hundredth anniversary of English Keswick in 1975. Two people attended that convention who carried great significance. The first was Dr. Steven Barabas, Associate Professor of Theology at Wheaton College. Dr. Barabas wrote the distinctive work on the history and message of the Keswick Convention entitled *So Great Salvation.*[1] In its more academic form, this "excellent piece of work" (writes W. Graham Scroggie) was his doctoral thesis at Princeton Seminary. It was Stephen's privilege to arrange and, with some help, underwrite the visit to Keswick for Dr. Barabas and his family. His welcome by the Keswick Council and speakers was warm and appreciative. Dr. Barabas was also asked to participate. The other distinguished guest and speaker was Dr. Billy Graham. No one there will ever forget the thousands who came to hear him, and the hundreds who responded to his call to full surrender and discipline.

Dr. Olford has been the guest teacher at many other conferences including the Mid-America Keswicks, when Alan Redpath was pastor of Moody Memorial Church, Chicago; the annual Christian Life Conventions at Calvary Baptist Church in New York City; the yearly Toronto Spiritual Life Conventions in Canada every January; the unforgettable conferences at Prairie Bible Institute with Principal L. E. Maxwell and Dr. Ted Rendall; the circuit of five cities in South Africa; and perhaps the most exciting and engaging, the Japan Keswick started and nurtured by Dr. Paul S. Rees for several decades. For the unity of believers, the purity of message, and the dignity of procedure, the Japan Keswick is hard to equal!

We could go on detailing the opportunities and extensiveness of this aspect of Stephen Olford's teaching ministry, but this must suffice. We have talked about the teacher. We have also invited the teacher to teach on the victorious Christian life. What better way could there be to demonstrate his skill than to let him go to work? Here are his notes on part of Romans 6 (NKJV)—one of the more difficult passages in that majestic Epistle over which theologians have traditionally locked horns. It is no small test of a Bible teacher's skill to see how he handles this explosive field of controversy! Stephen Olford does not flinch. With sure and certain steps he guides us through the minefield! Here, then, is the subject of the sermon:

A New Life in Christ
Romans 6:1-11, NKJV

It is one thing to be justified, but quite another to live the sanctified life. So the aim of the apostle at this point in the Epistle is to show the inconsistency of continuing in sin after being justified by grace. Newness of life and persistence in sin are a contradiction of terms. In developing his subject, Paul has shown in Chapter 5 how righteousness is received, but in the next three chapters he sets out to describe how righteousness is realized. In 6:1-11 we have a new life in Christ; in 6:12-7:6 we have a new loyalty to Christ; and in 7:7-8:30 we have a new liberty in Christ. Let us consider the first of these divisions.

The leading theme of these first eleven verses is identification with Christ or "newness of life" (6:4). The realization of this life not only brings deliverance from sin, but a dynamic to live for God through Jesus Christ our Lord. To realize this new life in Christ:

A. There Is a Redeeming Fact That Must Be Recognized

> What shall we say then? Shall we continue in sin that grace may abound? Certainly not! How shall we who died to sin live any longer in it? . . . Do you not know that as many of us as were baptized into Christ Jesus were baptized into His death? Therefore we were buried with Him through baptism into death. . . . For he who has died has been freed from sin (6:1-7, NKJV).

The redeeming fact is that identification with Christ in his death, burial and resurrection delivers us from the slavery of sin. So in verses 1-7 we have two movements in the apostle's argument:

1. FUSION WITH CHRIST

"Do you not know that as many of us as were baptized into Christ Jesus were baptized into His death?" (6:3, NKJV) In the closing verses of Chapter 5 Paul has reveled in the abounding grace of God. Before he goes any further, however, he anticipates the attitude of the antinomianists who argue that since grace abounds where sin abounds why not trade on the mercy of God? Paul exclaims, "Certainly not! How shall we who died to sin live any longer in it?" (6:2, NKJV) The very idea is despicable. What would we think of a son who continued to sin simply because he knew that he had a tender and forgiving father? This would be taking advantage of paternal love and would break the father's heart.

So Paul shows the inconsistency of continuing in sin on the part of those who are united with Christ in death. Baptism is breaking with sin forever. It is such an identification with Christ in His death, burial, and resurrection that no genuine believer will want to return to a life of sin. According to Bishop Hedlam, "Baptism expresses symbolically a series of acts corresponding to the redeeming acts of Christ: immersion symbolizes death; submersion burial, and emergence symbolizes resurrection."

Baptism is fusion with Christ in His *death* (6:3). Jesus spoke of His death as a baptism (see Luke 12:50). In that awful judgment which fell on our Substitute we were also judged. In the sight of God, therefore, our standing in Adam came to an end there and then. This means that we who in Adam were dead *in* sin are now, in Christ, dead *to* sin.

But baptism is fusion with Christ in His *burial* (6:4). To leave a dead body unburied was, to the Jew and Greek, the greatest possible indignity. When a man is buried he is out of sight and beyond all possibility of recognition or identification. Praying Hyde of India once said, "It is not enough to have the self-life crucified, it must be buried or the stench of it will drive souls away from Jesus."

Once again, observe that baptism is fusion with Christ in His *resurrection* (6:4-5). Resurrection can only follow where death has taken place. Such new life is wholly from God (2 Cor. 5:17). As the gardener plants his seeds in the earth and they spring up into life and beauty from a common grave, so we have been "planted together" (v. 5) with Christ and His death in order that we may share His resurrection life and fruitfulness (see John 12:24; Col. 3:3-4). On the basis of this fusion with Christ there is:

2. FREEDOM FROM SIN

"Knowing this, that our old man [the man we once were, N.E.B.] was crucified with Him, that the body of sin might be done away with, that we should no longer be slaves of sin. For he who has died has been freed from sin" (6:6-7, NKJV). This freedom from sin is described as *the termination of the former self* (v. 6). Anyone who understands what it means to be baptized with Christ is completely finished with the old life as it was in his unregenerate days. To return to that old life constitutes a repudiation of the redeeming work of Christ and a prostitution of the grace of God.

But this freedom from sin spells out *the domination of the lower self*—"Knowing this . . . that the body of sin might be done away with" (6:6). If the "old man" is the unregenerate life now terminated by union with Christ in His death, burial and resurrection, then "the body of sin" refers to that old nature within us which carries out sin's orders, as and when we give the permission. But through the redeeming work of Christ both the dominion of the devil and the dominion of the self-life have been broken or destroyed" (see Heb. 2:14). So while sin is dormant, it need not be dominant (6:14).

There is yet another point to understand in this verse. Freedom from sin means *the liberation of the higher self*—"Knowing this, . . . that we [the real you and me under the control of the indwelling Christ] should no longer be slaves of sin. For he who has died has been freed from sin" (6:6-7). The whole purpose of our baptism with Christ is that we should be delivered from sin in order to serve our Lord and Savior Jesus Christ. Galatians 2:20 (KJV) says, "I live; yet not I," because "Christ liveth in me." The human personality is never obliterated, but simply surrendered to the power of the indwelling Lord. When a believer reaches this point he comes into the good of the justifying grade of God and is gloriously "freed from sin" (6:7)

In Scotland, in the Middle Ages, the murderer who was taken red-handed was justified without any unnecessary or inconvenient delays of process. This was the Scottish way of saying that the murderer was executed. In this sense the justified man could not sin any longer. Similarly because the Lord Jesus has met all the demands of a broken law in His death on the cross, so we have been set free in order to serve our Master forever. The former self is terminated, the lower self is dominated, and the higher self is liberated to enjoy the glorious freedom of the children of God.

B. There is a Receiving Faith That Must Be Exercised

"Now if we died with Christ, we believe that we shall also live with Him, knowing that Christ, having been raised from the dead, dies no more. Death no longer has dominion over Him. For the death that He died, He died to sin once for all; but the life that He lives, He lives to

God" (6:8-10, NKJV). It is one thing to perceive a fact objectively; it is quite another matter to believe the fact subjectively. Most people know that Jesus Christ came into this world, died upon a cross, and rose again the third day, but relatively few have turned such historical facts into personal experience; that comes about through the exercise of receiving faith. Paul tells us there are two things that must be accepted by faith:

1. WE MUST ACCEPT THE FINALITY OF THE DEATH OF CHRIST

"Now if we died with Christ, we believe that we shall also live with Him, knowing that Christ, having been raised from the dead, dies no more. Death no longer has dominion over Him. For the death that He died, He died to sin once for all" (6:8-10, NKJV). There have always been people who believe that Jesus has to perpetuate His death in order for it to become a continual reality in their lives. The fact of the matter is that when our Savior died he dealt with sin once and for all; therefore, there is no need to repeat His agony on the cross. Jesus has done everything to make a life of victory possible. To accept the finality of the death of Christ by faith is to have both the authority and ability to deal adequately with the penalty and power of sin in our lives.

2. WE MUST ACCEPT THE VITALITY OF THE LIFE OF CHRIST

"We believe that we shall also live with Him, knowing that Christ, having been raised from the dead, dies no more. . . . the life that He lives, He lives to God" (6:8-10, NKJV). Just as truly as Jesus died, so just as vitally Jesus lives. To accept that resurrection life by faith is to know a counteracting power over the law of sinful gravity.

Sometime ago I boarded a plan for Dallas, Texas. The day was so foggy and wet I doubted we would take off at all. We taxied to the point of departure and waited for the 'all clear." Then with a mighty roar those engines carried the aircraft forward with such thrust and speed that we were thrown back in our seats. The law of gravity did its best to hold those tons of aluminum, baggage, gasoline and people on the ground, but another law came into operation—the law of aerodynamics—which canceled out the law of gravity, enabling us to rise above the fog and clouds into brilliant sunshine. One law had overcome another and we were free.

This is what is meant by accepting the vitality of life in Jesus Christ. Just as the law of resurrection life overcame sin, death, and hell on that first Easter Sunday, so that same resurrection life can overcome sin, death and hell in us and through us. This is the new life in Christ that Paul wants us to enjoy. So he concludes:

C. There is a Releasing Force that Must Be Utilized

"Likewise . . . reckon yourselves to be dead indeed to sin, but *alive to God in Christ Jesus our Lord*" (6:11, NKJV). While Paul has virtually said the identical things in the previous three verses he underscores the same truths with the key word *reckon*—"count it to be true and act accordingly." There is a personal involvement here in launching out on the redeeming fact with a receiving faith in order to experience a releasing force. In essence, Paul exhorts his readers to utilize what God has made possible through the death, burial, and resurrection of Jesus Christ, which he sums up in a two-fold way:

1. THERE IS THE AUTHORITY TO REPUDIATE THE LAW OF SIN

"Likewise you also, reckon yourselves to be dead indeed to sin (6:11, NKJV). Three times in eleven verses Paul has spoken of death to sin. Twice it refers to Christians (vv. 2, 11) and once it refers to Christ (v. 10). The purpose for which Christ experienced the passion and pain of the cross was that you and I might break with sin forever. This is how Paul starts the paragraph and this is how he concludes it: "How shall we who died to sin live any longer in it?" (6:2, NKJV) In the light of all that grace has done we must use our authority in Christ to repudiate the law of sin every time we are tempted to succumb to it. When sin in any form knocks at the door of our lives we should cry out "God forbid!" Failure to do this shows that we have never understood the meaning of God's redeeming act in Jesus Christ.

An evangelist tells of a young man who had entered into the knowledge and experience of identification with Christ in His death, burial, and resurrection. Shortly thereafter the young Christian was traveling by train between two cities in England. In the compartment opposite him was the only other passenger. He was a man who liked to indulge in every form of diversion during a long and tedious journey. After sitting in silence for some time, a conversation started up and the older man offered the Christian a cigarette. "No thank you," said he, "my lips are dead!" Without comment, the stranger withdrew his pack of cigarettes and smoked away in silence. A little later he ordered a drink, and looking across to his traveling companion he asked, "Would you like one?" to which the Christian replied, "No, thank you, my tongue is dead." Thinking that there was a screw loose, the older man refused to comment and finished his beer. An hour or two later he pulled out a deck of cards from his pocket and said, "You don't smoke and you don't drink, but how about joining me in a little gambling game?" Our friend once again confessed, "I'm sorry, but my hands are dead." This was too much for this sophisticated gentleman, so he burst out, "What do you mean, my lips are dead, my tongue is dead, my hands are dead? Explain yourself!" This was just the opportunity the Christian was waiting for, and for the next hour he expounded the sixth chapter of Romans. It was not that his lips were insensitive nor his tongue or hands inactive, rather it was the fact that he was morally and legally united with Christ in a death to sin that gave him every authority to say "God forbid!"

2. THERE IS THE ABILITY TO APPROPRIATE THE LIFE OF GOD

"Reckon yourselves to be dead indeed to sin, but alive to God in Christ Jesus our Lord" (6:11, NKJV) "Aliveness" to God is what redemption is all about; so when we have learned to repudiate the law of sin there is a "livingness" about our relationship with God which opens all the treasures of heaven for you and me. Paul says, "Eye has not seen, nor ear heard, nor have entered into the heart of man the things which God has prepared for those who love Him. But God has revealed them to us through His Spirit. For the Spirit searches all things, yes, the deep things of God" (1 Cor. 2:9-10, NKJV). But this secret revelation only comes to those who know what it is to die to sin.

A man appeared on television to tell of his visit to an isolated island where there lived two missionaries who had forsaken home, family, and country in order to identify themselves with a primitive tribe. They shared their lives, suffered their diseases, and saved their souls. In telling his story, this traveler and author was so emotionally affected that he had to pause several times to compose himself. The climax of his story was when he asked the missionaries where they got their money for support. Speaking for both of them, the husband said, "We have no concern about this. We talk to God about it and He tells us that he will take care of the situation." In that moment, commented the traveler, "I was so aware of God that it frightened me. Here were people who talked about God as if He were coming down the little dirt road at that very moment." I am sure this is what Paul meant when he said, "alive to God in Christ Jesus our Lord" (6:11, NKJV). Paul always climaxed every genuine experience of God with the words "in Christ Jesus our Lord." To know and crown Him as Savior, Sanctifier and Sovereign is to come into all the good of the new life in Christ.

We have seen what is meant by righteousness realized through a redeeming fact, a receiving faith, and a releasing force. This is not only life, but life abundant in Jesus Christ.

> We're dead to sin, through Christ our Lord,
> For in His death we also died;
> It's written clear in God's own Word,
> And, praise His Name, we're justified.
>
> We're dead to sin, thus we must live
> To Christ alone who gave His all;
> And for His love we can't but give
> Our lives and gifts, both great and small.
>
> We're dead to sin, so we must serve
> Our God and King each day and hour;
> What He commands we must observe,
> And seek to do with heav'nly pow'r.
>
> We're dead to sin, oh, blessed thought!
> We now can rest from care and strife;
> Our fight He has forever fought,
> And now we live His risen life.
>
> Stephen F. Olford

Stephen Olford was known for his authoritative, clear, and passionate communication of Biblical truth.

CHAPTER 11

The Contender

Earnestly contend for the faith.
Jude 3

Jude was a contender. He was the Lord's half brother and full brother of James, the prominent elder in the Jerusalem church. Jude told us he had planned to write to his readers about "the common salvation." We cannot help but wonder what he would have said about that. He is a colorful writer and doubtless he would have told us many interesting things. The human side of us makes us almost wish he had told us some stories from the well-remembered Nazareth days. He could doubtless have written as many volumes about that as he did verses in the memo that finally emerged from his pen.

Be that as it may, something Jude saw so greatly alarmed him as to drive all other thoughts from his mind. He saw inroads being made into the church, even in its very earliest days, by apostates from the faith. The Holy Spirit bore in upon his soul and urged him to warn God's people. He must exhort them to "contend earnestly for the faith." The word he used was *epagōnizomai*. It occurs only here in the entire New Testament. The Lord Jesus used a similar word when He told us to "strive [agōnizomai] to enter through the narrow gate" (Luke 13:24, NKJV). We can feel the throb of strife and agony in the very word. Jude was a contender. He lays the word upon us. We cannot take the inroads of the enemy complacently.

Stephen Olford's father was a contender, standing his ground every time divine truth was threatened on the missionfield, where he served the Lord for over twenty-five years. He urged his son to do the same as he grew up alongside him and later launched out into his own ministry.

"As a boy," Stephen said, "I had to read a sermon by C. H. Spurgeon every week; yes, and be questioned on the subject, the structure, and the substance of everyone of them! Even as a teenager, I was challenged by Spurgeon's distrust of modern Biblical criticism that led to his withdrawal from the Baptist Union in 1869. He was a contender for the faith."

The foundation was laid for Stephen to be a contender for the faith at a very tender age. At the age of seven he became a full member of Scripture Union (a Bible reading program based in Britain but known around the world). It followed a five-year plan that covered every book of the Bible. "I still treasure," he said, "the notes of some of the great expositors who wrote for Scripture Union at that time." This systematic and guided reading of the Scriptures exercised Stephen's spiritual senses "to discern both good and evil" (Hebrews 5:14). He recalled that even during the years of his wilderness experience, when he was walking "afar off" as a Christian, he would defend his faith from time to time before his classmates at the Devonport Technical College. He felt constrained to do so, perhaps, because there was one professor who took delight in poking fun at the Bible and other religious subjects.

The real tests, however, were to come after God called him to the ministry. One of the first occurred in Newport, South Wales. The issue at stake was that of Christian liberty—especially in the area of evangelistic outreach and service. He had completed his theological training and had volunteered to serve as an Army Scripture reader just as World War II broke out. He and his father established a center for servicemen and women in downtown Newport and ministered with great effectiveness during the war years.

It did not take Stephen long to realize that the spiritual condition of the churches in the area was very low. This was true of the church the Olford family and my own family attended at the time. As mentioned in the previous chapter, Stephen was concerned because his own brothers, Paul and John, were being starved for dynamic Bible teaching. So much that passed for preaching was both stereotyped, sterile, and frequently flawed by an undercurrent of strife in the church. The more Stephen looked around, the more he realized that there were very many young people his own age who were equally spiritually undernourished.

He started a young men's Bible class in his home. It grew rapidly and beyond all expectations. It was broadened to include young women and became the Young People's Christian Fellowship. Soon the Y.P.C.F. had to move to a spacious classroom above a tool shop which was made available by a kind Christian friend. His own church had refused to allow any of its ample facilities to be used. The reason for this "refusal" was one of the very issues for which Stephen was contending. Stated simply, it was the liberty to meet with believers outside of the Plymouth (Christian) Brethren who worshiped in that particular church building. Within that assembly was a vocal and formidable minority who carried the doctrine of "guilt by association" to such unbiblical extremes that even the use of church facilities was regarded as a serious compromise. The young people were not welcome as part of the body of Christ. Least of all was Stephen himself who believed that grace and peace from God the Father and the Lord Jesus Christ was to be shared "with all who in every place call on the name of Jesus Christ our Lord (1 Corinthians 1:2). So Stephen pleaded with the elders to incorporate this exciting venture into the work of the church. He met with them, listened to their objections and answered all their questions. He was simply told to disband the group altogether!

"To me," Stephen Olford said, "this was an affront on my liberty in Christian service. My fellow teammate, Bill Parry, and I requested that the matter be brought to the whole church for a public hearing and decision. With considerable reluctance the elders of the church acceded to this request. The meeting was convened. The elders argued for their position and Stephen for the Y.P.C.F.

"I will never forget what happened," he recalled. "Parents rose on the right and on the left to testify to the transforming work that had taken place in the lives of their teenagers. They told of reconciliations that had taken place in their homes. They rejoiced in the evangelistic fires that had been kindled in the hearts of so many. The battle was over! The overwhelming majority voted for the continuance of this ministry among the young people. The Y.P.C.F. went on to become one of the dominant factors in the evangelical life of Newport and that part of the world."

The Duke Street years were a relatively happy and harmonious period in Stephen Olford's ministry. But even in that church there was one issue on which he had to take his stand. It had to do with what was then called "ultra-Calvinism." Stephen's own background had always been in the Reformed tradition, a theological position he never abandoned. But during his early years at the Duke Street Baptist Church in Richmond, Surrey, a strain of extreme Calvinism pervaded many churches and some of the Christian Unions of Britain's leading universities. This extremism made an impact on Duke Street in an unexpected way.

From the very start of Stephen's ministry at Duke Street, Sunday evening services were held in the nearby Richmond Theater. These services were always evangelistic in character. The theater could not only hold bigger

Photo by Victoria Kuhl

*Sunday evening evangelistic services were held
in the Richmond Theatre during the Duke Street days.*

crowds than the church but was a more neutral meeting place, more likely to attract the outsider. Indeed, all kinds of young people and even celebrities were attracted to "the Church in the Theater."

The services were streamlined to fit within the one-hour time frame the theater was available. The closing invitation always included an appeal to seekers to come on over to the church hall which was just around the corner. Once the people had regathered (often braving inclement weather to do so) Stephen would give a word of welcome and then spell out the way of salvation, always making careful reference to the message he had just delivered. The very number of seekers who were always in the church hall mandated this after-meeting approach.

"After my brief instruction talk," he explained, "I invited those who meant business with God to remain for counseling. In most cases, decisions for Christ had already been made in the main service or during the prayer at the close of my after-meeting. Those were precious days of reaping and rejoicing!"

However the enemy was busy too. While this was going on, Stephen observed that a number of university students would sit at the back of the hall and would sometimes even talk to one another as he was conducting the crucial after-meeting. He conducted some discrete investigations and discovered they were there to examine and evaluate his message and his methods and to condemn his whole approach to evangelism. This they eventually did in no uncertain way by creating a confrontation with Stephen and a number of church members who eventually left the fellowship.

Stephen prayed much about what was going on. Then he looked around for spiritual counsel. First, he consulted with the church elders. Then he had a long talk with Professor E. M. Blaiklock of Auckland, New Zealand, who happened to be in England for special meetings at the time. He was encouraged by the words of this saintly scholar who assured him that the accusations being leveled against his evangelistic methods were wholly unfounded (he had been accused of grieving and quenching the Holy Spirit both in his proclamation of the gospel and in his invitation). Finally he shared his concern with Dr. Martyn Lloyd-Jones who listened carefully to Stephen's story and responded: "Stephen, have no fear, these pundits of extremism have out-Calvined Calvin!" Comforting words indeed!

But Stephen still had to face the church and contend for his stand and for his style as an evangelist. "Thank God," he said, "the church was with me, even though we lost some." About this time Stephen was especially blessed and helped by J. I. Packer's book *Evangelism and the Sovereignty of God,* which had just come off the press. Simultaneously, two booklets attacking Billy Graham, mass evangelism, and "the invitation system" were being widely circulated in Britain. Packer's book helped restore a measure of balance and tolerance when many were on witch hunts across the country.

Dr. Olford's own position on gospel preaching has been best stated, he said, in Dr. John R. W. Stott's book, *The Preacher's Portrait.* Dr. Stott said: "We must never issue an appeal without first making the proclamation. Much harm has been done to the souls of men, and much dishonor brought to the name of Christ, through neglect of this simple rule . . . The gospel is not fundamentally an invitation to men to do anything. It is a declaration of what God has done in Christ on the cross for their salvation. The invitation cannot properly been given before the declaration has been made. Men must grasp the truth before they are asked to respond to it." On the other hand, "we must never make the proclamation without then issuing an appeal. . . . it is not enough to teach the gospel; *we must urge men to embrace it*" (italics added).[1]

After six years at Duke Street, God called Stephen to Calvary Baptist Church in New York City (1959). On arrival he was approached by a number of deacons with the demand that he sign a document stating he would preach against Roman Catholicism from the pulpit and over the radio. He asked by what authority they brought this demand. Their answer was unconvincing. Even if it had been convincing it would not have changed his mind. He reminded those making the demand of Paul's words in 1 Corinthians 9:19-23, where the great apostle sums up his whole approach to evangelism in the glorious words: "I have become all things to all men, that I might by all means save some" (v. 22). He told them that one of the first laws of soul-winning was to resist cutting off people's ears before speaking to them.

Stephen Olford was fully aware that about forty percent of the New York population was at least nominally Roman Catholic. That, to him, was "a field white unto harvest." Having thus argued his case, he took the document and tore it to pieces before their eyes. This bold stand was to be more than vindicated in the days and years ahead as Roman Catholics were gloriously converted and added to the churches of the city as well as to the fellowship of believers at Calvary Baptist Church. This battle was won without compromise or controversy.

The next battle was a harder one. It centered on the issue of racism. When he went to Calvary Baptist Church he was dismayed to discover that it had a segregated membership. "Perhaps I had assumed too much," he confessed, "when making inquiries about the new pastoral charge from a place three thousand miles away." One thing he determined: the situation had to be changed or else he would not remain pastor of that congregation. He prayed much about the matter and then began an in-depth study of the problem. He discovered that eighty-five percent of the church members were against integration.

What made matters worse was that outside pressure was brought to bear on the young, new English pastor to act at once—or else! A black federal judge came to see him, convinced he was a racist. The judge argued that, since Stephen had not fought the issue to the point of splitting the church, he proved himself to be a racist.

"I pleaded with him for patience," Stephen said, "I explained to him that the answer to the problem would come through prayer, the preaching of the word of reconciliation, and the reviving of the Holy Spirit. Eventually the judge was persuaded when my secretary made him read one of my sermons on the race issue, while he waited for an interview. The interview never took place. The judge studied the manuscript, returned it to my secretary, and said, 'I am satisfied!' I never saw him again."

Time passed and Stephen began to sense a change in the spiritual climate of the church as the word of reconciliation was proclaimed in human weakness, as he said, but with divine unction. In fact, such was the moving of God that the provisional dateline he set for a church meeting on the race issue was advanced by six months.

"I shall never forget that night," he said. "Everybody was there, including many who should never have been present! I felt in my duty, on this occasion, to take a personal stand and not involve my officers, except as they spoke for themselves.

"The message I gave was bathed in prayer as I delivered my soul on this burning issue. I expounded the Scriptures and fielded questions from every part of the sanctuary. It is true that some used scathing language and that tense moments were experienced by all. But, when it came to the vote, the victory was practically unanimous. Only eleven raised their hands in opposition. Of these, seven assured me that while they did not agree with me on this matter, they were prepared to support the ministry. The remaining four were sovereignly removed from our midst in a manner that brought 'great fear upon the church.' One man died that very week!"

Stephen has often been asked how things worked out thereafter in the church. His answer: "God blessed us beyond all our asking or thinking. Even though we had the problems that are common to any inner-city church, the question of integration was not one of them. We found that the people who sought the right hand of fellowship at Calvary were those who were prepared to submit themselves to the disciplined training of our membership classes and accept the standard of ministry, the manner of worship, and the opportunities for service as structured within our church. We had black brethren and members of other minority groups represented on our boards, committees, the choir, and similar organizations—all working together for the glory of God."

"Dare to discipline!" That was another issue for which Stephen Olford had to contend. A prominent member of the church committed adultery. At first he would not admit his sin. The Biblical procedures of confrontation, condemnation, separation, and restoration were followed (see Matthew 18:15-20; 1 Corinthians 5:3-5,13; 2 Thessalonians 3:6-15; and Galatians 6:1). As a result the man demanded that he be allowed to have a private interview with Dr. Olford.

"As his pastor," Stephen said, "I consented, and endured one of the most horrific experiences of my whole ministry. I was trapped in my study, and this man (powerful both physically and mentally) presented me with an ultimatum. He stared me in the face and said, 'It is one thing for you to preach and teach in the pulpit, but quite another matter to deal with *me*. If you follow through with your so-called "Biblical discipline" you will pay for it!' At this point in the confrontation I feared for my life more than for my ministry. With an urgent prayer to heaven for anointed spiritual wisdom and Biblical authority I rebuked him in the name of the Lord for his sin and announced the procedures of discipline that would be carried out by our Board of Elders.

"The man had his right hand in his coat pocket while he tried to stare me down. Quite frankly, I thought it was all over. But God intervened in power, love, and victory! Suddenly this giant of a man fell to his knees and cried like a baby. I knelt with him and prayed that the spirit and substance of Galatians 6:1 would be worked out and embodied in all that would follow. The brother was disciplined and the church was cleansed and honored for the stand we had taken. It costs to contend. Indeed I was ill for days after that memorable evening."

One of the most unsettling things in the pastorate, Stephen admitted, is to know that you are being "gunned down" by someone who wants you out of the church or even out of the ministry. This happened on one occasion when a man with a powerful personality, who had been "converted" out of Roman Catholicism, took issue with Dr. Olford's style of leadership.

This man had developed a veritable aversion to what he called "one man ministry," or "Popery!" He expressed this by word and deed on a number of occasions. But things became worse when he launched a crusade to depose Stephen Olford altogether. The church elders knew about this and joined their pastor in prayer for God's intervention in the situation. Counseling sessions proved unavailing. The man was both hostile and adamant.

Matters came to a head at one unforgettable church meeting. Normally these annual church meetings were marked by what Stephen called "the two b's—business and blessing." The proceedings always closed with the singing of the Doxology. This time it was different. Some issue had been raised and this brother rose to his feet to attack Stephen Olford both verbally and unjustly. Dr. Olford did his best to answer the questions but the man was not satisfied. The church elders tried to silence him but that only enraged him the more. While all this was going on, Stephen was lifting his heart to the Lord for wisdom. The truth came home to him. He discerned that this was a satanic attack and that this individual was no fit person to be part of the church fellowship.

He stood to his feet and asked the man to be seated. The man shouted back, "Not before I pray for you." "We bowed our heads for prayer, Stephen said, "and what followed cannot be printed. The man let out one of the most vitriolic tirades I have ever heard—and all this under the pretense of prayer. I was still standing. I was pleading silently with God for the anointing of the Spirit and for the correct attitude and authority to deal with this demonic confrontation. As soon as he said his amen I pointed my finger at him and declared, with a holy unction: 'I rebuke your sin before all so that all may fear, and I expel you from the membership of this church. And may God have mercy on your soul.'"

With that everyone present rose to their feet and applauded. The man left the church immediately. When order had been restored Stephen explained to the people why he had acted as he had, quoting 1 Timothy

5:20. He then led his people in prayer for the brother's repentance and restoration. The man, however, never did return and refused visits and ignored letters. This was an instance of contending for order in the church.

This is a classic example of what Paul meant when he wrote, "We command you, brethren, in the name of our Lord Jesus Christ, that ye withdraw yourselves from every brother that walketh disorderly . . . and have no company with him, that he may be ashamed. Yet count him not as an enemy, but admonish him as a brother" (2 Thessalonians 3:6, 14-15).

One morning Dr. Olford was faced with a different kind of situation, but one that also called for a willingness to contend for the faith. The crisis came with a phone call. It was from one of Calvary's television supporters, a man who contributed something like fifty thousand dollars a year to help keep "Encounter" on television.

"This was our most powerful and profitable evangelistic outreach," Stephen said, "for reaching the metropolitan area. The program was designed for the unbeliever and was used by God to reach thousands for Christ."

When the phone rang, the voice at the other end said, "Is your seatbelt fastened?" Dr. Olford, somewhat apprehensive said that it was. The man continued: "I understand you are vice-chairman for the upcoming Billy Graham crusade New York City [1969]." Stephen agreed that this was indeed so, adding that the church was solidly behind him in this. Then came the bombshell. The man on the other end of the line issued an ultimatum: "I want you to resign from that position," he said, "or I will cease to support your television program."

Stephen Olford was not for sale. "I sent up a quiet prayer for wisdom," he said, "then I answered: 'My dear brother, with all my love for you, I want you to know that my convictions are not negotiable. Cost what it may, I will not be bribed.' We lost fifty thousand dollars a year—which God made up through other channels. And we had our Billy Graham crusade!"

What emerges from a consideration of these stories is the picture of a champion, the portrait of a man who could neither be bought or bullied. Here was a man of God. He hammered out his convictions in long hours of Bible study and prayer. He put them to the test in many an arena, time and time again. He knew where he stood. Behind that charming smile, that warm handshake, that attractive personality, that cultured English accent, and that jovial laugh was a man who knew what he believed and why. Neither fear nor favor could sway him. He was not hasty to make up his mind. He listened, discussed, sought counsel, took his time, waited upon God, read, studied, and prayed. But once he knew what the Word of God said, and what the will of God was, there he drew the line. He was a man in the tradition of Daniel and Paul, Martin Luther and John Knox.

One more story will illustrate this. Some years ago Stephen Olford was invited by Mrs. Anne Lotz, Billy Graham's daughter, to take a series of meetings in the fashionable Hayes Barton Baptist Church in Raleigh, North Carolina. Through her own effective teaching, Mrs. Lotz had already made a considerable impact in that extremely liberal church. Billy Graham himself took time to plead with Dr. Olford to accept the invitation. Later on Stephen learned that quite a battle had taken place over his nomination as the evangelist; indeed, it hastened the resignation of the pastor.

Arrangements for the series of meetings in Raleigh went forward. Ron and Patricia Owens, good colleagues in the ministry, were to provide the music. Dan and Anne Lotz mobilized supporters to pray. The meetings were to run from Sunday through Wednesday. Opposition arose from every quarter.

On the first Sunday morning the church was packed. The service was "stone cold," to use Stephen's own words. He was told he could preach for twenty minutes—"and not one minute more."

He chose as his text: "For to me to live is Christ" (Philippians 1:21). "God gave me great liberty," Stephen recalled, "in spite of the local circumstances and the frigid spiritual climate. I gave the invitation—and not a soul stirred. Then something happened. I sensed a holy boldness that almost frightened me. I stepped down from the pulpit and addressed the congregation. 'The message I have just delivered will bear fruit,' I said. "God's Word will not return void. Tonight this place will be packed, and at the invitation seekers will fill the altar.' Then I pronounced the benediction." It might be added, here, that no evening services were held in this church and for fourteen years, not a soul had ever walked the aisles to confess Christ as Lord!

Sure enough, that night the church was full. Stephen Olford preached with a sense of anointing and gave the invitation. The altar was filled with seeking men and women. The meetings continued with power and blessing from then on.

The pastor had resigned. In his absence, a professor of systematic theology was asked to chair the meetings. This he did on the first Sunday and on the final meeting on Wednesday. On that closing evening Stephen preached on the power of God's inerrant Word to change lives.

"I knew I was in a church and an area noted for its liberalism," he said. "Already I had been challenged as to my stand on the Holy Scriptures. But I could not compromise—something that became very evident as my expository sermon unfolded. Suddenly, right in the middle of a sentence, the chairman-professor stomped off the platform in a rage and, in order to vent his protest, walked down the center aisle of the church on his way out. Not a soul followed him. On the contrary, a chorus of amens from the congregation gave voice to their oneness with me. It was tough going but, glory to God, souls were saved and the work goes on in Raleigh to this very day."

Stephen was often asked to give his statement of faith. During the course of his ministry, he often shared it with churches, committees, and clergy alike. It is as follows:

> I believe that the Holy Scriptures, consisting of Old and New Testaments, were originally and inerrantly communicated by God and, therefore, are verbally inspired, and constitute the infallible and final authority in all matters of faith, life, and conduct.
>
> I believe that there is one true God, subsisting in three persons: the Father, the Son, and the Holy Spirit, the same in essence and equal in wisdom, goodness, power, and glory.
>
> I believe in the essential deity of our Lord Jesus Christ; in His virgin birth; in His sinless life; in His inerrant teaching; in His substitutionary and expiatory death by which we have redemption through His blood, even the forgiveness of sins; in His bodily resurrection from among the dead; in His ascension into Heaven; in His present priestly session; in His personal return at the end of the age to raise the dead, glorify the church, judge the earth, and reign as King of kings and Lord of lords.
>
> I believe that man was created innocent and in the spiritual image of God; and that he was tempted by Satan and fell; and that through his sin, his posterity thereby incurred not only physical death but also spiritual death, which is separation from God.
>
> I believe that the salvation of lost and sinful man comes only through the regenerating work of the Holy Spirit, as the sinner repents toward God and exercises faith in our Lord Jesus Christ.
>
> I believe in the present ministry of the Holy Spirit to convict the world of sin, of righteousness, and of judgment; and to indwell and enable the Christian to live soberly, righteously, and godly, in this present age.
>
> I believe that the church on earth consists of believers

in our Lord Jesus Christ who are dedicated to the
worship and service of God through the proclamation of the Word, the observance of the
sacraments, and the administration of discipline.

I believe in the bodily resurrection of the just and the
unjust—the just to everlasting life and bliss, the unjust
to everlasting shame and perdition.

To this doctrinal statement Stephen Olford appended these words: "As
far as I have been enabled by the Holy Spirit, I have sought throughout my
ministry to 'contend earnestly for the faith which was once for all delivered
to the saints' (Jude 3). To me, the matter is once and for all settled. God's
inerrant Word affirms the finality of the divine revelation in Christ in
redemptive history. This revelation is fixed and non-repeatable. We need not
look outside the covers of the Bible to find our infallible rule for all matters
of faith and practice."

Part Three

THE MENTOR

*Whenever possible, Stephen Olford made himself available
to people at the Stephen Olford Center for Biblical
Preaching. Many sought his counsel and received it.*

CHAPTER 12

The Counselor

Without counsel, plans go awry, But in the
multitude of counselors they are established.
Proverbs 15:22, NKJV

In the course of his long and distinguished career as an evangelist, a pastor, and a teacher, Stephen Olford counseled many thousands of people. I recall three pieces of advice he gave either to me or to those who were close to me.

There was my father, for instance. My father was a businessman in South Wales. At the end of the Second World War he was contemplating selling his business and going to the missionfield. He was a gifted Bible expositor whose teaching was much appreciated over a wide area. A missionary from the West Indies suggested to him that there would be great scope for his Bible teaching on one of the islands. He suggested Barbados as a possible sphere of activity. My mother, who had always wanted to be a missionary, was enthusiastic. My father's business was prospering. I was in the army, and he had three teenagers at home. He prayed about it, sought guidance from the Word, faced the pressure of a man who had spent much time in the West Indies and who urged him to go. He corresponded with an old missionary on the field. Then he decided to seek spiritual counsel. He set out the facts, his feelings, his doubts and hesitations to Stephen Olford. The advice he received was short and to the point: "If you don't know what to do, don't do it, Leonard." In other words, as long as my father had mental reservations and doubts he shouldn't go. It was sound advice. In the end my father sold his business, received the blessing of the church were he had been known and respected for half a lifetime, packed his bags, and headed for the missionfield with his wife and two of his children.

It was a disaster. He was not wanted on the little island. Indeed, the senior resident missionary perceived him as a threat. He received not a penny of financial support all the time he was there. My younger brother rebelled outright at being imprisoned on a small, tropical island. My younger sister became desperately ill, and it soon became evident the climate would kill her. My mother was worn out by nursing the sick child, worried by the financial strain, and harassed by the mean-spirited behavior of the missionary in whose home they were forced to live. She finally collapsed herself. In desperation, my father decided to return to England while he still had enough money left to pay their passage.

His troubles had only just begun. When he arrived home the people in his former circle of fellowship labeled him a quitter. Doors that had once opened to his ministry were now firmly closed to him. He discovered he was now as likely to starve at home as he was on the missionfield.

Many years later, when he was a loved and honored fulltime minister of the gospel in Canada and the United States, he opened his heart to me about that disastrous trip to Barbados. "Your mother always wanted to be a missionary," he said, "ever since she was a little girl. After her youngest sister became a missionary there was no holding her. I finally gave in and we went. I should have listened to Stephen Olford."

About the same time, Stephen gave similar sound advice to a young woman I knew. This young woman was dating a young man. Her parents decided to go abroad and told her, since she was not yet of age, that she was to accompany them. She dug in her heels and flatly refused to go, fearful she might lose her boyfriend. Her father suggested she seek counsel from Stephen Olford. She did. She went to him and poured out her heart. Yes, she loved her parents. No, she did not want to go abroad. She loved her young man. She intended to marry him the moment she turned eighteen. Her love for her boyfriend was more important to her than any other consideration. Stephen's comment was short and sharp: "Love that cannot be crucified," he said, "is not love, but lust."

The third example of Stephen's sound counsel was advice given to me. The 1950's found me in Canada. I had been with the Bank of Montreal for some years, but had left to become an accountant for a lumber company. The town where we lived was a lumber town and a wild enough place in those days. My wife and I were unable to find a compatible church so we began teaching a home Bible class to a small handful of interested people. It prospered and blossomed into a church. As the church began to grow, a building was erected and souls were saved. We kept busy. I worked as an accountant and pastored a church.

Then I received a letter. It was an invitation to join the staff of the Correspondence School of the Moody Bible Institute in Chicago, some three thousand miles away. I was torn between two desires. I felt the local church still needed me. On the other hand, I felt the opportunity to serve the Lord at Moody was one that I could not afford to miss.

About that time an opportunity arose that enabled me to visit the Institute and then go on to England for a brief vacation. While in England I went to Richmond, a London suburb, to seek counsel from Stephen Olford, who was pastoring there at the time. I put the issues to him.

He did not hesitate for a moment. "Go to Moody Bible Institute," he said. I asked, "What about that infant church?" "God will take care of that," he said. "If that work is of God it will stand; if it is of John Phillips the sooner it falls, the better!" Blunt words! I went back to British Columbia and, within the year, had moved to Chicago and had joined the staff of the Moody Bible Institute. It proved to be one of the most important and far-reaching decisions of my life. And that church? Well, that was thirty-six years ago. It is still there and still flourishing.

Over many years Stephen counseled countless people. He had a rare gift for going right to the heart of a problem. He dissected it, saw it in its context and from the proper perspective, and put it back together again. He spoke directly to the issue with an assurance and an authority that derived from his knowledge of the Word of God and his personal yieldedness to the Spirit of God.

Many years ago I heard him tell the story of a concerned young man who came to him because of his inability to witness for Christ. Seemingly changing the subject, Stephen said to the young man, "What is your favorite hobby?" "Motorcycles," said the young man. "How interesting!" Stephen said, "I went in for motorcycles myself years go. What kind of bike do you have?" For the next few minutes the words flowed as the young man described his motorcycle—the make, the model, the horsepower, the compression, how it handled on the road, how fast it would take a curve, how long he had owned it, what it could do on a race track. Stephen stopped the flow. He said, "Young man, when you spend as much time thinking about Jesus Christ as you do thinking about your motorcycle you won't have any trouble talking to people about Him."

When I was putting this chapter together, the Lord put it into my mind to ask Stephen a series of questions and let him answer them for himself. These included everyday questions and some very thorny questions. I asked him, when answering, to amplify the answers to explain his spiritual philosophy and the Biblical convictions on which they were based. In addition to the questions I posed there are a few more taken from the thousands of actual letters he has received over the years. Counseling others entails awesome responsibility. Think of the terrible advice Naomi, in her backslidden condition, gave to Orpah and Ruth—advice Orpah took to the loss of her own soul (Ruth 1:8-14). Contrast that with the godly counsel she gave to Ruth when, at last, she was right with God (Ruth 2:19-20; 3:1-18).

Here, then, is Stephen Olford, the counselor.

Dr. Olford, you are a prayer warrior. Would you please tell us how to maintain a prayer life? How does one actually pray all night—or even for a solid hour, for that matter. Most of us are plagued by wandering thoughts and restlessness. What do you do and say?

The first thing to recognize is that prayer is a convictional discipline and not an emotional one. I heard Dr. W. Graham Scroggie once say, "Pray when you feel like it; pray when you don't feel like it; pray until you do feel like it!" The Lord Jesus put it plainly and finally when He declared, "Men always ought to pray and not lose heart" (Luke 18:1, NKJV). With that I mind, here are some simple suggestions that have helped me.

1. *Pray in the Spirit* (see Romans 8:26-27; Ephesians 6:18; Jude 20). Without a conscious dependence on the Holy Spirit, prayer becomes nothing but a formal or farcical exercise.

2. *Pray with the Scriptures* (see John 15:7). George Mueller used to say "soul nourishment first." Take time to read and ponder God's Word before going to prayer. Sometimes it is helpful to read while praying. I have prayed using the psalms or other appropriate scriptures. In fact, the use of a prayer book (such as *A Diary of Private Prayer*[1]) or the prayers of great saints of the past can serve as an aid to praying.

3. *Pray with a System.* When Paul exhorts, "Let your requests be made known to God" (Philippians 4:6) he is implying system (and this does not negate spontaneity or sincerity). The model prayer (Matthew 6:9-13, NKJV) is God's pattern for us all:

Adoration—"Our Father in heaven, Hallowed be Your name." Here is reverence and penitence in prayer.

Dedication—"Your kingdom come. Your will be done." Here is allegiance and obedience in prayer.

Supplication—"Give us this day. . ." Here is trustfulness and thankfulness in prayer.

Intercession—"Forgive us our debts, as we forgive our debtors." Here is confession and concern in prayer.

Preparation—"Do not lead us into temptation, But deliver us from the evil one." Here is contest and conquest in prayer.

Veneration—"For Yours is the kingdom and the power and the glory forever. Amen." Here is wonder and worship in prayer.

Study also 1 Timothy 2:1-7. Have a prayer list for saints, sinners, subjects, and situations.

4. *Pray with Sensibilities.* Make sure you are physically ready for prayer. If you are dead tired you cannot concentrate (Mark 14:34,37; 1 Corinthians 9:27a). Make sure you are morally ready for prayer. If there is unconfessed sin in your life God will not hear you (Psalm 66:18). Make sure that you are spiritually ready for prayer. If the Word of God is not dwelling in you, prayer will not be answered (John 15:7). Posture in prayer is important. Sometimes it is best to kneel (1 Kings 8:54; Ephesians 3:14). Other times it is good to sit (2 Samuel 7:18). I often stand or walk when praying. Be comfortable before God. Praying aloud is a good antidote to wandering thoughts.

You are internationally known as "an expository preacher." Exactly what is an "expository" sermon? Often we hear preachers rambling from verse to verse down a passage of Scripture, commenting here and there along the way. Are they expositors? What are the essential ingredients of an expository sermon? What pitfalls should a person avoid who is new to the process?

Exposition simply means detailed explanation. The exposition of God's Word is the Spirit-enabled explanation and proclamation of the text of God's Word with due regard to the historical, contextual, grammatical, and doctrinal significance of the given passage, with the specific object of invoking a Christ-transforming response from the hearer. An expository sermon is normally based on a complete "unit" of Scripture (usually distinguished by paragraph marks). This passage is then analyzed to reveal three essential elements: first, the dominating *theme*; second, the integrating *thoughts*; and, third, the motivating *thrust*. The integrating thoughts are the points of the sermon (taken from the text) that support the theme and lead to the thrust of the final piece of workmanship (the sermon) of a preacher who rightly divides the Word of Truth (2 Timothy 2:15). Pitfalls in sermon construction are deviations from the simple principles stated above. How the main and subpoints are set forth depend on the artistry of the preacher, but they must be biblical, logical, practical, and memorable without doing violence to the facts or flow of the text.

How would you advise a person to go about discovering God's will for a specific, important decision? For instance, how do you decide which of the hundreds of invitations you receive to speak here, there, and everywhere, is God's will for you to take?

Knowing God's will (divine guidance) is something discerned retrospectively rather than prospectively! But having said that, I also hold that God has a plan for our lives that we can find, follow, and finish (Ephesians 2:10). I would say that guidance can be regarded as general and special.

General guidance comes through walking in the Spirit and living in the Word. In any given situation we can count on a promise like Proverbs 3:5-6—"Trust in the Lord with all your heart, And lean not on your own understanding; In all your ways acknowledge Him, And He shall direct your paths" (NKJV). The word *direct* means "to make plain (or straight)." As long as we desire God's will in any matter, disregarding our own wishes or desires, He will lead us to do the right thing. If, on the other hand, we are governed by self-will or personal ambitions, God may permit what we have chosen, but we cannot say He has directed it (Psalm 106:15). Hundreds of times a day we make decisions on the phone, in letter writing, or in business matters. How important, then, to walk in the light under an unclouded heaven with the ungrieved and unquenched Holy Spirit filling our lives. Only then can it be said, "For as many as are led by the Spirit of God, they are sons of God" (Romans 8:14).

Special guidance needs more time. It may relate to a life's partner, a career, the call to the missionfield, and so on. I believe the Bible gives us three guiding principles for discerning God's will. The first is the *warrant of the Scriptures* (see 2 Timothy 3:16). "Instruction (or discipline) in righteousness" includes doing things righteously or rightly. God's guidance never contradicts His Word. The second is the *witness of the Spirit* (see Romans 8:14,16). Just as the Spirit witnesses to our relationship to God as Father, so he witnesses to everything that reflects the Father's will for us. As we pray, the witness of the Spirit will affirm a "yes" or confirm a "no." The third is the *wisdom of the saints*—"Without counsel, plans go awry, but in the multitude of counselors they are established" (Proverbs 15:22, NKJV; see also Proverbs 11:14; 24:6). The apostle Paul echoed the same principle in 2 Corinthians 13:1 (see also Deuteronomy 19:15). When we stand before a court or a church, it is good to have the objective confirmation (or condemnation) of others. Now anyone of these guiding principles may not be sufficient, but when they all point in the same direction, and God fills the heart with His peace (Philippians 4:6-7), I believe we can claim to know the guidance of God.

As to the matter of invitations to speak here, there, and everywhere, that is another question. It is amazing how often a dozen pastors or conference directors will write and say that, after much prayer and consultation, they have been led to invite me for a series of meetings, and then propose exactly the same dates! I can honestly say that this kind of thing has puzzled and even pained me over the years of ministry. My approach to the problem, after prayer and discussion with my wife and staff, has been to ask two questions:

1) *What are my priorities?* This is very important to me. At every stage of my ministerial life there have been certain priorities to which I give first consideration. Right now (1994) pastors' meetings or preaching institutes have priority. Next would come missionary conferences, and on an equal footing I would list conventions for the deepening of spiritual life. At one time, it would have been evangelistic crusades—all within the context of church life.

2) *What are my capacities,* in terms of time, strength, and ministerial gifts that God is at present using?

When I prayerfully apply these two tests I make what I would call a sanctified, common-sense decision. This comes under the category of general guidance.

How would you define the difference between the baptism of the Spirit, the gift of the Spirit, and the filling of the Spirit? Also, what is meant by the anointing of the Spirit? Is the anointing a special ministry of the Holy Spirit for all believers?

It is of first importance to use and interpret the biblical terms on any subject mentioned in the Word of God. This is especially true when dealing with the person and work of the Holy Spirit. Take the four words in question:

Baptism. The baptism of the Spirit is the act of our risen and exalted Lord in which He imparts the Holy Spirit to those who believe in Him, in fulfillment of such promises as Mark 1:8 and John 16:7. This baptism is described in 1 Corinthians 12:13 where the apostle declares that "by one Spirit we were all baptized into one body." This epistle was addressed not only to the believers in Corinth, but also to "all that in every place call upon the name of Jesus Christ our Lord" (1 Corinthians 1:2). The baptism of the Spirit is not an experience subsequent to believing the gospel, nor is it predicated upon any other condition than repentance toward God and faith in Christ as Lord and Savior. Every true believer is baptized in the Spirit, and is therefore united in the Body of Christ.

Gift. The gift of the Spirit is essentially the person of the Holy Spirit received at conversion. Peter made this clear when he exhorted those who "were cut to the heart" (convicted of the sin of rejecting and crucifying Christ) to "repent, and . . . receive the gift of the Holy Spirit" (Acts 2:37-38, NKJV). Every believer has the gift of the Spirit indwelling him.

Filling. The filling of the Spirit is not strictly a Biblical term. At the same time, believers are said to be "filled with the Spirit" (Acts 2:4; 4:8,31; 9:17;

13:9). The key verse, of course, is Ephesians 5:18 where the apostle Paul commands his readers to "be filled with the Spirit." Being filled with the Spirit means more than being indwelt by Him. It is possible for the Holy Spirit to be present in the life without being president! Paul is urging the believers at Ephesus—and you and me today—to be under the undisputed control of the Spirit. This is why the verb is in the imperative mood, the passive voice, and the present tense. That calls for obedience and allegiance to, and dependence on, the Holy Spirit every day of our lives.

Anointing. In Old Testament times, people—and sometimes things—were anointed with oil to set them apart for special and sacred use; e.g., patriarchs (1 Chronicles 16:15-17), priests (Exodus 29:1-7), prophets (1 Kings 19:16), and kings (1 Samuel 10:1) were anointed. In the New Testament, Christ (which title means "anointed One") was anointed by the Holy Spirit. This was predicted (Isaiah 6:1), fulfilled (John 1:32-34), and explained (Luke 4:18). This prepared our Lord for His messianic ministry. Christians (like you and me) may know this anointing, unction or enduement with power (see Luke 24:49; Acts 2:1-41; 2 Corinthians 1:21-22; 1 John 2:20,27).

I believe the filling of the Spirit is for normal Christian living, for wives, husbands, parents, children, servants, masters, members, and pastors (see Ephesians 5:18-19). The anointing of the Spirit is for special Christian service, for all believers who will appropriate "the promise of the Father" (Acts 1:4). In particular, the anointing (or unction) enables us to appreciate the Word of God (study 1 John 2:20,27). This "unction" *(charisma)* from the Holy One is God's safeguard against error, in the light of His inerrant word. Both are received at conversion. Notice: you heard the Word, and you received the Spirit. The Word is the objective safeguard, while the Spirit is the subjective safeguard. What is important to observe and obey is the command to "go on abiding" in the Anointing (who, of course, is the Holy Spirit). Underscore those words, "you will abide in Him (1 John 2:27). This is an imperative action verb. Jesus employed the same verb when speaking of Himself (John 15:4).

The other important verse is 2 Corinthians 1:21-22. In these verses Paul defends his authority in preaching the gospel (without any trace of fickleness) and affirms that this cannot be achieved without the anointing of the Holy Spirit. The anointing enables us to communicate the Word of God. God anoints all Christians, provided they fulfill the conditions. These conditions are beautifully exemplified by our Lord at His own anointing (Luke 3:21-22). There was the life of holiness. God could declare, "Thou art my beloved son; in thee I am well pleased." Jesus was "holy, harmless, undefiled, separate from sinners" (Hebrews 7:26). So must we be. There was the life of yieldedness. Addressing John the Baptist, Jesus said, "Permit it to be so now, for thus it is fitting for us to fulfill all righteousness" (Matthew 3:15, NKJV). God only pours out His Spirit upon those who obey Him (Acts 5:32, N.B., present tense). There must be the life of prayerfulness. Luke records that Jesus went down into Jordan "praying" (3:21). Later He taught His disciples to pray with persistence (Luke 11:5-13). Commenting on verse 13 Dr. Leon Morris said: "The reference [here] is . . . to the Spirit's work in the Christian's life generally."[2] Therefore, without the anointing of the Spirit there can be no authority in living or preaching the Word.

Your circle of fellowship is much wider than would be allowed, for instance, by so-called "fundamentalists." They would label you a "neoevangelical." You must have decided before God many years ago the terms and scope of your cooperation with groups, some of which hold views contrary to your own basic convictions. What criteria do you use for determining which churches or denominations you can cooperate and have fellowship with?

I call myself a "conservative evangelical." My basis for fellowship with a Christian or a church is oneness in Christ—"the unity of the Spirit" (Ephesians 4:3), rather than "the unity of the faith" (Ephesians 4:13). All of us are on the road to "the unity of the faith," but no one has yet arrived! This is why Paul expressly states, "Till we all come to the unity of the faith."

When my sons were little boys they had every right to share all our family privileges on the basis of life, rather than light. Since then, as they have matured, they enjoy oneness—not only of relationship, but also of knowledge. In a similar way, I can have fellowship with a brother or sister because of the common life we possess in Christ; but, by the same token, that brother or sister may not be knowledgeable in "the deep things of God." These believers are on the road of faith, but they have not traveled very far. Like Apollos, they need to be taken aside to be taught "the way of God more accurately" (Acts 18:24-28, NKJV).

While I would not tolerate fellowship with anyone who espoused false doctrine it has been my earnest prayer, throughout my Christian ministry, to "comprehend *with all the saints* what is the width and length and depth and height—to know the love of Christ which passes knowledge" (Ephesians 3:18-19, NKJV, italics added).

In my early crusades in Britain I used the thirty-nine Articles of the well-known statement of faith of the church of England to reflect my evangelical position. Those who could not subscribe to these tenets would not qualify to serve on committees.

At the same time, I will preach anywhere—even in "Satan's synagogues"—as long as my message is not compromised. On the other hand, I would not allow anyone with false doctrine to use my pulpit.

All converts in my crusades were followed up carefully and linked with evangelical churches.

How do you handle the issues when you are speaking in a church or to a group with which you have some basic theological differences? For instance, you are speaking on the campus or at a conference of a group which holds a radically different view from yours on the person and work of the Holy Spirit or to those who embrace a covenant position, or whose eschatology conflicts with yours. What do you do? Do you studiously avoid the controversial issues and speak on "neutral" subjects?

As a matter of Christian courtesy, I have always sought to speak on "neutral subjects," when invited to preach outside of my denominational circles. Within "the faith which was once for all delivered to the saints" there is more on which to agree than to disagree. Of course, there are those whose attitudinal idiosyncrasies make them professional controversialists. I am not one of them.

Throughout your ministry you have emphasized teaching on the so-called "higher life" or the "Keswick message," as it is sometimes called. I have known you for a long time and know that, from the very earliest days back there in Newport, you have practiced what you preach. Many have studied the liberating truths of Romans 6–8. Few have put them into practice. You have learned how to translate doctrine into a moment-by-moment experience. How can we translate the "theory" of victorious Christian living into a continuous present-tense experience?

It is true that I have often preached at conventions and conferences for the deepening of the spiritual life. I prefer to welcome such opportunities as occasions for expounding the Word of God on what I call "the normal Christian life." We are exhorted (indeed, commanded) to be consciously, continuously, and conspicuously filled with the Holy Spirit (Ephesians 5:18). Failure to live this way is sin—period! (James 4:17)

To turn theory into practice here must be determined discipline, on the part of a truly yielded (surrendered) Christian.

1) He must have a daily quiet time. This is not for sermon preparation, but for "soul nourishment" (see my booklet, *Manna in the Morning*).

2) He must depend moment by moment on the Holy Spirit to enable him to die to self and live for God (Romans 8:13; Galatians 5:16-26; Ephesians 5:18).

3) He must confess sin at once, when conscious of broken fellowship with God (1 John 1:9).

4) He must witness to Christ at every God-given opportunity (Acts 1:8). Spiritual sensitivity will signal the right moment to say a word for Jesus. Failure to witness is sin.

5) He must become involved in a Christ-exalting and Bible-preaching church (Hebrews 10:25)

6) He must seek to know and do the will of God concerning some "specific service" at home or abroad (Ephesians 2:10).

7) He must live out the simple, but vital, principles set forth in the Scriptures for his home life (Ephesians 5:18–6:4; 1 Peter 3:1-7).

What are your views on divorce? Is divorce and remarriage ever permissible? Is a divorced and remarried couple living in adultery? Can a Christian who divorced and remarried hold any kind of office in the local church or engage in active Christian service in the local church? Where would you draw the line? What counsel do you give to people contemplating divorce; people who have been divorced and are seeking remarriage; people who are divorced and remarried, but who are facing discrimination?

The multiple issues raised by this question are supremely important, but scripturally intricate. Able students of God's Word differ in their respective interpretations. Years of pastoral work have taught me, therefore, not to generalize, but to deal with each situation in dependence on the Holy Spirit and the appropriate application of relevant Biblical teaching.

1) *Marriage* is God's creation ideal, which Jesus affirms, and is a life-long, exclusive union that should not be broken (see Genesis 2:18-24; Matthew 19:6; Hebrews 13:4).

2) *Divorce* is "hated" by God and should be hated by Christians (Malachi 2:14-16). The only "exception" to this holy covenant of love is stated in Matthew 19:9, where the Lord Jesus specified "sexual immorality" as the only reason for divorce. Even when such sexual immorality is committed, however, there is still room at the cross for repentance, forgiveness, and reconciliation (see Hosea 3:1-5; 1 Corinthians 7:10-16).

3) *Remarriage.* Our Lord appealed to the Old Testament passage in Deuteronomy 24:2 to show that a divorced person (presumably the innocent party) is free to remarry. But His teaching clearly implies that such a marriage can only take place when reconciliation is morally and totally impossible (see Matthew 19:8-9; Mark 10:1-2; Luke 16:18; and 1 Corinthians 7:15).

4) *Acceptance.* When there is a genuine repentance and forgiveness after moral breakdown, there is restoration of fellowship, but not necessarily of leadership in the church. In a day of eroded standards, we need to ponder a passage such as Proverbs 6:30-35—"Whoso committeth

adultery . . . his reproach shall not be wiped away." How can anyone with such a "reproach" meet the qualifications delineated in 1 Timothy 3:1-13? God can certainly use such forgiven offenders in other areas of Christian service, but not as pastors, elders or deacons.

What advice would you give to newlyweds for keeping their love fresh and making their marriage work over a lifetime?

There is a simple acrostic that I like to share with young couples and it's all summed up on one word C-A-R-E.

C – stands for *commitment—love's commitment.* It is a significant fact to observe that love, in Scripture, is legislated. Jesus said, "You shall love the Lord your God" (Matthew 22:37); and Paul added, "Husbands, love your wives" (Ephesians 5:25). The delight of love can never be enjoyed until the duty of love is fulfilled. It isn't how we feel about our love life that matters, but what God says about our commitment. When we do our part God will see to it that the pleasures of a true love life follow.

A – stands for *adjustment—love's adjustment.* When Peter addressed husbands and wives in 1 Peter 3:1-7 he said in effect, "Learn how to dwell with your wives in an understanding way." This calls for adjustment at every stage of married life. Of course, this is an important principle in all human relationships. Even our relationship with the Lord is dependent on our daily adjustment to His will. This is why we should have our daily quiet time so that our lives are more closely adjusted to "that good and acceptable and perfect will of God" (Romans 12:2). Unless this matter of adjustment is studied and practiced, disaster is bound to follow.

R – stands for *restatement—love's restatement.* When you made your vows in the presence of God on your wedding day you expressed statements of utmost importance and meaningfulness; but what is so often forgotten is that those statements need to be *restated.* Once again, this is true in the Christian life. We repeat the Lord's Prayer in public worship. We repeat the words of communion in the Lord's Supper, and so on. The fact that we affirm these truths helps us to understand the meaning of our relationship with Christ. So it is in marriage. I think one of the saddest things is to visit young couples who once were so endearing in their references to each other and now are using terms that convey anything but warmth or tenderness. Carefully examine this aspect of love in your own life.

E – Stands for *enjoyment—love's enjoyment.* Marriage is not only for procreation, but also for pleasure. The Westminster *Shorter Catechism* says "Man's chief end is to glorify God and to enjoy Him forever." This applies to all relationships of life—including marriage. What are you both doing to ensure total enjoyment of one another in the Lord?

I suggest you review this acrostic very carefully in the light of such passages as 1 Corinthians 7:1-16, Ephesians 5:18-33, and 1 Peter 3:1-7.

How does one overcome bodily temptations in order to be one's best for God?

The Bible has much to say about the body (see 1 Corinthians 6:19-20; Romans 12:1-2; 13:14; 1 Corinthians 9:27; 2 Corinthians 6:16-18). It is a hellish lie to believe that the body is merely for selfish satisfaction. The body is God's because He created it, indwells it, and directs it.

Therefore, there must be the *dedication* of the body (Romans 12:1). Have you ever surrendered your body—your eyes, brain, ears, hands, feet, sex life, emotions—on the altar of God's acceptance and offered it totally and worthily to Him? To do this means keeping your body in tiptop shape for Jesus Christ.

The body also involves *diet*. The Bible says, "Therefore, whether you eat or drink or whatever you do, do all to the glory of God" (1 Corinthians 10:31, NKJV).

The body further calls for *discipline*. The body should be our servant, rather than our master (1 Corinthians 9:24-27). There should be the right development through exercise, the right mental stimulation through reading good books and having the proper attitudes (see Philippians 4:8).

The body is to be dedicated to God's use alone. We were bought with the precious blood of Christ; so to hold anything back from Him is wrong. One day we will appear before the judgment seat of Christ to give account for the things done in the body, whether good or bad (see 2 Corinthians 5:10). I urge you to live in such a manner that you will hear His "well done" and receive the crown of life promised to those who endure temptation (James 1:12). Look up the verses I have quoted. Make them the controlling principles of your life. If you know Jesus Christ as your personal Savior you have the indwelling Holy Spirit to enable you to overcome temptation. Follow the divine formula of James 4:7—first, "submit to God"; then "resist the devil and he will flee from you." Hallelujah! Through Christ it is possible to be more than conquerors!

In Mark 8:34 we read that we are to deny ourselves, but often you talk about "death to self." This expression is not found in the Bible. Isn't it dangerous to use terms that are not expressly stated in Scripture?

Let me try to answer the question you have raised in the following manner. The fact that the phrase "death to self" is not a Biblical quotation does not mean that it is not a Scriptural expression of truth. For example, we use the word *trinity*, but it is not found in the Bible and yet can be supported by such verses as Matthew 28:19 and 2 Corinthians 13:14. The same applies to "the fullness of the Spirit" (see Ephesians 5:18); "the second rest," taken from Charles Wesley's hymn "Love Divine" (see Matthew 11:29); the "second coming."

I hold that, positionally, our self-life was crucified with Christ some two thousand years ago. That is why we use the past tense in quoting Galatians 2:20; but, experientially, we are exhorted, by the power of the Holy Spirit, to "put to death the deeds of the body" (that ever-emerging and troublesome self-life). A key verse in this regard is Romans 8:13. Bishop Handley Moule in his commentary on Romans renders this verse as follows: "If you are living flesh-wise you are on the way to die. But if by the Spirit you are doing to death the practices, the stratagems, the machinations, of the body, you will live."[3] Observe that the verb rendered "doing to death" is in the present tense in the Greek. The process is a continuing one.

It is important to point out here that the practices of the body cannot be disassociated from the self-life. It is the I or self that chooses to act. This is brought out very clearly in Colossians 3:9-10, NIV: "Do not lie to each other, since you have taken off the old self with its practices and have put on the new self, which is being renewed in knowledge in the image of its Creator."

As for Mark 8:34, I take this even further. To deny one's self involves far more than the forfeiture of some small luxury "for the Lord's sake." Jesus' words, "take up his cross, and follow me," support my point. The cross was an instrument of death, and for the Lord Jesus it meant the denial of His rights, His reputation, and His resources (see Philippians 2:5-11). If we are to follow our Lord in self-denial then we must be willing to be "obedient to the point of death, even the death of the cross," and that will cost everything.

What advice do you give to a new convert who comes forward at one of your church services or evangelistic crusades and wants to follow Christ?

Each individual is referred to a counselor who explains from Scripture how to receive Christ and go on with the Lord. A follow-up letter is sent from my office within a day or so with some further pointers on how he can effectively live the Christian life. I tell the new convert that if he is going to trust the indwelling Christ to live His life through him he must have:

1) *The Right Christianity.* I advise him: Never take your Christianity from other Christians; you might be bitterly disappointed. Keep your eyes focused on the Lord Jesus Christ. Make the motto of your life "Looking [off] unto Jesus, the author and finisher of [your] faith" (Hebrews 12:2).

2) *The Right Confidence.* For your assurance of salvation and progress in your Christian life, always rely on the Word of God, rather than on your own

feelings, someone else's opinions, or the devil's doubts. Remember that your faith grows by daily hearing the voice of God through His Word (Romans 10:17).

3) *The Right Communion.* Spend time daily in prayer and the reading of His Word. In prayer we speak to God, and through the reading of the Bible God speaks to us (Luke 18:1; Matthew 4:4).

4) *The Right Cleansing.* Never hide sin nor excuse it. When you sin, confess it at once to God and believe that He has forgiven you (1 John 1:9).

5) *The Right Corrective.* When in doubt as to whether anything is right or wrong for you as a Christian, test it by asking yourself three questions:

    a) Can I ask God's blessing on it? (Colossians 3:17)

    b) Will it help me in my new life? (1 Corinthians 6:12; 1 Thessalonians 5:21-22)

    c) Will it be a stumbling block to others? (1 Corinthians 8:9)

6) *The Right Companions.* Be careful to seek friends among those who know and love the Savior (2 Thessalonians 3:6).

7) *The Right Church.* If you do not already belong to a live, Christ-exalting church, seek one as soon as possible. If you are already in fellowship with a local church then give yourself wholly to the teaching and the opportunity of service offered by the church (Acts 2:42; Hebrews 10:25).

8) *The Right Consecration.* Do not be satisfied with half-heartedness in your Christian life. Let your consecration to Christ be full, glad, and free. Constantly remind yourself that He gave His all for you; therefore, you must give your all for Him (Romans 12:1-2; 2 Corinthians 5:14-15).

I encourage the individual to look up these references, study each point prayerfully, and make them controlling principles in his life.

There seems to be so little discipline nowadays in our churches. We allow lax morals, heterodox teaching, and personal quarrels without taking steps to purge the church of such evils. To what extent should church discipline be exercised today?

The Bible teaches quite clearly that "the time has come for judgment to begin at the house of God" (1 Peter 4:17). Without question, the waning authority in the church of Jesus Christ is reflected in our inability to act decisively on the matter of discipline.

There is no question as to what the believers did when deceitfulness reared its ugly head in the early church, as recorded in Acts 5. Peter acted decisively in discipline, resulting in the death of both Ananias and Sapphira. The fact that people don't drop dead today in no way minimizes what God thinks of deceitfulness in the church of Jesus Christ. Whether people die physically or not doesn't alter the essential reality that something dies in the church when sin is not dealt with.

In the case of incest, Paul had to rebuke the church for not judging this sin. He commanded them to put the man out of fellowship. Indeed, the language is strong and clear: "In the name of our Lord Jesus Christ, when you are gathered together, along with my spirit, with the power of our Lord Jesus Christ, deliver such a one to Satan for the destruction of the flesh, that his spirit may be saved in the day of the Lord Jesus" (1 Corinthians 5:4-5, NKJV). Immorality had to be dealt with in the church.

In 1 Timothy 1:20, Hymenaeus and Alexander were "delivered to Satan that they [might] learn not to blaspheme."

The early church enacted discipline in three areas: spiritual impropriety, sexual immorality, and theological infidelity. These passages are for our instruction. Pastors and lay leaders should follow through on this instruction with wisdom, love, and anointed authority; otherwise God cannot possibly bless the ministry of the local church.

What advice do you give to one who feels led to go into evangelistic work? How can he be sure of his calling?

The answer is not simple, since God does not deal with every person in the same way. There are, however, certain important questions that one should ask himself?

1) *Do I meet the qualifications of an evangelist, as set forth in the Word of God?* When God called Paul to be an evangelist He clearly delineated what was involved and required (see Acts 9:15-16, 20; 22:14-15; 26:16-18). You cannot study these divine instructions without discerning both the qualifications and responsibilities of an evangelist.

2) *Have I the witness of the Spirit in my heart that God has called me?* The same Holy Spirit, who witnesses with our spirits that we have been born of God, also witnesses with our spirits that we are called of God to be evangelists or any other calling of ministry (Romans 8:14). As you pray earnestly about the matter, "the sense of call" will either come alive or die altogether. When Paul prayed, "Lord, what do You want me to do?" he received the answer.

3) *Has the gift of the evangelist become evident in my life and service?* 1 Corinthians 12:7 declares that "the manifestation of the Spirit is given to each one for the profit of all" (NKJV). The "manifestation" is not human ability alone, but rather the indwelling and infilling power of the Holy Spirit. Every gathering together of God's people constitutes an opportunity for the exercise and ministry of a gift for the profit of all.

4) *Has my church recognized and confirmed my evangelistic gift?* 1

Timothy 4:14 and 2 Timothy 1:6-7 give a significant object lesson in the divine/human recognition and confirmation of a person's gift and ministry in the early church (see also Acts 13:1-4).

5) *Has God used my evangelistic gift to the salvation of souls?* Writing to the Corinthians, Paul could affirm with confidence, "You are the seal of my apostleship in the Lord" (1 Corinthians 9:2, NKJV). Can you point to converts and say the same things?

How do you advise someone struggling with depression? Where is God at such times?

My heart and prayers go out to one who is struggling with depression. I thank the individual for sharing the pain through which he or she is passing at this time. I offer the following advice.

From a negative standpoint:

1) *Stop being introspective.* Introspection is a violation of the truth of Romans 6. When you died with Christ everything and anything that troubles you was condemned, put to death, and buried. Therefore, you have no right to visit the cemetery and dig up the old bones. The day God showed me this wonderful truth I was gloriously set free! I saw so clearly that there is nothing that people or the devil can say about me that God hasn't said already; but at the same time God has condemned and put my past out of sight.

2) *Do not read or discuss subjects or materials that tend to depress you.* Romans 13:14 says, "Make no provision for the flesh, to fulfill its lusts" (NKJV). It is amazing how this principle works, even with such a problem as depression.

3) *Avoid people or places that adversely affect you.* In saying this I am not asking you to be an escapist, but just to be sensible.

4) *Refuse to pity yourself.* The martyr complex can be detrimental to your healing and restoration.

From a positive standpoint:

1) *Quietly realize that whatever has been your experience in the past or however you feel at the present time, God is love.* During a period of illness when I could not pray, read my Bible, or even listen to music without triggering a paroxysmal tachycardia episode, I laid hold of Deuteronomy 33:27a: "The eternal God is [my] refuge, and underneath are the everlasting arms." Remember that however low you may feel or fall, the everlasting arms are still under you. Let this truth be a pillow at night and a power by day.

2) *Recognize that your experience is not unique and that what God has done in restoring others He can do for you.*

3) *Get involved in some hobby or work that is manual or physical.*

During the months of my illness I remember building a rock garden that proved to be occupational therapy for me. It took my mind off the problems and pressures of the ministry and accelerated the healing process.

4) *Remember that suffering is not a curse, but a blessing.* Read carefully what St. Paul had to say regarding his "thorn in the flesh" (2 Corinthians 12:7-10). Whatever agonies Paul had to pass through he came to the place where he could rejoice in his infirmities because he found that through suffering the power of God rested upon him.

5) *Finally, if the symptoms persist, seek the help of a Christian doctor of clinical psychologist.* There may be medical or psychological reasons for your condition.

You emphasize the importance of belonging to a local church. What guidelines would you give for selecting a good church? What should a person do if no such church exists in their neighborhood?

I believe that the Scriptures teach very clearly that, when and where possible, God's people should not only belong to a local church, but seek to function within that church as active members (read carefully Acts 2:42; 13:2; Hebrews 10:25). The tendency today among so many Christians is to be nothing more or less than church tramps. According to the great Puritan John Calvin, the church of Jesus Christ exists for "the ministry of the Word of God, the administration of the sacraments, and the discipline of its members." Where these three essentials are not operative we cannot call any group a local church. Here are five directives I give people who are looking for a good church:

1) *The Directive of Doctrine.* This is most important. Is the church Bible-based, Christ-exalting, and soundly constituted?

2) *The Directive of Devotion.* Are the members in love with Jesus, the pastor, and with one another? Are they friendly? Do they love souls and are they eager to win them?

3) *The Directive of Discipline.* Does the church demand everything I am and have? Does it involve people, their service, their money, and their time? Does it have high standards of purity, loyalty, and honesty?

4) *The Directive of Denomination.* While this is not all-important it is a consideration. Upbringing, background, and religious orientation do play a part in being "comfortable" in a church fellowship.

5) *The Directive of Distance.* This makes a difference if you have a family and you want your children to be involved in church activities.

If there is no local church to meet these criteria, move to another location. Your church life is as important as your home and even more important that your place of business.

Jesus loved His church and gave Himself for it, and He is building His church on earth and will one day present her without spot and wrinkle before the glory of the Father. What He thinks of the church is what you should think of the church, and seek to support it in every way possible (see Ephesians 5:25b-27; Hebrews 10:24-25).

What do you think about the "prosperity" teaching of today?

I am very disturbed by it. I believe that God intends His people to be successful in the "faithful" sense, e.g., God is going to judge me by my faithfulness to my own ability. God has prospered many businessmen, and I thank God that He has, for they have been the undergirders of missionary work and all manner of Christian service throughout the centuries. But I do not see from either the Old or New Testament that by becoming a Christian one is going to prosper materially. America has always been a great and prosperous country, but now inflation has hit and living is hard—especially among the poor (the same applies to Britain and other countries, of course). Then along comes somebody with the gospel of prosperity. One almost feels it is an ingenious method to gain a following and to gather funds. Jesus promised that in the world we would have tribulation. He said, "If any man will come after me, let him deny himself, and take up his cross daily, and follow me" (Luke 9:23). The early church faced immense poverty; the saints shared everything in order to help a church that was really on the rocks (Acts 2:44-45; 4:32-35). Paul had to make a strong appeal to the Macedonian churches for their brethren in Jerusalem (2 Corinthians 8). Study the lives of great Christian leaders over the centuries. Apart from some of the sharks who made money at the expense of the gullible, very few were rich and famous in the worldly sense. Material prosperity is a gift from God to those who can be trusted to use it in the work of God; but, generally speaking, it is the simpler lifestyle that God has called us to live. Our task today is not to invest in big buildings, big programs, etc., but rather to win souls and so hasten the coming of the King. Our day for prosperity is going to be in Heaven!

Do you think there is an undue emphasis these days on experience at the expense of doctrine?

Yes, we are facing the danger of over-subjectivism, where the emphasis is being placed on experience instead of truth. Everywhere I go it seems to be that people are seeking "an experience." If I understand the Word of God aright, we should move from truth to experience not from experience to truth. When experience is all that matters we manipulate truth to support our experience. Romans 6:17 appeals to me: "You obeyed from the heart [that's experience] that form [or pattern] of doctrine to which you were delivered" (NKJV). You don't change the pattern, you fit the pattern, and that pattern is truth. If you don't fit the pattern your experience can be suspect.

What do you see in the life of the church that causes you concern?

Very simply, it is that few pastors seem to be engaged in the expository preaching of God's Word. Preachers are without a message, without the authentic note of "thus saith the Lord." They don't know where they are or where they are going. They're aimless and frustrated, and this concerns me a great deal. I don't believe Biblical preaching is ever going to be substituted successfully. As someone has said, "There is only one thing that will ever take the place of great preaching and that is greater preaching." My greatest burden is to restore anointed expository preaching to the pulpits of our land.

What is the greatest truth God ever taught you?

There are many important truths that I have learned from my wonderful Lord over the years, but I feel that one of the most precious is this: *There is no demand made upon my life that isn't a demand on the life of Christ in me.* Hallelujah, Jesus is alive; He's available; He is adequate!

Photo by Victoria Kuhl

The Olfords with three of their grandchildren—
Jeremy, Justin, and Lindsay

CHAPTER 13

The Man

A man greatly beloved
Daniel 10:11

It is Shakespeare, of course, who has immortalized the name of Brutus. Marcus Junius Brutus, son-in-law of Cato the Roman philosopher, was an important man in Rome. He became the close friend of Julius Caesar. When it became evident that Caesar's ambitions threatened the Roman republic, Brutus allowed himself to be persuaded by the Roman General Cassius to join a conspiracy to murder Caesar. The murder was successful, but the conspiracy failed. The conspirators were defeated in battle by Marc Antony and Augustus.

Shakespeare quickly exposed the character of the envious Casca and the self-seeking of Cassius and the others. Octavius (Augustus) leaves us cold. Even Marc Antony, for all his brilliant oratory, does not move us – perhaps because we know too many of his weaknesses from history. Brutus, however, was different. Shakespeare, indeed, lets us shake our heads over the singular lack of common sense of Brutus in allowing Antony to speak at Caesar's funeral. Cassius saw the folly of it but was overruled. But Brutus was Shakespeare's hero. What made the man was his integrity. It comes out in full color in Antony's eulogy over the dead body of his fallen foe:

> This was the noblest Roman of them all.
> All the conspirators, save only he
> Did that they did in envy of great Caesar;
> He, only in a general honest thought
> And common good to all, made one of them.
> His life was gentle, and the elements

so mixed in him that Nature might stand up
And say to all the world, "This was a man!"

Thus it was with Stephen Olford. Here was a man! The thing that
persuades us, with all such men, is what accountants call "the bottom line,"
the line on the balance sheet that shows just how things really are. The
bottom line is integrity. We ask the question "Is this man for real? Is his
character mingled with alloy or is he for real?" All who knew him well will
say of Stephen Olford, "This man was solid gold."

We soon got past the handsome features, the cultured English accent,
the glowing personality, the enthusiasm, eloquence, and keen intelligence.
We found that underneath all these outward things was absolute integrity.

Several years prior to Stephen's death I asked a variety of people who
had known Stephen Olford over the years to share their memories. What
follows are the reminiscences of those men and women whose lives have
crossed that of Dr. Olford. We could easily fill a book just with these
testimonies. Often I found the various testimonials awakening an echo in
my own memory of this extraordinary man.

One test of a man's character is the impact he makes on children.
Children's likes and dislikes are frequently definite and passionate. When it
comes to other people, they go for the jugular or the heart. One of the most
attractive pictures we have in the Gospels is that of the Lord Jesus taking
little children up into His arms in order to bless them, as their admiring
mothers stand by.

Children's letters to their pastors can be very revealing. Here is a note
written when Stephen was pastor of Calvary Baptist Church from one of his
youthful admirers:

> Dear Pastor Olford,
>
> I like this church just because of you. You make it
> very, very, very, very, very good to come to church. My
> family and I love you so very much. And I love Jesus
> because He loves you, And you love Him.
>
> > Love,
> > Kathleen Brooks

The same youthful admirer likewise eulogized Stephen's wife:

> Dear Mrs. Olford,
>
> You are a very sweet and kind woman. My family and
> I love you as much as we love Pastor. We love you so

very much, from the tip of your head, to the bottom
of your toes. And, I love Jesus because He loves you,
And you love Him.

Love,
Kathy Brooks

Stephen's impact was just as great on little boys as on little girls:

> July 11, 1966
> Dear Dr. Olford sir,
>
> My Daddy has gotten a job at last. I am sure it is
> because God answers prayers. I must leave the church.
> My Daddy's job will be in San Diego. Please tell Mrs.
> Olford I loved listening to her play the piano. I was too
> shy to speak to you but I like you. Thank you for smiles.
>
> > Your pal,
> > Gordon Scott

Another clue to a man's character is to be seen in his influence on
young people, though their acceptance or rejection of another person is
much more complex than that of little children. Stephen Olford was always
able to impact and influence young people, as borne out by the following
letter received after a three-week lectureship at Columbia Bible College
(now Columbia International University, Columbia, SC) in December 1974:

> There is no way for me to express my sincere thanks
> and appreciation for your ministry to my own life
> while you have been here at school. It seems like
> these three weeks have gone so fast. Of everything
> that ministered to my needs, the Tuesday and
> Thursday evening voluntary sessions and the personal
> friendship I enjoyed with you stand out the most.
> Even when in a hurry and with much on your mind,
> you seemed to always find a moment to be kind to me
> and to say a friendly word.
>
> I come from a broken home myself, and you are like
> the Christian Dad I would have wanted. If ever I have
> a family I would like to love them and take the
> personal interest in them as you do your own. Your
> life is your testimony of Christ to others, and you have

> an abiding place in my heart. I think I will always remember you as a man who lived out his message of Christ, and in the midst of being involved with so many matters had time to be my friend.

Another clue to man's reality is seen in his impact on his peers. As a general rule, there is no group of men more critical of another man than those in the same class or profession as himself. Often envy and jealousy raise their ugly heads among peers. Nor are ministers of the gospel exempt. Doubtless, Stephen Olford had men in the ministry show him their ill-natured rancor, but they were far outweighed by the mighty chorus of those who called him blessed. One voice in that mighty chorus is that of Dr. Billy Graham, the world-famous evangelist who has spoken to more people concerning Christ than any man in history. He cheerfully acknowledged his debt to Stephen: "You will be remembered as a great pulpiteer, a great statesman in the Kingdom of God, and a compassionate friend who was a pastor in the highest sense of the word. Your ministry has been a blessing to my own life."

In the Foreword to *The Secret of Soul Winning* (1963), Dr. Graham said: "Stephen Olford is not only one of the greatest Bible preachers I know but one of the most successful soul-winners I have ever met . . .We have ministered together on three continents. He is unquestionably one of the most refreshing, radiant Christians I know. He exemplifies in his personal life everything the apostle Paul meant when he spoke of 'the fruit of the Spirit.' He is also a man of great compassion, carrying a burden for the lost."

Another voice is that of Dr. Charles Stanley, pastor of the prestigious First Baptist Church of Atlanta, Georgia. Known to millions, he is one of the "chief among the brethren" in Southern Baptist circles. Of Stephen he declared: "Dr. Stephen Olford [was] one of the greatest expositors of our time. He [was] a preacher's preacher, and a man used of God – probably more than any other single preacher today – to motivate, to stimulate, to stir, to bring conviction, to bring a deeper spiritual walk to the preachers of our nation. As I think about my relationship to him, God used Dr. Olford in a special way in two of the most important spiritual turning points in my life. One of these, I am sure, saved my life and my ministry, and therefore Dr. Stephen Olford will always have a very special place in my life – not only as a dear friend, but also a vital part in my ministry."

Cliff Barrows, the song leader and choir director in Billy Graham's great crusades, added his own tribute. He first met Stephen in 1946, shortly after the war. He described him as "a man who has meant more to us as a team than any man I know." Then he added, "His knowledge of the Word created in our hearts a desire to know Christ in the same manner. It was during this time [1946] that Stephen's interest and love for two Americans [Cliff's wife

Billie was with him] who hardly knew what to do in England meant more than we could ever say."

Jim Duffecy, an Australian, was head of the Open Air Campaigners in Glen Rock, New Jersey when he first met Stephen at Calvary Baptist Church in New York City. Jim allowed the church to use its specially-equipped van for the church's open-air meetings at Columbus Circle in Central Park. When he heard that Stephen Olford had been invited to come to Sydney, Australia to participate in the 1968 centennial celebrations of the Baptist Union, he sent a letter to Bruce King, then Secretary of the Baptist Union of New South Wales. He had nothing but praise for Stephen: "He is an evangelist," Jim wrote, "a Bible teacher, deeper-life speaker, a young people's man, and a minister to ministers. He will challenge every audience to the depth of their being by confronting them with the need of an all-out commitment to Christ as Lord. He himself is his best sermon. You meet Christ when you meet Stephen Olford. Expect great things."

Bellevue Baptist Church in Cordova, Tennessee is one of the truly great churches in the Southern Baptist Convention. When they built their new seven-thousand-seat auditorium the pastor, Dr. Adrian Rogers, hoped to get away from the burden of having to preach three times every Sunday to the vast crowds that packed the old sanctuary. He had not been in the new sanctuary long before it, too, was full to overflowing and he was back to preaching twice every Sunday morning to ever-growing crowds. Dr. Rogers was himself a gifted and eloquent pulpit orator with a tremendous soul-winning, church-building ministry. He testified, "Dr. Olford's dynamic ministry has enriched my own preaching, and that of thousands of other Southern Baptist pastors. He has given his life to preaching the gospel. His reputation and character are impeccable. In my estimation, Dr. Olford has no peer as a preacher of the Word and as a teacher of teachers."

The tributes from other pastors follow in an endless stream. One pastor, who confessed to being utterly defeated and out of the ministry, told of hearing Stephen speak: "I saw for the first time," he said, "that the deeper Christian life could be lived; for I saw something in [Dr. Olford] that I have never seen in another human being: I saw a life dedicated to God, filled with the Holy Spirit, and a man who totally believed and accepted the Bible as God's Word. I left that meeting that Wednesday night of February 8 knowing that I could never again live as I had lived."

D. Merrill Evert, Assistant to the Director at the Billy Graham Center in Wheaton, Illinois sent an unusual testimony. "When I was a little boy on a farm in Minnesota, my dad used to listen to Dr. Olford's messages while we milked the cows. Dad would often write down things he heard that he did not want to forget. Since the barn door was the nearest writing surface, we have a record of how God spoke to him over the years, even though he is now with the Lord. Some of those thoughts came through Dr. Olford's messages!"

Norman Vincent Peale, who was senior minister of Marble Collegiate Church in New York City for many years, is best known for his book *The Power of Positive Thinking*. Both Dr. Olford and Dr. Peale pastored New York churches and corresponded on occasion with each other. Following a trip to England in 1968, Dr. Peale thoughtfully wrote:"You may be interested to know that recently when Mrs. Peale and I were at Chartwell, the home of the late Winston Churchill, we were pleased to see one of your books on his shelf. So, you see, your writing has reached to the very highest level, and justifiably so."

But what about those who knew Stephen Olford on an everyday level as friend, colleague, and employer? A man may grace a pulpit yet in his daily life fall lamentably short of the ideals he proclaims. Here is another way to test a man to see if he is, indeed,"for real."

Few men, perhaps, have known Stephen intimately for as long as the late Dr. J.C. Macaulay. At the time of Dr. Olford's resignation from the pastorate of Calvary Baptist Church he spoke of the warm relationship that existed between Stephen and himself for nearly thirty-five years. "I am not one to express my emotions," he said,"or to give vent to my sentiments. . . . I don't believe that I have known an affection for any man equal to that which I have known for Stephen Olford."

Colin Jackson, Chairman of the Deacon Board at Calvary Baptist Church, once said this of his pastor:"He came to us full of the Holy Ghost and of power, and he has maintained that fullness throughout [his] years of dynamic ministry. He has been faithful in his proclamation of God's Word in this changing world. We have witnessed a man in action, completely dedicated to his high and noble calling, and a man completely dominated by the living God."

Ellie Carman was Dr. Olford's personal secretary for thirty-four years. She told how working with him blessed her heart, stretched her mind, revived her soul, and encouraged her spirit. She summed him up as "a man of prayer" and as "a man of perfection and purpose."

"I remember my first day of dictation" she said."He opened with prayer! This was new to me, and has left an indelible impression on me as to how important prayer is, not only in his private life but in his work life.

As to his being a man of purpose she stated:"He sets goal and carries them out. He is unflinching in determination." She knew him as a man who delegated work and who expected his subordinates to follow through with equal thoroughness and determination. "He works hard and has more energy than many people half his age."

Commenting on his standard of perfection she added:"He always strives for perfection and has challenged me to do the same." She recalled some of his written guidelines on how to get work done more efficiently and effectively – "even on how to answer the phone properly."

She summed it up by paraphrasing Romans 13:7, "Render honor to who honor is due."

Vicky Kuhl, who worked closely with Stephen Olford for over forty years as his Homiletical secretary, had ample opportunity to observe him in the office, in the study, in the pulpit, on the crusade platform, in radio and TV studios, and on his knees in prayer. Several years before her death, she remarked, "I have seen him sick, I have seen him well; I have watched him laugh, I have seen him cry. In all the years I have known him he has never wavered in his character or in his commitment to the Lord. Ever and always there has been that eager pursuit after more holiness and conformity to Christ. You can't be in his company long before you sense 'an other Presence.' It is no wonder that the 'shekinah' shines through his face and comes through his message. He makes you want to stretch spiritually – and in every other way – and to emulate his example, even as he has followed his Lord."

On the occasion of the twenty-fifth anniversary of Stephen Olford's years in the ministry, his staff at Calvary Baptist Church wrote this tribute: "Ours is a unique position. We say a hearty amen to the expressions of much blessing from your pulpit ministry – the strong salvation messages, the edifying teaching and the inspiring deeper-life instruction. To us is given the privilege of saying, 'We thank God for what we have seen of the Lord Jesus in your life.' The harmony and consistency between your public ministry and your private, daily life among us have been to us the greatest impact of all. Truly, you have been a living epistle, whose example has spurred each of us to more consecrated service."

The integrity of the man can be seen in what he says about himself in his preaching. "Time and time again," he confessed in one of his sermons, "I have been tempted to quit the ministry, to go back to engineering; but thank God, I have never done it, and God helping me, I'll never do it. Why? Because there's no greater calling in all the world. God had only one Son and He made Him a preacher. There's nothing more wonderful in all the world than to follow in His train.

"Having crisscrossed the world again and again, having had the joy of preaching to literally millions, having had the thrill of every possible experience any person could wish for, I want to say all that fades into insignificance. All that really matters is just this: *to be like Jesus*. The longer I live, the longer I read my Bible and pray; yes, and the longer I sense the strivings of the Spirit of God in my life, the more I say, 'Lord Jesus, if anything should ever happen to me, and my boys look upon their father's life, I would be heartbroken if they said, 'Dad was an evangelist,' 'Dad was a radio speaker,' 'Dad was a conference speaker,' 'Dad was a pastor.' I hope and pray that they will say, 'Dad reminded me of Jesus.' I hope that my wife – should I precede her to Heaven – will look back and say the same thing – that she had a husband who reminded her of Jesus."

There was also Stephen's younger brother, Paul. Many a time he, his parents, and his brothers Stephen and John sat at our table for a Sunday meal. My father taught Paul to drive. It was wartime. Car headlights had to be masked so that only a sliver of light showed. Paul remembered a three-hundred-mile round trip (a considerable journey in wartime Britain, mostly on narrow and winding roads) with him, a learner, at the wheel, undertaken to bring Stephen home from a tent mission.

He said, concerning his brother: "As a man, Stephen [was never] satisfied with anything but the best." He recalled the others, after a game of golf, being content with brushing off the odd blade of grass. "Not Stephen!" he said, "Out would come a little yellow duster, and a whole cleansing procedure would follow!"

He remembered him, too, as one who "always had to lead." He recalled many a rough and tumble when they were lads together. Stephen was smaller than his younger brother, yet "he would very often win the day – such was his desire to win." This was part of the rigorous family training received at home. "We were taught that determination not desire controls our destiny."

"One of the days I shall never forget," Paul recalled, "was when I went to the Labor Exchange with Stephen. He handed over his insurance card stating that he was stepping out in faith to serve the Lord. Mad? Not really. When Jesus called, 'Follow Me' he responded!"

Stephen's youngest brother John captured several incidents from boyhood days in Africa. He wrote: "When I was six years of age I was on the threshold of death with malaria. Dad was knocking up a box for me as burial could not wait in those days. Of course, I knew nothing of it at the time, but I was told later on that Stephen (then about twelve) mounted a protest to the Almighty on the veranda of our house at Luma Cassai."
John added that "Stephen was a fine marksman; he took over from Dad. On one occasion he was about to shoot a duck for dinner. To steady his aim, he put his foot on a log in the marshy grass. The log slithered away: it was a dozing crocodile!"

Much later, following his marriage to Heather, Stephen and John were out together duck hunting near Heather's home in Lurgan, Northern Ireland. John "carried a loaded 4.10 single bore shotgun and was following Stephen through the reeds. "I tripped," he said, "the gun went off, and the shot entered the ground about ten inches from Stephen's foot – a merciful escape." John confessed, "I've never touched a firearm since that day."

When the family lived in Plymouth, Devon, England before World War II, Stephen was employed as an apprentice motor mechanic. One night, after working late, Stephen was speeding home on his powerful motorcycle, thereby attracting the attention of the police who gave chase. Not to be outdone, Stephen "switched off his lights where the streets were lit and made for Dartmoor. In the darkness he needed his lights, but obscured his license plate with the tail of his great coat. The police never caught him."

John remembered that Stephen "showed his skill in handling a car after the family bought its first one – a Morris 8. Father, already suffering from angina, was being taken out for a ride. I was sitting beside Paul in the rear seat. Suddenly, out of the corner of my eye I saw a wheel overtaking us and realized that it was the one that should have been underneath me. Stephen brought the car to a halt safely."

Another who knew Stephen Olford in his early days was Dan Maynard. I knew Dan well. He assisted at my baptism. Like so many others he was a member of the Young People's Christian Fellowship in Newport during the war years. He, I and the Olfords all attended the same church. He bore witness to the impact Stephen had on his life. He came into our rather dull town like a breath of wind from heaven. "In 1939," Dan recalled, "he formed and led the Young People's Christian Fellowship, bringing together separate groups of young people and uniting them in a common cause. It proved to be a source of rich spiritual blessing to literally hundreds of young people during the war years and in the period immediately afterwards. Many . . . became leaders of young people's groups themselves. Others took up positions of church leadership in Britain and overseas." Dan himself was no exception. He served as an International Trustee of the Gideons International in Christchurch, England.

He recalled a humorous Olford anecdote. "Stephen," he said, "was mindful of his physical aliments. During a visit to his home in the mid-seventies he was describing how he felt during a recent serious illness and finished by saying, 'I have said good-bye to the family on three occasions!' Even during the ensuing laughter it was good to realize he had been somewhat premature!"

Mention has been made elsewhere of Philip P. Gammon who was Stephen's boyhood friend in the Angola days. He became Dr. Olford's first assistant pastor at Calvary Baptist Church in New York. He said: "Probably the first sound I ever heard (other than the initial birth-cry of my own voice) was the shattering explosion of an old double-barreled shotgun being discharged by Stephen Olford." He explains: "In that part of the world it was the custom in those days to announce to the small missionary community and larger African population, that another 'missionary kid' had seen the light of day." He adds:"I do not know if it did much more than scare away a flock of birds in the tall eucalyptus trees in front of our house, but [I] told him . . . that I'm glad he missed me!"

On a more serious note Philip Gammon remembered an early experience in their new partnership at Calvary Baptist Church. Stephen said to him,"Let's go away somewhere and plan and pray for the great work that is before us." Accordingly, they found a quiet spot in upper Manhattan overlooking the Hudson River."There," he said, "we discussed every aspect of that challenging ministry and then cried out to God for His power and blessing to make an impact for God on that vast metropolis. The result of that get-together was an all-night prayer meeting for the first Friday night of every month for all who felt constrained to pray. We also embarked on a television ministry when few religious broadcasters used that medium."

Another whose association with Stephen Olford went back a long way was Frank Lawes, a British pastor and evangelist, now with the Lord. He worked with Stephen in the war years, among the troops, and co-authored with him the book *The Sanctity of Sex*. He recalled his first encounter with Stephen Olford around the year 1938 when Stephen was still working as and apprentice motor engineer. "We talked long into the night," he said, "about the restlessness of adolescence, through which he had just passed. Stephen had lived for fast cars and girls . . . Those three nights were to be the beginning of a new vision given by the Spirit of God. The man was emerging – with hands, feet, heart, and mind all surrendered to the Savior who has ever captivated youth. As for love and marriage he said,'I have, like Adam, gone to sleep in the will of God.'"

Later they met again. "I had already written two chapters on a proposed book on sex problems. Stephen, unknown to me, had also prepared some material. We pooled our ideas and the book, *The Sanctity of Sex,* was born. In those days the subject was taboo. Both of us found ourselves in hot water. Someone said recently that it was book forty years ahead of its time. God blessed the work and it went into several editions and a few languages."

Another incident he recalled with a smile illustrated Stephen's ready wit and love for a good joke. During the war years in Britain clothes were rationed. "Most men," Frank Lawes recalled, "bought with the frugally allotted coupons a pair of corduroy trousers, because they were so hard wearing, even though the material had a pronounced musty-fusty smell." Frank Lawes arrived at the Olford home and was met at the door by Stephen, bravely decked out in a pair of the fusty pants."He saw me looking at them. 'Frank,' he said, 'they are scriptural. It says "Provide yourself with bags that wax not old."' [*Bags* is an English synonym for trousers.]"

Frank remembered another incident of a more poignant nature.

"Stephen's father who had spent years in Angola as a missionary had painstakingly translated the New Testament into the Chokwe language. He had that day received the first copy from the Bible Society. He, with tears of joy in his eyes, held the copy for me to see. He handled it like the jewel it was. Stephen was present and I thought the two would dance around the room."

Then there was the time when Stephen Olford, Jack Nickless, Arthur Gove and Frank Lawes banded together to conduct a campaign at Clumber Hall in Nottingham. Someone volunteered the loan of a good piano but transportation was a problem. "Then a coal merchant offered to move it to the hall, if we four would lift it." The monster was loaded on board the truck and the quartet of young evangelists climbed up beside it. "When the driver took off," Frank Lawes said, "a cloud of coal dust swirled around us as we sat in the back of the truck anchoring our treasure. Our eyes became gummed, our faces begrimed, our white collars blackened, and our pockets full of coal dust. On our return we looked like four chimney sweeps! How we laughed!"

Jack Nickless, an early friend of Stephen Olford, gave us a glimpse of Stephen's prankster qualities when they were young classmates at the Missionary Training Colony. "We first met," he said, "in a quiet Devonshire village overlooking beautiful Dartmoor scenery when he was about twenty years old. He was inquiring about life at the Missionary Training Colony where he was to join us. His earnestness, mingled with a strong sense of humor, won our confidence from the first. During the year at Upper Norwood, living in rough wooden huts, I recall one of his occasional pranks. He climbed on to the roof of our hut to pour water down the hot stovepipe in retaliation for our failure to invite him and his hut-mates to a 'midnight feast.'"

Like so many others, Jack Nickless bore testimony to Stephen's emphasis on prayer. "*Dynamic* was one of his favorite words, and it was descriptive of his life and ministry. One product of his own rich prayer life was his ability to encourage other young Christians to pray – not the wordy 'prayer-meeting killers,' but brief, specific petitions that would inspire praise and expectation of God's positive answers."

Perhaps the man Stephen knew longer than any other American was Jack Wyrtzen, founding director of Word of Life Fellowship, Inc. "We [were] personal friends since 1946," said Jack, "when Stephen was chairman of some evangelistic meetings he had arranged for me in Wales. When we arrived in Newport by train we didn't know what he looked like, but all of a sudden we heard someone shouting 'Praise the Lord!' 'Hallelujah!' 'Glory be to God!' 'Amazing!' 'Terrific!' He was a Spirit-filled, enthusiastic preacher of the gospel and we fell in love with him at first sight."

Jack recalled how Stephen quoted that phrase "only one life" the first time he heard him speak. "Stephen told how God shook the life out of him, and he went from being an engineer to one of the world's great preachers – a prophet, expositor, evangelist, etc.

"The next year Stephen came to America to speak at our Word of Life Camps at Schroon Lake, New York. What a blessed time we had! Shortly thereafter," said Wyrtzen, "I broke my hip and ended up in the hospital; so Stephen not only spoke at the rallies in Times Square to over one thousand young people, but he took the nationwide broadcast for us each Saturday night, along with Carlton Booth." He was a young British evangelist with no experience in radio work, but God graciously overruled and poured out His blessing beyond all measure. What is more, it exposed him to the Christian world in America.

Later, Stephen went on to Minnesota where Jack believes Billy Graham had booked him at the First Baptist Church of Minneapolis. "No one had ever heard of Stephen Olford, so they said, 'Oh, you will really enjoy him. He's a bell-ringer!' They took that literally and thought that meant he rang bells in a morning church service as a musician. When he arrived and was coming up the steps the pastor met him and said, 'Where are your bells?' Stephen didn't know what he was talking about. What a surprise!

"I remember how we encouraged Stephen to come to Calvary Baptist Church in New York City. God used him like very few men have ever been used in New York."

Elton Irwin, once Chairman of the Board of Elders at Calvary Baptist Church, remembered Stephen Olford's golf prowess. One incident that took place at a golf club on Long Island came readily to mind. "We often took him there to get some fresh air and exercise," he said. "Eager to get into the game, having missed playing for several weeks, he made a powerful swing at the ball. It hit a tree, bounced to the club house and rolled back to the place where it was hit. We all had a good laugh! However Stephen had the last laugh – he ended up with the best score!"

In a different and enlightening vein, he recalled taking Stephen home on one occasion after a lengthy church business meeting. "The traffic was heavy and it was a bitterly cold night," he said. "As we approached the apartment building in which he lived, I slowed down. It was then that a taxi rammed the rear of my car, causing damage to both vehicles and pain to Dr. Olford. We learned that the driver of the taxi was intoxicated. We both talked to him, prayed with him, and invited him to our church. Despite Pastor Olford's pain, his deep concern for this man both spiritually and physically was very much in evidence."

Dr. Roger Willmore, pastor of Deerfoot Baptist Church, Trussville, Alabama and minister-at-large for Olford Ministries, considered Stephen Olford his mentor and friend for over 35 years. He wrote of Dr. Olford's ability to impact lives for God: "In 1977 the Lord blessed my wife, Sandra, and me with a son. Prior to his birth his name was prayerfully selected. We named him Stephen in recognition of Dr. Olford's ministry to our lives." Reflecting on Stephen's ministry after his death, Willmore said, "Although he had his arms around the world, he never lost his ability to put his arms around the individual."[1]

Bill Ridley, a Christian layman, told what happened when Stephen came to the small Maranatha Baptist Church he was attending in Detroit, Michigan in the late forties. He preached at both Sunday services, but what Bill and many other young people remembered was the "squash' held afterward in the living room of the pastor's house. Young people filled the chairs, overflowed onto the floor, all ears to hear the dynamic visiting preacher one more time. Stephen preached on how one can find the will of God for his life – "a perennial question for serious young people of senior high school and college age." Bill Ridley still remembered the main points: The *Word* of God, the *witness* of the Spirit, and the *warrant* of circumstances. He said: "A number of those young people became active in Christian service," and he went on to give example after example.

Rev. Edwin H. Mitchell was led to Christ by Stephen and later became an Associate Minister at Calvary Baptist Church in New York. On the personal level, he recalled many hours the two families spent together. "They were happy times," he said, "offsetting the great social problems that beset New York City. Heather, Stephen, and their two boys were great role models for our children." One of his responsibilities at Calvary Baptist Church was to "protect" Stephen Olford from bizarre and eccentric individuals who walked into the church sanctuary off West 57th Street. He recalled that, over the years, Stephen was visited by women claiming to be "'the Mother of God' not to mention individuals claiming to be 'Jesus in the flesh.'" He recalled one such pretender, a certain "Major Arnold from Vietnam." He wanted to cash a fifty-dollar check because the banks were closed. The check was "as phony as the four-thousand-dollar check he gave us representing his accumulated tithe from the time he was wounded in Vietnam. He even showed his 'wound'"!

When Edwin Mitchell was invited to be Stephen's associate he was given this word by a friend: "At best the task will be relieving a great man of God so he can exercise in larger measure the great gifts God has given him. At its worst, you may feel you are 'Joe boy' for Stephen Olford." Looking back he said, "Stephen Olford, the man, never caused me to feel I was a 'Joe boy.'" On the contrary, Edwin Mitchell bore witness to the fact that Stephen's "support of men and women in the ministry with him" was one of his strengths. One of his great personal attractions, as a man, is his charisma. He has a way of giving the person to whom he is talking his undivided attention and making that person feel like the most important person in the world.

What Ted S. Rendall, Chancellor Emeritus of Prairie Bible Institute, remembered about Stephen was an amusing incident involving his late wife Norline. "We have a son whose name is Stephen," Ted said. "When Stephen came to give the message at our Founder's funeral service, he stayed with us." At times Dr. Olford had occasion to call the Rendalls' home from a campus telephone. "At that time our son, Stephen, was in the stage of humorously mimicking preachers." So it was that when Stephen Olford called the Rendall home he announced himself as "Stephen." Mrs. Rendall thought it was her own son Stephen and bantered with him in a light vein. When Dr. Olford finally asked if Dr. Rendall was home she suddenly realized her mistake. Embarrassed, she plunged into explanations. Stephen Olford took it good-naturedly.

Dr. Carl F.H. Henry, author, theologian, scholar, lecturer, and former editor of *Christianity Today* recalled another humorous incident. He and Dr. Olford were to share some meetings in Yugoslavia on one occasion. Through a chain of circumstances Stephen arrived late in Belgrade and missed an outdoor picnic arranged with some of the local pastors. On the menu was soup, served domestic style. The whole chicken, including the feet (to give it special flavor) was in the pot. When the group went to the airport to meet Dr. Olford they decided to prepare some sandwiches for him. Dr. Henry volunteered to prepare them. And so he did! When Stephen seized one of the sandwiches, served on the delectable local bread a couple of chicken feet fell out! "At that moment I caught the look on his face," Dr. Henry said. "I thought he might be on the verge of translation to another world! He was a good sport, however, and offered to try everything, which was a diplomatic way of excusing himself from the sandwiches and concentrating on the potato salad and dessert."

Dr. Gerald B. Griffiths, Pastor Emeritus of Calvary Church, Toronto recalled an incident that took place at Zurich, Switzerland. He and his wife were on their way to the Holy Land. Because of fog at Amsterdam they had been diverted to Zurich and were being accommodated for the night in a hotel. Mrs. Griffiths decided to contact a Zurich listener to her radio program. When the contact was made the lady insisted on coming to the hotel to see them early the next morning.

She had a story to tell. She was attending an evangelical church, and also a home Bible study with a husband and wife who were both employees of Swiss Air. The wife was an air hostess who had come to faith in the Lord Jesus Christ through a passenger on a Swiss Air flight from New York. She had never heard the gospel until this passenger spoke to her, shared his own testimony, and God's way of salvation through faith in Christ and His atoning death. The passenger gave her a booklet to read. She was regenerated, and soon afterward led her husband to faith. Both husband and wife were now keen Christian workers in Zurich, said the Griffiths' early morning visitor. The name of the passenger, she added, was Stephen Olford. Did they know Stephen Olford?

The Griffiths had known Stephen since their student days in Cardiff, South Wales. The story stuck me as being typical of Stephen Olford, the man. The man cannot be divorced from the message and the mission. He lived to win people to Christ.

Dr. Eric G. Crichton, Pastor Emeritus of Calvary Church, Lancaster, Pennsylvania and formerly associate to Dr. Alan Redpath at Moody Church in Chicago, said: "There are few men who have left a deep spiritual imprint upon my life . . . Stephen Olford was one of the most influential of these."

He referred to Stephen's friend, A. Lindsay Glegg. "Mr. Glegg wrote a book which he entitled *Life with a Capital L*. By that title Mr. Glegg was portraying the life we have in Jesus Christ. In that life there is a vertical line that reaches up to touch the very life of God. But there is also a horizontal line that is lived out in demonstration before men. That title, *Life with Capital L* aptly describes what I observed in Stephen Olford."

Rev. John Caiger, minister for fifty years at Gunnersbury Baptist Church, London, England and a former assistant minister at Duke Street Baptist Church, Richmond, Surrey, added his testimony. He recalled an incident that took place when he and Stephen went together to attend the inaugural luncheon in preparation for Billy Graham's first London Crusade.

"Stephen and Billy were old friends," he said, "and they were looking forward to seeing one another again. About eight hundred of us were standing behind our chairs at the tables, waiting for the arrival of the party at the head table. As they passed us Billy spotted Stephen and immediately stopped to greet him. Stephen graciously introduced me, and Billy, in turn, graciously acknowledged my greeting. Then he turned once more to Stephen and said to him in a tone of great urgency: 'Stephen, pray for me! I am frightened to death!' His audience included several bishops, members of the aristocracy, and members of Parliament; hence his understandable fear, which was gloriously overcome by the grace and power of the Holy Spirit.

"To me, this incident was a striking testimony to the stature and quality of Stephen Olford, that among all those hundreds of distinguished ministerial figures, it was to Stephen that Billy turned in the urgency of his need."

Miss Mary Beam and Miss A. Elizabeth Cridland were veteran missionaries associated with the Africa Inland Mission. They remembered when the Olfords came to live next door to them in Florida. Stephen had been ill and the doctor had insisted that he must have a six-month's rest. The home of Dr. and Mrs. G. Allen Fleece was made available to them. Heather flew back to New York to honor a commitment to play the piano at a Christian Life

Convention. The missionaries offered to keep an eye on Stephen and make sure he had a good evening meal – at least until Heather could get back.

"That was God's provision for us to be wonderfully renewed in the Spirit," they said. "Every evening we had our own private victorious life conference, when we could ask all the questions that had piled up in our years away in the bush. We will never forget how we were lifted to the very heights of Heaven!"

"So far as we can remember," they declared, "we … never left the Olfords after a visit, a meal in their home, or at some conference, without Stephen placing his arm around Heather, and his other hand on one of our shoulders, committing to the Lord everything said during the conversation, and asking blessing from the Lord on the names that were mentioned."

Rev. John Balmer, head of Training Pastors International, was Encounter Ministries' first intern. He traveled much one summer taking care of the incidentals of Dr. Olford's ministry. He said: "I heard seventy-two messages from Dr. Olford that summer and only one time did I hear a message repeated – and that was because there was not enough room to get everyone in at a particular convention.

"Many times, after everyone had left and I had already packed up all the literature, I would find Dr. Olford leaning over and listening intently to a man who had just surrendered to Christ."

On these trips John Balmer would usually have a room next to Dr. Olford's so as to be readily available should he be needed. John recalled that one night after a very busy day, he was worn out and soon fell asleep. "About three o'clock in the morning," he said, "I was awakened by what I thought was someone crying out for help. It was Dr. Olford next door. He was crying to the Lord that He would come down and have mercy on the people. I was so moved I got down on my knees and prayed with him for nearly two hours. Was it any wonder that the next day, when he stood up to preach, that God sent revival to that meeting?"

Dr. W.F. "Chubby" Andrews was an outstanding surgeon, layman, and former Vice-Chairman of the Board of Encounter Ministries. He told how he was drawn into the Olford orbit by the bonds of friendship between his son Steve and David Olford. The two young men were roommates at Wheaton College for three years. "Steve spoke of David Olford as a man who, more than anyone he had known, allowed the Lord Jesus to be visible in his life."

Several years before Stephen Olford's death, Dr. Andrews gave his impressions: "Stephen's walk with the Lord," he said, "is not by any means just a casual thing. It is a consuming, passionate walk that rarely ever breaks contact. His love and respect for his wife, Heather, is a thing of beauty. Closer contact with this beloved couple revealed to me why their son David was a vessel through whom the Lord shone in His loveliness."

On a practical note, Dr. Andrews recalled that, on a number of occasions, funds for Encounter Ministries were low. "He refused his salary," he said, "that others on the staff might not suffer. Only after some searching by the Board was this made known."

Returning to his memory of the man, Dr. Andrews mused, "In the lives of so many great preachers we usually find some weak areas, such as weakness in family relationships, lack of love for the masses, a sense of being too busy to care, and sadly, in so many today, marital infidelity. Praise the Lord, I have never seen any of these things manifested in the life of Stephen Olford. He not only has a great heart for God, but a tremendous love for all people, regardless of their position in life. He is indeed one of God's great men."

I have kept for last the words of Mrs. Marjorie Redpath, the widow of the man who was about as close to Stephen as any man could be. Both were gifted evangelists. Both pastored great churches on both sides of the Atlantic. Both preached and practiced the "higher" life.

"My husband and I," Marjorie Redpath recalled, "met Stephen and Heather at Hildenborough Hall before they were married. Later, Alan took part in their wedding in Norhern Ireland. In the late forties Stephen and Alan were sometimes asked to take evangelistic missions together preaching on alternate nights. They incorporated a cricketing term to assess the evening's impact: 'LBW' (the initials stand for 'leg before wicket'). With Alan and Stephen, however, they stood for 'lash! bang! wallop!' In other words, there had been an outstanding presentation of the gospel message, bearing fruit in changed lives."

Both Alan Redpath and Stephen Olford were often speakers at the annual Keswick Convention in England, though rarely at the same time. "One year," Mrs. Redpath wrote, "Alan occupied a single room in the tower of the hotel, and during that time our second daughter was born. The next year Stephen had that room and Jonathan was born. We all wondered who would be there the following year – and with what results!"

The last time the Olfords and the Redpaths were together was in 1989, when Alan was in his final illness. "He was at home between two hospital visits and, although he had Alzheimer's disease and had suffered a stroke, the Olfords were amazed at the way he conversed, remembering their boys and many things in the past. Before they left they were even more amazed at the intensity of his prayer for them all.

"A few weeks later the Lord called Alan 'Home.' The one person my girls and I wanted to take the memorial service was Stephen." She summed up her remembrance of Stephen Olford, the man – "He has been a friend who is even closer than a brother." The same thing has been said of the Man, Christ Jesus. What greater testimony could there be to anyone than that?

Heather and Stephen Olford in 1999.

CHAPTER 14

The Dreamer

by Stephen F. Olford

As he approached his late seventies, Stephen Olford, in what might be considered a personal letter to the reader, expressed his dreams and goals for the remaining years of this life. What follows is an extraordinary glimpse into the expectations, energy and emotion of a man who would gracefully and faithfully serve the Lord until the day of his home-going some ten years later.

Your old men shall dream dreams.
Acts 2:17

The day of Pentecost was the fulfillment of Joel's prophecy concerning "the age of the Spirit," which stretches between the two comings of Christ – an age when sons and daughters, young men and old men, servants both men and women, can know the abundant fullness of the Spirit (Acts 2:17-18). In the power of this fullness, young men will see visions, while old men will dream dreams. We attribute "visions" to young men in the vigor of their strength and wide-awake activity; and "dreams" to old men, with the calmer and less active and excited mindsets! The two categories, however, are not to be regarded as mutually exclusive. What is important is that we test all visions and dreams by the Word of God. Every vision or dream in the book of Acts (eleven references) bears directly on the missionary work of the church and so has both a spiritual and an evangelistic value (see Acts 2:17 and Acts 11).

We associate "dreams" with one who sleeps or reflects. As years advance "old men" do more and more of this! I shall limit my "dreams" here to three longings I have cherished and nourished in my heart for years.

First, I dream of *revival in the church*. It has been my privilege, throughout my life, to experience Heaven-sent local revival at Wheaton College, Nyack Missionary College, Moody Bible Institute, Providence Bible Institute (as it was known then), Prairie Bible Institute and other schools. I have also witnessed revival in local churches and conference centers. The lasting results of these holy events have been felt around the world. To God be the glory!

Throughout my ministry, however, my dreams and earnest prayers have been focused on an outpouring of God's Spirit church-wide. Let me borrow from my book *Heart Cry for Revival* and summarize what I mean by revival:

"Revival is that mysterious and sovereign work of God in which He visits His own people, restoring, reanimating and releasing them into the fullness of His blessing. Such a divine intervention of the Holy Spirit always issues in evangelism. In the first instance, however, it is a work of God in the church and among individual believers. Once we understand the nature of heaven-sent revival we shall be able to think, pray and speak intelligently of such 'times of refreshing . . . from the presence of the Lord' (Acts 3:19).

"There has never been a time, in the history of the church, when God's people have not had a heart-cry for revival. Even in times of appalling moral darkness and spiritual declension there have always been those whose heart-cry to God has been:

Oh, that you would tear the heavens open and come down
– at your Presence the mountains would melt,
as fire sets brushwood alight,
to make known your name to your enemies,
and make the nations tremble at your Presence,
working unexpected miracles
such as no one has ever heard of before
(Isaiah 64:1-3, *The Jerusalem Bible*)

"I see no hope for our time outside of a mighty spiritual awakening. This conviction was vividly expressed sometime ago in an open letter published in the *Harvester* magazine. Ponder this appeal:

It is doubtful whether, in this history of the world,

there has previously been a period of difficulty so complex in character and so wide-spread in effect as that through which we are at present passing. A feeling of uncertainty and instability prevails in every circle, and the future seems to hold no sure promise of either peace or prosperity. It was never more true that "upon the earth" there is "distress of nations, with perplexity; . . . men's hearts failing them for fear, and for looking after those things which are coming on the earth."

In the midst of change and unreliability, spiritual values alone remain immutable, and there never was a greater need for the reminder of their reality, security, and stability. Yet the Church, which should be proclaiming the glorious news, seems totally inadequate to meet the need. Generally speaking, the lives of Christians do not differ, to any great extent, from the lives of other folk around them. They share the same fears, express the same doubts, feel the same uncertainty, show the same disconcertion. The peace of God and the joy of Christ are little in evidence. The dynamic power of the Holy Spirit is not appropriated.

Unparalleled opportunities present themselves, but there seems a moral and spiritual inadequacy to respond to their challenge.

If there is to be a revival of spiritual life and power, it must originate with the individual believer, and there is a great need for a personal searching of heart and exercise of soul in this matter. The sin, which is spoiling the life of the Christian, must be judged, and put away. The selfishness, which is robbing Christ of the love and devotion which are His due, must be confessed and removed. The ambitions and desires, which are hindering the work of God, must be uprooted and thrown on the refuse heap. A renewal of blessing is dependent upon the restoration of communion and the reconsecration of heart and life.

"Many of God's people, longing for a reawakening of the Church and for a revival of the work of God, . . . are praying that the . . . difficult conditions of the present day may lead to a reassessment of values, a fresh stirring of love for the Lord and an amazing harvest of souls.

"The contemporary scene . . . closely resembles the days of General William Booth, founder of the Salvation Army, when he analyzed the chief dangers of the twentieth century. As I review his words, I am struck by their aptness and accuracy. He enumerates six dangers:

1. Religion without the Holy Spirit

2. Christianity without Christ

3. Forgiveness without Repentance

4. Salvation without Regeneration

5. Politics without God

6. Heaven without Hell

"William Booth saw that these dangers would affect the twentieth century – and how right he was! The question arises, then, as to how these trends can be reversed. Very simply, the answer is revival. Yes, we need revival.

"I can remember the spiritual awakening which visited the Hebrides in 1949. God's servant used in this gracious moving of the Holy Spirit was the Rev. Duncan Campbell. In recounting the story of God's dealings with His people, Mr. Campbell stated: 'I personally believe in the sovereignty of God in the affairs of men, but I do not believe in any concept of revival that eliminates man's responsibility. Here were men and women who believed in a covenant-keeping God, who believed that the God to whom they prayed could not fail to fulfill His covenanted engagements; but they also believed that they too had to do something about it. God was the God of Revival, but they were the instruments, the agents through which revival was possible.'"[1]

I know that God will not disappoint me, even if I have to witness a mighty revival from Heaven's perspective! But revival in the church is my dream. Second, I dream of *repentance in the world*. Of course, when there is genuine revival in the church there will be corresponding repentance in the world – but we need to see repentance. There is no sense of sin and no fear of God in our land today. Romans 1:18-32 depicts the state of affairs all around us. Someone has recently stated that now it is sin to call anyone a sinner!

All this troubles me deeply. I long for men like Jonah who will emerge from the deep waters of purging and preparation to stride across our cities until it can be said that "the people . . . believed God, proclaimed a fast, and put on sackcloth, from the greatest to the least" (Jonah 3:5, NKJV). One man, truly revived, crying out in God's name for repentance, can bring a Nineveh to its knees.

The same thing happened on the day of Pentecost, when Peter thundered out those words: "Let all the house of Israel know assuredly that God has made this Jesus, whom you crucified, both Lord and Christ." The crowd was "cut to the heart, and said to Peter and the rest of the apostles, 'Men and brethren, what shall we do?'" (Acts 2:36-39, NKJV). It has happened under the preaching of the Reformers and revivalists – men like John Wesley, George Whitefield, Jonathan Edwards, Charles Finney, and a host of others. I dream of biblical preaching like that today. God has not changed; His Word has not changed nor has man and his sin changed. We need repentance in the world, if we are going to avert the sword of divine judgment.

Third, I dream of *rapture in the air!* As a boy, I was brought to faith in Christ through the message of a soon-returning Lord. That same message has inspired purity of life and urgency in my service ever since. First Thessalonians 4:13-19 is one of my favorite passages. I dream of a day or night when death will be cheated because of the "shout," "the voice of an archangel" and "the trumpet of God." Rapture in the air, that is my dream. Until Jesus comes, my dream is to be busy. Jesus said, "Occupy till I come" (Luke 19:13).

Dr. Vance Havner, that great proponent of righteousness and revival, was an encouragement to me on this matter of growing old and keeping busy. We often talked together about this. He wrote in his book *Threescore and Ten:*

> Some old preachers keep silent in an evil time. They say, "This is the day of youth – I've had my say." But Rehoboam would have saved the kingdom if he had listened to the sober counsel of the elders instead of the rash advice of the younger set. Age has a word for any day and generation. Some things would be in better shape today if some older men had spoken out a few years ago. No prophet was ever meant to be superannuated into silence. As long as he can speak he should speak without apology. The Scriptures tell us that when the Spirit is poured out, young men shall see visions and old men shall dream dreams. It is as proper for an old preacher to be a dreamer as for a young preacher to be a seer, so long as his dream is not a nightmare![2]

A study of "old men" in biblical literature and daily life makes it evident that aging is not so bad! We have the acceptance of old age. It was with confidence that the psalmist prayed: "Do not cast me off in the time of old age; Do not forsake me when my strength fails" (Psalm 71:9, NKJV). The Levitical laws governing day-to-day life taught that the younger generation should rise before the aged, and defer to the old (Leviticus 19:32). Where great truth and good taste are nourished, this kind of respect is demonstrated today. Even in some cultures where the Bible is not widely read and studied "old age" is still venerated. I love to travel to Japan and enjoy their reverence for old age. A white head of hair will get you anywhere in Japan!

We find this "honor" for old age all through the Bible. "The elders" in Paul's day were "worthy of double honor" (1 Timothy 5:17). In Old Testament times, God visited Abraham and Sarah when they were 90 and 100, respectively (Genesis 17). The divine visitation was to announce the birth of their son Isaac "from whom, according to the flesh, Christ came" (Romans 9:5, NKJV). Despite his initial hesitation, Moses led the people of Israel through forty years of wilderness wandering to the outskirts of the promised land. He was 80 when God called him and 120 when God buried him! Zechariah is described as an "old man," and Elizabeth as a woman who was "getting on in years," when they were caught up in the events that led up to the Messiah's birth. Simeon and Anna, two elderly saints, waited and prayed for the coming of Jesus.[3] The apostle Paul put great importance on the fact that he was "Paul the aged" (Philemon 9). And so we could go on exemplifying that "old men shall dream dreams." We also have the importance of old age. "They shall still bring forth fruit in old age; . . . To show that the Lord is upright" (Psalm 92:14-15).

Some years ago, *Eternity* magazine published an article listing some statistics that are pertinent to our theme of old age:

> Many of the prominent careers in our day exact a short span of youth and then eject their subjects as has-beens, consultants, or ex-celebrities. Most of the sports stars are finished by their 30s or 40s. Among many working artists the assumption is that the early years, the 20s, are the most creative, after that, the talent evolves into management. And the homemaker, one of the largest professions, often feels washed up at 50 when the last child leaves home.

But there is another side to all this –

At 53 Beethoven wrote the Ninth Symphony. At 57 Handel wrote "Messiah." Walter Reed found a cure for Yellow Fever at age 50, and Louis Pasteur discovered the vaccination for rabies at 62.

All the U.S. Presidents in this century have been over 50 except Theodore Roosevelt and John Kennedy [and we could add Bill Clinton].

Michelangelo didn't begin his work on St. Peter's cathedral [in Rome] until he was over 70 and kept working on it until his death at 89. Frank Lloyd Wright designed New York's Guggenheim Museum in his 90s. and of course Grandma Moses didn't take up painting until she was almost 89; she kept at it until 100.

Among writers age knows no limits. Tolstoy, Shaw, Victor Hugo and Bertrand Russell all did their best work after 75. Within the Christian world, John Bunyan wrote *Pilgrim's Progress* at age 50. Francis Shaeffer's first widely read book was during his 53rd year. Prolific Herbert Lockyer, in his 90's, had a new book out almost every year . . . Frank Gaebelein [in his seventies] . . . [found] time to edit the *Expositor's Bible Commentary* for Zondervan and to serve as a consulting editor for . . . other publications.

For ventures, you have to credit C.T. Studd for tackling Africa at age 50. That must have been comparable to J. Howard Pew of Sun Oil tackling the Alaskan oil fields in his 80s. Col. Sanders hardly sold any chicken until he was forced to "retire" at age 65 by a new highway that closed his roadside restaurant. Gutenberg got his press to work when he was 50.[4]

As Richard L. Morgan has put it, "As long as we keep our hopes and dreams alive, as long as we stay involved in life, our spirits will be renewed. There should be no wrinkles on the soul."[5]

While I wait for the rapture in the air I will "dream dreams." Among personal dreams, I want to major on the following:

To the end of my pilgrimage, I want "no wrinkles on my soul." With the apostle Paul, I am determined to "run, . . . fight . . . and [train] . . . lest, when I have preached to others, I myself should become disqualified" (1 Corinthians 9:27, NKJV). Contrary to popular opinion, the race becomes more exacting and the fight more intense as the years come and go. I am often asked by pastors and others whether having my daily quiet time is easier now than when I was a young man. My answer is always "it's tougher now." The devil knows that what counts costs and what costs counts! My devotional life is vital. I am only as tall in the pulpit as I am on my knees in the study. I must walk with God under an unclouded sky with the ungrieved, unquenched Holy Spirit filling my life. This will mean discipline and dedication until my journey is done. Needless to say, when I pay the price of fellowship with my Lord I experience "joy unspeakable and full of glory" (1 Peter 1:8). So I want more Bible, more prayer and more fullness in the Holy Spirit.

*Next, I do not intend to retire unless the Lord compels me to do so! Projects and possibilities storm my mind – especially when I'm relaxing or trying to sleep. I want to do more writing; I must keep on preaching; and of course, I will continue to "equip and encourage pastors and laymen in the art of expository preaching and exemplary living to the end that the church will be revived and the world will be reached with the saving Word of Christ."

With this in mind, I have great dreams for the Stephen Olford Center for Biblical Preaching here in Memphis, Tennessee. I want to see the work well established under the able leadership of our beloved son, Dr. David Olford, and the capable Board of Directors that God has raised up over the past years. I thank God for every one of them. Whether at board meetings, ministry occasions, the golf course, or vacations together, they have been wonderful. They have enriched and encouraged our lives – more than they will ever know.

Finally, I want to spend more time with Heather, my sweetheart and companion throughout nearly fifty years. I have never allowed the ministry to take first place. She comes first in human relationships, but she deserves more of me in these sunset years! Our wedding motto has never been abrogated: "together with God" (1 Corinthians 3:9a). She has been all and more than a man, husband, or father could ever hope for. Our oneness is sweeter and stronger as the days go by.

I want to enjoy the family in a more intimate and involved program of reunions and celebrations. Our sons Jonathan and David, with their precious wives, Catherine and Ellen, and our grandchildren are a rich heritage from the Lord. God has blessed us with a family in Christ and, therefore, a family in love.

I also want to enjoy the fellowship of our faithful staff and those who serve us by prayer and support. As emigrants from Britain, Heather and I have very few relatives in the United States. Our larger family consists of our board members, whom we love deeply, and our immediate staff - two of whom have been with us for over thirty years (Vicky Kuhl and Ellie Carman). Their loyalty and fidelity can never be truly rewarded until they stand before the judgment seat of Christ.

These, then, are my dreams until Jesus comes or calls. So to conclude:

> I'm heading for the summit,
> I've hear the call to climb -
> To heights that have no limit
> In heav'nly realms sublime.
>
> I'm heading for the summit,
> I see the prize ahead;
> I'm pressing on to win it,
> As I am daily led.
>
> I'm heading for the summit,
> To see my Savior's face;
> To be, through endless ages,
> A trophy of His grace.
>
> Stephen F. Olford

Stephen enjoying and sharing in some relaxed moments with granddaughter, Stephanie, and grandson, Jeremy, and others. Such times were very special to Stephen and to all the Olfords.

CHAPTER 15

The Afterword

by David L. Olford

r. Stephen F. Olford drew his last breath just after 11:15 p.m. on Sunday, August 29th, 2004, at the age of eighty-six. My father used to refer to Sunday as "King's Day," and it was near the end of a King's Day that he went to see the King.

In an interview the following day with Baptist Press, Dr. Adrian Rogers, pastor of Bellevue Baptist Church in Memphis, said, "The Christian world has suffered a great loss in the homegoing of this man, but I can say without a shadow of a doubt he finished well. He stayed on course and came across the finish line with a torch ablaze."[1] At the memorial service, Dr. Rogers gave us the key as to how Dad finished so well, "How did [Stephen] do it? Looking unto Jesus. . . . He was a man who kept his eyes on the Lord Jesus Christ. He never got sidetracked . . . He was a Jesus man."

It was my father's stated intention to never retire, but to press on in effective ministry – and, indeed, the last ten years of my father's life were characterized by continued spiritual vitality and fruitful activity. This meant, first of all, that he gave himself to the disciplines, the duties, as well as the delights, which were the fabric of his own walk with God. My father always taught that a personal walk with the Lord had to precede and, indeed, be the foundation for public ministry. Daily devotions, private and corporate prayer, and good reading were all part of his lifestyle. My father always valued and enjoyed hearing the preaching of the Word, especially in the context of a worship service. He and my mother were members of Bellevue Baptist Church in Memphis, Tennessee, and they appreciated greatly the preaching ministry of Dr. Adrian Rogers.

There was a dynamism to my father's life that can only be attributed to his "freshness" in the Lord. He knew what it meant and what it took to remain fresh in his spiritual life. He believed that you must "walk in the light with the ungrieved, unquenched Holy Spirit filling your life." This was my father's experience, and this was the reason for his constant impact on the lives of others. Those closest to him, especially family members, often benefited from that freshness when he shared a verse, an encouraging word, a devotional thought, or a written note. Those working at Olford Ministries International were frequently blessed by his study of the Word when he spoke at staff devotions. Whether you were a beloved Board Member on the phone or a visitor to the Olford Center, very often a conversation with my father would include a thought from the Word of God and prayer. When the word of Christ indwells and the Spirit of Christ fills, ministry takes place moment by moment, person by person, and situation by situation. This was his experience.

In his public ministry, my father maintained a very full schedule during his last ten years. Only twice was my father's speaking ministry briefly sidelined – by quadruple by-pass surgery in January of 1997 and by his bout with cancer in the Fall of 1999. However, for Dad, this was an opportunity to focus on his writing ministry. Yes, there were the signs of wear and tear, especially from the cancer and chemotherapy, but the determination to "keep on keeping on" was true to the end. A good friend once asked my father to share with others in the ministry the answer to the following question: "Why do you still do it?" Why did he still study to produce new sermons? Why was he in his study late at night? Why did he still work so hard? The answer went back to the sense of call and commitment to the task of "rightly dividing the word of truth." The answer, also, must include a reference to the disciplined lifestyle that was such a part of my father's walk with the Lord. Dad knew nothing other than working hard for the advancement of the Word of God and for the greater glory of God. This discipline included time set aside and planned for family, rest, recreation, and other priorities, but it certainly was true that my father was a hard-working, devoted servant of the Lord.

It was my father's practice for many years to present an annual report to the Board of Directors of OMI, reviewing the previous year and looking ahead to the next year. The following report, prepared for the Annual Board of Directors Meeting (January, 2002), presents a "snap-shot" of the various ministry activities that my father gave himself to in his later years. My father was eighty-two at the time of this report.

Beloved brethren:

The year 2001 was launched under the banner "FORWARD WITH GOD" – and what a year it has been! Despite the fact that America was plunged into war, following the September 11th attack on the World Trade Center, spiritually speaking it was one of my best – and busiest – years, in terms of ministry and outreach.

I ministered in seven countries – Japan, Honduras, Nicaragua, France, Wales, England, as well as our beloved United States.

I preached seventy-eight times, over and above radio, institutes, and writing commitments.

I lectured sixty-four times at fifteen Institute events – most of them at the Stephen F. Olford Center for Biblical Preaching in Memphis – but also at Liberty University, Lynchburg, Virginia; Calvary Baptist Church, New York City, and Tabernacle Baptist Church, Penarth, Wales. Permanent videotapes in English/Spanish were produced for the ongoing training of pastors and bi-vocational leaders in Central America during our visit to Honduras and Nicaragua. In October and November we were host to internationals from ten different countries during three weeks of back-to-back institutes. Testimonies, emails, and letters all spoke of "times of refreshing from the presence of the Lord," as well as appreciation for the food, fellowship, and blessing received. Guest lecturers included Dr. Gene Getz, Dr. John Phillips, Dr. Wayne Barber, Dr. Jonathan Olford, the Rev. Bob Sorrell, Dr. Alan Streett, Dr. Ted Rendall, and the Rev. Ron Owens.

Two new books came off the press – *The Sword of Suffering* (AMG Publishers) and *Windows of Wisdom: Devotional Studies in Proverbs* (Ambassador-Emerald International). . . . Some twenty radio and TV interviews gave wider exposure to the books. In addition, I gave a radio interview to promote my book, *The Grace of Giving.*

Twelve articles were written for my column, "Points

to Ponder" in *Pulpit Helps,* a publication for preachers of all denominations. Nine articles were produced for *Evangelism Today* (UK) – a publication to which we have been contributing articles since 1972. Four articles were submitted to our in-house publication, *Angelos.* I wrote blurbs and book endorsements for at least nine new books. OMI also gave permission to publish excerpts of *Manna in the Morning* to numerous nationals in Asia and Africa, as an outcome of Amsterdam 2000 (BGEA).

Four radio tapings of Encounter took place throughout 2001 . . . All in all, forty-nine programs were produced last year. I also produced a Christmas cassette . . . which featured seasonal and other piano selections by my wife, Heather (side one) and a message from me on 2 Corinthians 9:15 (side two).

E.K. Bailey Ministries presented me with their 2001 Living Legend Award at a special banquet . . . [in] Dallas, Texas for "proclaiming the gospel of Jesus Christ throughout the world, and assisting African-American preachers in developing their skills for expository preaching."

Truly, it has been a banner year. To God be the glory, great things He has done!

What the future holds for us as a nation is uncertain, but "Jesus we know, and He is on the throne." As for the ministry, we can testify "Hitherto hath the Lord helped us," and this gives us confidence as we move into the uncharted months of 2002. Meanwhile, my sincere thanks to each of you on the Board, who have helped by prayer and support, to enable this ministry to go forward under God's good hand.

Respectfully and affectionately,

Stephen F. Olford

Stephen Olford with the late Dr. E.K. Bailey on the occasion of receiving the "Living Legend Award," July 12, 2001 in Dallas, Texas. The award was presented by E.K. Bailey Ministries, Inc.

Over the last decade, my father devoted much of his time to enriching the ministry provided by The Stephen Olford Center for Biblical Preaching. The program of study at the Center expanded to seven different training events all committed to calling pastors and laypeople, men and women, to faithfulness in preaching or teaching the Word of God. As the ministry grew both domestically and internationally, participants from around the world arrived at the Center to receive practical training, as well as spiritual challenge and encouragement. And, through partnerships with various seminaries and Bible colleges, many theology students found they were able to receive academic credit for the Institutes.

My father described the ministry at the Center in the following way:

> I feel that this ministry is first of all dynamic. It is dynamic because it's charged with a word called "preach" . . . Dynamism is anointed expository preaching. . . . Secondly, the ministry here under God is absolutely distinctive. We are not a seminary. We are not a Bible college. We are not a church. We have a distinctive and that distinctive is "Jesus is Lord," "Be Ye Holy," and "Preach the Word." Our task is to teach men how to preach in the power of the Holy Spirit. . . . But, . . . the ministry which is dynamic and distinctive, is dependent. This is a dependent ministry. We are utterly and totally dependent upon the Lord for the supply of our needs."

These words were shared in 1999, as the construction of a new Ministry Center project began. Added to the Welcome Center, the Emmaus Lodge, and my parents' home, this 23,000 square foot building would include a chapel/lecture room, library space, forty-three bedrooms, a studio, as well as other facilities. The dedication of the Bethany Ministry Center, on October 19, 1999, was a bittersweet day for my father. Due to his bout with cancer, my father was confined within his own home just yards away from the Bethany Lodge where the Dedication Service was taking place. He was, however, able to share his heart with those at the Dedication Service by recording his thoughts on audio tape. Hearing his voice and his specific words to us was very meaningful on that occasion, but his absence was deeply sensed. Through God's healing grace, he was soon able to preach and teach again, and to participate in events in our newest campus venue.

Ultimately, my father's passion was for people's lives to be touched and changed at the Center. It was his prayer that preachers and teachers would leave with a new or renewed resolve to proclaim the Word of God in the power of the Holy Spirit. After one of our Essentials of Expository Preaching

Institutes, a gentleman had this to say:

> For me it is one of the high watermarks of my life to be around people who love God and want to teach the Word. I have always been a fan of expository preaching, but [I] never have . . . had it explained to me. . . . It has been a blessing to me and I am looking forward to seeing how the Lord is going to use it in my life and the life of my church.

A participant from Central Africa said, "When we were here in 1999, I went back to my church. I [went] to help my people in leadership in expository preaching. I saw eight Muslims come to Jesus." Other people have come to the Center seeking a refreshing and renewed vision. From one such person came the following testimony:

> These last three weeks have been an absolute godsend. This past year has been a difficult one for me. I was becoming so dull and dry in my own spirit and wasn't having the fellowship I had enjoyed in other years. The future looked bleak. I didn't want to do anything else but preach the Word of God. God blessed me by bringing me here. He revived my heart and my vision by revealing Himself to me in a new way. I thank Him for that, and I thank you and all the staff here for how you have contributed to that.

Central to each training event was a series of sessions by my father himself. His classic series on "The Essentials of Exposition" was featured in the training event more recently called "Rightly Dividing the Word of Truth." Other lecture series included "Evangelistic Preaching," and "Lessons in Leadership," not to mention various powerful individual messages. Also offered at the Center were practical preaching workshops. Each participant delivered a sermon here at the Center and received a constructive critique by my father and our ministry team. Another special event we developed featured preaching on the victorious Christian life and sessions on how to preach and teach the Word for spiritual growth.

In his later years, my father's messages and lectures blessed thousands of people who attended these training events in Memphis and other locations around the world. In his characteristic foresight, video and audio recordings were made of his core messages for future use at the Center. Today, these recordings continue to allow people to benefit from my father's teaching and preaching.

In 1996, a group from Birmingham, Alabama came for a weekend retreat

The group picture of the attendees and speakers of the "Essentials of Expository Preaching" Institute (June 7-10, 2004).

based on the "Keswick" message. This event became the providential inspiration for our biannual Christian Life Conventions. These meetings were an opportunity to challenge believers to new commitments and a more meaningful walk with the Lord by focusing on a sequence of Biblical teaching dealing with sin, sanctification, surrender, Spirit-fullness, and service. Dr. John Phillips, Dr. Tom Elliff, Dr. Crawford Loritts, Dr. Eric Crichton, Dr. Wayne Barber, Dr. Jim Shaddix, and Dr. Ted Rendall were among those who joined my father to minister at these meetings.

In and around regular Institute events, Dad mentored many in the ministry, through counseling, consultations, and correspondence. Over the years, a number of people in ministry came for extended times of internship. Two men who spent extended times learning from my father were Paul Ndungu from Kenya, and Edgar Sathuluri from India. "Pastor Paul," who was led to Christ through my brother, Jonathan and his wife, Catherine, in Kijabe, Kenya, became a missionary to the Masai. Paul's ministry over the years has seen the hand of God at work in amazing ways as thousands have been reached with the gospel. The latest word indicated that some fifty-two churches have been established. Also, leadership training has taken place. Edgar Sathuluri heads up a ministry called NATIVE that disciples and trains village evangelists in Hydrabad, India. Edgar spent hours of personal time with my father, as well participating in the formal teaching sessions. Since his time here, God has used Edgar remarkably and his ministry has multiplied in growth and impact. Edgar's ministry is based on the process described in 2 Timothy 2:2, which is also the Biblical text behind the philosophy of ministry at the Center.

My father's ministry in Japan and Italy deserve special note. Due to the special relationship they had with the Japan Keswick movement, my parents traveled to Japan at least seven times over the last twelve years. Much of his time was spent in convention ministry, but there were also specific sessions planned for training pastors and preachers. In July of 2005, Olford Ministries was blessed to host a group of thirty-seven Japanese pastors, leaders, and spouses, at one of our training events in Memphis. This was anticipated prior to my father's death and was the result of his ministry in Japan and the attendance of various Japanese pastors at the Institutes in Memphis over the years.

In association with Gaetano Sotille and Italy for Christ, several trips to Italy were made as well. Training events and special preaching commitments took place in Italy, and in May of 2005, a large contingent from Italy came for training at the Center in Memphis.

These special events are a testimony to the global vision and impact of my father's ministry. And yet, despite the magnitude, he gave himself personally and with incredible intensity to any individual who came to receive counsel, prayer, or to discuss some aspect of their life or ministry.

As my father looked ahead to his final years, he expressed the desire for quality time with his wife, his family, and his friends in the Lord. This was not because he had neglected these relationships, but because these relationships meant so much to him. My father and mother were very close, and this was true as much, if not more, in their last few years together. Through the challenges of life and ministry, and through the specific challenge of aging and illness, my folks were inseparable. Not only were my parents in ministry together, they really shared in all things. They planned together. They did things around the house together. They traveled together. My folks enjoyed times of relaxation and refreshment together, playing golf right up to the last weeks of my father's life.

My father did much to encourage and bless both my brother and myself. Special family vacation times were planned to be together. When meetings or responsibilities brought us together, time was taken to catch up on the latest news. Times with the grandchildren were precious indeed, especially because the family was two thousand miles apart. Despite the busy schedule of the last few years, my father always seemed to be available. This was something that was true of him throughout his life. As far as "the boys" were concerned, he was available. He often taught at our Center the need for fathers to be accessible, available, and adaptable. By accessibility he meant simply that fathers could be reached by their children. The routine commitments of life were not to be a barrier for their children. This was true of my father. As children, as boys, as sons, we always knew that we could get through, we were priority. But, my father defined "availability" a little differently. Availability is more than being in the same room at the same time, or being on the phone together. Availability has to do with focus, with an intentional commitment to hear, to listen, to engage with your children and their needs. My father was one of the most "available" people I have ever met. This was true in our relationships with him as sons, but it was also true for others who spent time with him. I believe this was one of the "engaging" things about being with my father. You sensed that you were really with him and he was really with you. I am sure that people who had the opportunity to spend time with my father would testify to this quality of "attention" that he would give. What a quality! What a discipline! What a gift to others! What a gift to us!

As far as adaptability is concerned, we as sons were the beneficiaries of sensitivity rather than rigidity in the practical matters of life. What do I mean? Well, picture an English father and an Irish mother trying to raise two boys in an apartment building in New York City in the 60's! What about devotions, schooling, play time, recreational activities, sporting events, concerts, entertainment, or special events in the city? There were definitely non-negotiables in terms of behavior, personal habits, church involvement, schooling, and playing an instrument! But, what I want to stress is the fact that there was an openness on the part of my parents to allow us to experience those things that were not deemed harmful, but helpful for the overall well-being of two boys who couldn't just "go outside and play in the backyard." Yes, there were rules. I knew I had done wrong when I threw a baseball through the fourteenth floor window. But, I don't remember being "exasperated" by unreasonable rules, some type of unexplained rigidity, or the lack of personal involvement in our lives. Some of my best childhood memories are devotional times we spent together, especially in the evenings when we were on vacation. It was then that conversation moved beyond the devotional thought itself to issues and questions about life that either my brother or I were asking. Much was communicated in these "unstructured" moments when accessibility, availability, and adaptability were displayed. Questions were welcomed. Wise counsel was given. Sleep was delayed!

I had the privilege of working with my father for over 19 years. My father truly had a heart for God, His Word, and His work. The sheer authenticity and intensity of my father in the "things of the Lord" was such an example and challenge to me. In his personal life, he was a man who pursued and practiced holiness. In terms of ministry, he had a vision as big as the world and a jealousy for the Lordship of Christ. He had a heart for people: individuals, preachers, churches, and the nations. My father was burdened not only to see people come to Christ through a sound, steadfast, and saving faith, but also to experience more and more the fullness of life in Christ. He believed firmly in the sufficiency of the Word of God and in the power of the Spirit of God to change lives for time and eternity.

My father was, also, a man who displayed balance in his life. This balance revealed itself in his ministry as well as in his personal life. He had strong convictions, but he would not let differing views on non-essentials hinder fellowship with other believers. He was able to hold in tension various doctrinal positions that received Scriptural support, without having to reconcile what he believed to be "mysteries" of the faith or complementary truths. My father had a great sense of humor and he laughed at lot. He enjoyed life. He enjoyed the good things in life. This enjoyment should be viewed in contrast to his hatred of evil and the sins that not only displeased God but ruined people's lives. Those closest to my father witnessed this balance in thinking and living that enabled my father to be both approachable and helpful to so many people.

My father consistently encouraged me personally, and in the ministry. He had the right word in season. He always had a "good word" to share on a birthday card, at a birthday party, at Christmas time, at an anniversary or some other special occasion. Gifts were rarely given without a special note being written or at least words of love shared in his beautiful handwriting. Certainly one of the personal highlights of my life was my service of ordination which took place on Sunday, November 23rd, 2003 at the Calvary Baptist Church in New York City. My father delivered the ordination message and spoke on the same text that he had given me many years before when I was baptized at Calvary, "You therefore, my son, be strong in the grace that is in Christ Jesus" (2 Tim. 2:1, NKJV). These words from 2 Timothy really became a life's message from my father to me, and what could have been more appropriate? I cherish these words, I cherish this text, not only because it is in the Word of God, but because it has been expounded and applied directly to my life. It has been passed on to me in a real sense as a life's blessing and a life's exhortation from my own father.

I know that I am not the only one who has received the right word at the right time through my father. Hundreds, even thousands of people, can recall a specific occasion, a specific message, a specific challenge that they received from the Lord through His Word by my father. Over the years I have heard or read numerous testimonies from those whose lives were impacted through the preaching of the Word by my father. People have come to Christ in saving faith. People have repented of specific sins and experienced a fresh cleansing and commitment to live holy lives. People have surrendered to the Lordship of Christ in a specific and personal way. People have yielded their lives to the control of the Holy Spirit. People have said "yes" to

God in terms of service and missions – "anywhere, anytime, at any cost." People have committed themselves or recommitted themselves to Biblical ministry and the preaching of the Word of God in the power of the Holy Spirit. Lives have been touched and changed in so many places and on so many occasions as my father just preached the Word.

My father aged gracefully. This was seen especially as he dealt with the illnesses and weaknesses of the last few years of his life. He handled the pain well, embraced his own frailty, and sought the Lord for strength and insight. He certainly faced the psychological depression that went hand-in-hand with such illnesses and treatments. But, in facing and not denying his humanity, he looked to the Lord to grant grace and healing. He accepted the help and prayers of others, and valued most of all the constant care of my mother, who has always been quick to say that she is not a nurse. And yet, she did everything that needed to be done to see my father through these "valleys." The cancer experience was indeed "a valley of the shadow of death," but God granted recovery and healing. My father, as far as I know, never struggled with the relationship between medicine and miracle. The sovereign God over medical practice is the supernatural God who is able to help and heal with or without human means. So, thanksgiving was offered to God for recovery in both these situations and others. Thankfulness, I know, was also expressed to the doctors, nurses, and technicians that helped along the way. Not forgotten either were the prayers and thoughts of countless people praying for God's servant. Incredible stories could be told of church leaders, international guests, and personal friends who joined in prayer on my father's behalf. It takes grace to receive such ministry, admitting your own need and weakness. This only goes to show that my father's life verse, Galatians 2:20, was lived out in the practical and personal details of life.

I view the by-pass surgery of 1997 and the cancer experience of 1999 as somewhat analogous to the Apostle Paul's imprisonments. My father had so much he wanted to do but was unable to during those periods. Instead, they became times of learning from the Lord and occasions to write and share truth with others. Instead of getting frustrated by the physical limitations, my father did what he could to maximize the time for God.

My father was a student of revival and there was a deep desire for revival that remained in him to the end of the journey. In times past, he had experienced powerful interventions of God in ministry and he longed for that supernatural reviving presence and power of God that would cleanse and energize the church afresh and issue forth in a great movement of God for His glory and the further evangelization of the world. While he looked for "rapture in the air," he longed for the work of God on earth. Only a true sovereign work of God, my father would say, would "stem the tide of evil," revive a complacent church, and make the church the pure bride and empowered servant for Christ that it needs to be. "Lord, do it again," was his prayer as he thought of the previous great movements of God in this country and overseas.

It is of significance that one of his last projects was the re-publishing of the book, *Heart Cry for Revival.* This book expresses my father's heart cry – his longing for God's powerful intervention in His church as He has done in times past. We praise God that with the assistance and hard work of Dr. Ted Rendall, this book has now been revised and released. It is, also, of significance that one of the last "video" interviews that my father did was on the subject of revival. It is my understanding that the interviewer gave a few suggestions or questions to get things started, and then my father just took off. He shared Biblically, personally, and practically concerning what revival is, what revival looks like, and our responsibility as believers in relation to the sovereign working of God in revival. This interview was done for Bellevue Baptist Church, but it has also been a blessing at our own Center.

My father and mother came to the United States in the summer of 1959. The invitation had come from the Calvary Baptist Church in New York City to be the Senior Minister. One of the factors in sensing the call of God to the United States was the opportunity to be involved in media ministry. Calvary Baptist Church had one of the longest broadcasting ministries in the States at that time. My father was interested in using the airwaves for the gospel and the preaching ministry. Throughout my father's life in the States, he was involved in radio ministry and for fifteen years he had a television program. It was his passion to preach the Word and to reach the world. The four walls of a church were not the extent of his ministry. He wanted to reach "Jerusalem . . . all Judea and Samaria, and to the end of the earth" (Acts 1:8, NKJV).

As was my father's custom, following his final radio recording session in the summer of 2004, he led us in a brief prayer. Unknown to us at the time and not discovered until after his death, the tape was still recording when my father prayed, "Lord, we thank you for the grace given to handle some very powerful, mighty spiritual truths. . . . May they reach hearts and do the miracle that we long for in our own lives – to live righteously before men. We ask it for Jesus sake, Amen." This prayer expresses the heart of a man committed to the incarnational ministry of the Word of God with a passion to see lives changed for the glory of God!

My father would, indeed, want all the glory to go to His Lord, and so it must. We know that God brought all this to pass through His grace and by His power. My father was the earthen vessel holding the treasure of "the knowledge of the glory of God in the face of Jesus Christ" (2 Cor. 4:6-7, NKJV). So, to God be the glory!

In a day when we tend to celebrate trivial things, it is worth celebrating a life lived to the glory of God, and a life that was characterized by faithfulness to the end. The suddenness of my father's death allowed no time for a bed-side meeting with family and friends. But, in a real sense, my father didn't need such an occasion. There were no wrongs to be put right. There was no need for parting words because he had shared the truths of his life with us constantly and consistently. There was no need to make sure we knew of his love, for he had loved us all until the end. Such an occasion may have been very moving and meaningful, but it was not necessary.

Faithfulness speaks for itself. My father was faithful as a husband, as a father, as a servant of the Lord and as a preacher of the Word. His passion was the will of God; His confidence was the Lord Himself. Ultimately, as Dr. Rogers said, Stephen Olford "was a Jesus man," and to Jesus, His Lord, he remained faithful.

Chronology

1889

July 12 — Stephen's father, Frederick Ernest Samuel Olford, is born in Plymouth, England.

1893

January 22 — Stephen's mother, Elizabeth (Bessie) Rhoden Santmire is born in Buffalo, New York.

1902 — Bessie is saved.

1905 — Bessie is baptized.

October 12 — Fred Olford makes a public profession of faith at an R. A. Torrey evangelistic mission.

1906

January 21 — Fred is baptized.

1912

September 1 — He enters Livingstone College for medical training for the mission field.

1913

April 23 — He goes to Portugal to learn Portuguese.

June 28	He leaves for Central Africa.
1914	Bessie Santmire goes to work with "Sister Abigail," caring for the sick. She subsequently attends Toronto Bible College (now Ontario Bible College).
November 16	He arrives at Luma-Cassai in Angola.
1915	
June	She leaves for Africa with the Gammons.
1917	
May 15	She marries Fred Olford.
1918	
March 29	Stephen Olford is born in Northern Rhodesia.
1920	
August 5	Paul Olford is born.
1924	
March 2	Heather Brown is born in Northern Ireland.
December 12	John Olford is born.
1925	
March 29	Stephen is born again on his seventh birthday.
1930	
July	Nellie Sawyer meets the Olfords in England and agrees to come to Africa to tutor the boys.
1931	
January 5	The Olford boys commence school with Miss Sawyer as their tutor.
1932	
June 26	Stephen is baptized at the age of 14.

1934

March	Heather Brown is led to Christ by her mother Barbara after hearing Tom Rees preach.

1935

May 24–June 27	The Olfords travel to England.
July	Stephen is confronted for the first time with the message of Keswick.
1935	He enrolls at Devonport Technical College to study mechanical engineering.
1937	He enrolls at St. Luke's College, Mildmay, London.
1938	He enters the Missionary Training Colony and studies under Dr. W. Graham Scroggie.
March 25	The Olford family settles in Newport, South Wales.

1939

October 3	World Word II breaks out September 1939. Stephen is appointed an Army Scripture Reader, and with his father operates a Christian servicemen's center in Newport.

1940

May 17	Stephen launches the Young People's Christian Fellowship in Newport.
1941	Heather makes a total commitment of her life to Christ
1942	Heather takes up social work with evacuees in Ireland.
1945–1953	Stephen begins campaigning in earnest. One of his first crusades is in the Brethren hall in Wallington.

1945

June	Stephen and Harold Wildish conduct tent mission in Cardiff, Wales.

August	Stephen and Harold Wildish conduct Christian Challenge campaign in Bournemouth, England.

1946

March 3-15	Stephen conducts campaign in Llandrindod Wells in Wales.
April 27–May 8	Manchester Evangelistic Campaign at Houldsworth Hall and St. Ann's Church.
May	Heather is invited to come to England by Tom Rees to be his crusade pianist.
Summer	Years of constant ministry to the troops and the demands of crusading leave Stephen totally drained and desperate for a new touch from God. Canceling all engagements for two weeks, he seeks the liberating power of the Spirit upon his life and ministry.
September	Stephen's message, delivered at the Royal Albert Hall in London, finds its way into booklet form—*Becoming a Child of God.*
September 27	Stephen speaks to crowd of 6,500 at Belle Vue Stadium in Manchester, England. 200 respond.
October	Stephen speaks at Hildenborough Hall, where he meets Billy Graham. Stephen shares with Billy Graham the secrets of the quiet time and the Spirit-filled life. It is the turning point in Billy Graham's life and ministry.
October 21-29	Stephen conducts crusade in Barking (New Park Hall).
Late 1946	He receives invitations from Jack Wyrtzen, Moody Bible Institute and Youth for Christ to come to the United States for meetings.

1947

Spring	Stephen and Heather become engaged to be married.

April 4-19	Stephen shares platform with Arthur Wallis at Christian Challenge Convention in Pontypridd, Wales. An overwhelming response to the challenge to confess Christ as Savior and Lord.
June 25	Stephen and Heather, accompanied by Stephen's father, sail for America.
July 1	Heather enrolls for courses at Moody Bible Institute while Stephen goes to Schroon Lake, New York to speak at a Word of Life Bible conference.
July–August	Each Saturday night finds Stephen preaching on radio at Word of Life rallies in New York's Times Square area, substituting for Jack Wyrtzen who has broken his hip in a water-skiing accident.
October	Stephen commences travel under the auspices of Youth for Christ, visiting Toronto, Ottawa, Smith Falls, Arnprior and Pembroke in Ontario, Canada.
October 17-20	Stephen conducts special services at Moody Bible Institute. Revival breaks out.
November	Stephen holds meetings in the American Northwest.
December 1-20	He preaches at rallies, schools, and clubs in southern states.

1948

January 1-5	He speaks at Moody Memorial Church, at the Chicago Gospel Tabernacle, and at Youth for Christ World Congress rallies.
January 6-10	He continues rallies in the American Midwest.
January 11-18	While conducting meetings at Wheaton Bible College, revival breaks out and spreads to Wheaton College. Jim Elliot (later martyred in Ecuador) is moved to begin recording his spiritual experiences in a journal.

February 2-8	Stephen speaks at the Founder's Week Conference at Moody Bible Institute.
February 17-22	He flies to Rhode Island for chapel meetings at Providence Bible Institute and evening evangelical meetings. Revival breaks out.
March–April	Surgery forces Stephen to cancel his activities and eight weeks of meetings.
May 7	Stephen and Heather return to Britain to prepare for their wedding.
	The 11-month tour of the United States and Canada has taken him over 34,000 miles to 100 major cities. He has held 1,096 meetings and has spoken to some 132,000 people. Over a thousand conversions have been recorded and others have made fresh commitments to Christ.
June 30	Stephen Olford and Heather Brown are married in First Lurgan Presbyterian Church in Northern Ireland.
July	The Olfords take up residence in Newport, South Wales.
October 31–November 21	Stephen continues crusading throughout Britain, including Northern Ireland.

1949

March	He holds intensive 10-day Methodist mission in Nelson, Lancashire, England.
April	He conducts evangelistic rally in the largest hall in Manchester, England.
Summer	The book *I'll Take the High Road* is published.
July 19	Stephen speaks at English Keswick Convention for first time.
November 26–December 5	He conducts "Christ is the Answer" campaign at Corporation Road Baptist Church, Newport, South Wales.

1950

January 18-31	He holds evangelistic campaign in Bedwas, South Wales.
March	He leads month-long ministry at Toxteth Tabernacle, Liverpool, England.
October-December	Stephen conducts evangelistic campaigns in Winnipeg, Manitoba, Canada; Wheaton, Illinois; and Providence, Rhode Island.
December 12-15	Stephen holds rallies in New York in connection with Jack Wyrtzen and Word of Life Fellowship.

1951

March 31–April 27	Manchester citywide campaign at Houldsworth Hall with final rally at King's Hall, Belle Vue Stadium. Ex-Communist is converted.
June 4-8	Carlisle Keswick Convention.
October 14-31	Mansfield Evangelistic Mission.
November 19–December 6	Birmingham citywide crusade. Civic life affected, good reception from the press. B.B.C. promotes effort through two broadcasts.

1952

February 2-10	Belfast Young People's Convention in Northern Ireland. News is received of the death of King George VI.
March 1-17	Stephen shares 17-day mission with Alan Redpath at Cardiff, Wales.
April 24–May 5	Stephen conducts Sunderland Campaign at Bethesda Chapel.
June 21-28	He speaks first time at Portstewart Convention in Ulster—the equivalent of English Keswick in Northern Ireland.
July 16	He speaks at English Keswick.

July 17	His first son—Jonathan MacGregor—is born in Northern Ireland.
September 25-27	He holds converts' reunion rallies in Manchester and Birmingham, England.
October 2	Stephen returns to Plymouth to speak at Keswick Convention.
October 11–November 1	He conducts "This is the Way" Campaign in Norwich, England.
October 22	Fred Olford called home to be with the Lord.
December 13-14	Stephen spends weekend in Richmond, Surrey addressing a young people's rally and full day of ministry at Duke Street Baptist Church.

1953

January 10	He holds devotional meetings and reunion rally in Cardiff for crusade converts.
June 10	Stephen accepts invitation to become the pastor of Duke Street Baptist Church for a three-year period.
August 1-5	Stephen speaks at Llandrindod Wells (Keswick in Wales) Convention
August 28-30	He conducts Norwich campaign reunion weekend.
October 7	Stephen is ordained by Thames Valley Baptist Association and is installed as minister of Duke Street Baptist Church, Richmond, Surrey, on the outskirts of London.

1954

May	He supports the Billy Graham Harringay Crusade in London and devises "Operation Andrew" plan as a means of bringing the unsaved and unchurched to the crusade.

June 26	Duke Street Baptist Church hosts first welcome meeting for 100 converts from the Harringay Crusade.
November 9	Missionary challenge presented to converts of Harringay Crusade. The substance of that address—"Missionary Preparation" is published the following year.

1955

October 2-5	Duke Street Baptist Church celebrates 85th anniversary.
October 17-21	Stephen conducts a week of meetings at Chicago's Moody Bible Institute and Mid-Atlantic Keswick Convention. Returning home to Britain, he is invited to share ship's stateroom with Billy Graham and be "chaplain to his soul" as Billy faces upcoming mission at Cambridge University.
December 14	The Olfords accept church invitation to continue at Duke Street for an indefinite period on the condition that Stephen be allowed certain periods away each year for crusade ministry.

1956

January 14	Mr. Richard A. Bennett, a "son in the faith," is welcomed to the pastoral team at Duke Street.
February 4	Stephen speaks at evangelistic rally at Houldsworth Hall, Manchester.
February 23	Negotiations get underway for a new and larger church building to accommodate growing congregation.
May 2	The Olfords rejoice in the birth of their second son—David Lindsay, 6 lbs. 7 oz.
May 6	The joy is tinged with sadness with the homecall of Heather's father, Cecil Brown. Stephen attends funeral in Ireland.

October 20–November 4	Stephen conducts Harrogate Evangelistic Campaign which is attended by many V.I.P.'s.

1957

January	Duke Street launches house-to-house visitation effort called "Operation Andrew" throughout borough of Richmond.
March	Duke Street begins broadcasting "A Voice of Cheer"—30 minutes of recorded music, prayer and ministry for shut-ins.
April 7–June 6	Stephen is involved in two evangelistic campaigns in the United States—First Covenant Church, Minneapolis (Pastor: Dr. Paul Rees) and Billy Graham's New York Crusade at Madison Square Garden. During New York Crusade Stephen preaches his first sermon at Calvary Baptist Church, resulting in a later invitation to become its pastor.

1958

March 1-17	Stephen conducts Derbe Christian Challenge Crusade.
April 8-13	Stephen returns to New York to conduct a week of deeper life meetings at Calvary Baptist Church.
June 11	He is officially called to become the pastor of Calvary Baptist Church, New York City.
July 20-27	He speaks at Mandeville Keswick Convention, Jamaica, West Indies as a deputation speaker from English Keswick.
September 27-28	Stephen and Heather Olford celebrate fifth anniversary at Duke Street.
	Christianity and You is published (British edition).
	Successful Soul-Winning is published in the U.K.

1959

January 4	Having accepted the call to Calvary Baptist Church, Stephen announces his resignation to Duke Street congregation, effective June 21.
February 23–March 17	He conducts "This Is Life" Crusade in Lurgan, Northern Ireland.
April 6-17	Stephen holds "Tell London" campaign.
April-June	Farewell services for the Olfords are held in Manchester, London, and Richmond.
August 27	The Olfords arrive in New York.
September 10-16	Stephen is installed as pastor of Calvary Baptist Church, New York City
October 21	An eight-week Discipleship Class course is introduced, obligatory for all members.

1960

	Becoming a Man of God and *Becoming a Servant of God* are published (USA edition).
January 24	Calvary Baptist Church begins broadcasting its evening service, designed to be evangelistic in content.
March 13-19	First annual Christian Life Convention at Calvary Baptist Church with Rev. Alan Redpath, Dr. G. Allen Fleece, Major Allister Smith and Mr. C. Stacey Woods as speakers.
June 27–July 1	Stephen participates in Baptist World Alliance Congress in Rio de Janeiro, Brazil.
September	"The Calvary Church Hour" begins broadcasting over Trans World Radio, Monte Carlo, Monaco; and Station ELWA, Liberia, West Africa.
October 9	First "Encounter" telecast airs in New York metropolitan area on WPIX-TV, Channel 11, at 12:30 p.m.

1961

June 1	*Encounter* magazine is launched.
June 4-18	Stephen conducts evangelistic crusade at the Queen Elizabeth Theater in Vancouver, British Columbia, Canada.
July	Monthly half-nights of prayer are introduced at Calvary Baptist Church.
September 10	Morning and evening services resume live broadcasting from Calvary's sanctuary.

1962

January	Stephen speaks at first "Keswick in Kingston" (Jamaica, West Indies), sharing the ministry with Dr. G. Allen Fleece.
	Heart-Cry for Revival is published. Also two booklets: *Manna in the Morning* and *Meeting My Master.*
July 14-21	Stephen speaks at Canadian Keswick.
August 11-19	Commences summer ministry at Ben Lippen Conference, Asheville, North Carolina.

1963

	Three books are published this year: *The Secret of Soul-Winning, The Living Word,* and *The Sanctity of Sex* (the latter co-authored with Frank Lawes).
March	Stephen is voted one of the ten most effective preachers in the United States and Canada today (Boston University School of Theology).
March–April 6	He holds evangelistic crusade at Fairfield Halls in Croydon, Surrey, England as part of civic celebrations marking the borough's thousand-year anniversary.
June 5	Forty years of broadcasting from Calvary Baptist Church are celebrated at a Partnership rally.

July 28	Audio portion of "Encounter" telecasts are adapted for use on "Encounter" radio.

1964

January 20-24	Stephen ministers the Word at first Southland Keswick Convention, Dallas, Texas.
	Calvary Baptist church participates in New York World's Fair outreach.
May 10	Commencement of visitors' reception following Calvary's morning worship service.
May 24	"Encounter" Radio goes on the ABC network, adding 68 additional stations in 30 states where the broadcast can be heard.

1965

May 3-7	Stephen and Allen Fleece establish a Keswick Convention in Birmingham, Alabama.
July 18	The first of two open air rallies are held at Columbus Circle, Central Park, New York City.
October 9-30	Stephen holds evangelistic crusade in Usher Hall, Edinburgh, Scotland.

1966

January 28	He receives honorary Doctor of Divinity degree from Wheaton College.
May 7	Stephen is honored at banquet celebrating 25 years of preaching.
May 16-22	He speaks at Mid-South Keswick Bible Conference, Memphis, Tennessee.
June 5-6	He receives an honorary Doctor of Letters degree from Houghton College.
September	The Olfords move into the 14th floor "parsonage" in the Hotel Salisbury.

October 26–November 4	Stephen participates in World Congress on Evangelism in Berlin, West German.

1967

March 5	Rededication of refurbished sanctuary.
April 4-5	Stephen delivers Swartley Lectures at Eastern Baptist Theological Seminary, Philadelphia, Pennsylvania.
May	Closed-circuit TV ministry begins in bookstore window and Hotel Salisbury.
October 9-13	Stephen preaches at Spiritual Emphasis Week at New York's Nyack Missionary College. God moves in revival blessing.
	The "Shepherd Plan" is implemented to strengthen the unity of Calvary Baptist Church.

1968

January 8-12	The Olfords minister at first Keswick Convention in Montego Bay, Jamaica, West Indies. Dr. Billy Graham pays surprise visit on closing night.
	Stephen serves as vice-chairman of the Executive committee in preparation for 1969 Billy Graham Crusade in New York City.
June 27	American edition of *I'll Take the High Road* is published.
September–October	Stephen makes a preaching tour to Australia, the Philippines, and Vietnam. Here he distributes copies of his booklet, *God's Answer to Vietnam,* published earlier this year. It is also put on tape and sent to civic and government leaders.
October 20	President-elect Richard Nixon and Dr. Billy Graham attend morning worship service at Calvary Baptist Church.

December	"Encounter" telecast begins taping in color.

1969

January	The Olfords attend the inauguration of President Richard Nixon in Washington, D.C.
January 29-30	Stephen speaks fot the first time at National Religious Broadcasters' convention in Washington, D.C.
April 6	Calvary Baptist Church conducts Easter sunrise service in Central Park, New York City.
June	The church participates in the Billy Graham Crusade at the new Madison Square Garden.
August 10-21	Stephen and Dr. and Mrs. Carl Henry speak at first Pastors' Workshop ever held in Yugoslavia.
	Calvary Baptist Church begins supporting national workers.
September 12	Stephen delivers address at U.S. Congress on Evangelism in Minneapolis, Minnesota.
October 11-12	The Olfords mark their 10th anniversary at the church. Mr. and Mrs. A. Lindsay Glegg and Dr. and Mrs. Paul S. Rees are surprise guests in a "This is Your Life" presentation.

1970

April 30–May 3	The Olfords minister at Christian Leaders Conference in Madrid, Spain.
June 1	Encounter Ministries is incorporated.
June	"Encounter" telecasts are taped in Toronto, Canada, utilizing the modern facilities of CFTO-TV.
September	The Olfords attend Filey Conference in England and speak at 100th anniversary of Duke Street Baptist Church, Richmond, Surrey.

1971

January 25-29	Stephen speaks at Keswick Convention in Bridgetown, Barbados, West Indies.
February–September	Ill health forces Stephen to take a leave of absence from Calvary Baptist Church.
September 12	He returns to the pulpit and an outpouring of affection at a welcome home service and reception.
September 27	The interdenominational New York School of the Bible is launched at Calvary Baptist Church with Dr. Joseph C. Macaulay as dean.
November 8-12	Stephen speaks at Gulf Coast Keswick in Houston, Texas.
November	Loizeaux Brothers, Inc. publishes *The Tabernacle: Camping with God. The Secret of a Happy Home* is also published that year.

1972

	Christian Citizenship, a booklet attacking the lethargy of Christians in the area of civic duties, is published.
February 27	Calvary Baptist Church begins 125th anniversary year celebration.
May 8-12	Stephen speaks at Keswick Convention in Knoxville, Tennessee.
July 1-16	As part of the 125th anniversary celebrations, members and friends enjoy motorcoach tour of England, Wales and Scotland, including a week at English Keswick, at which Stephen is a speaker.
September 9-15	Stephen speaks at Filey Holiday Crusade (England) on "The Christian Message for Contemporary Man." These Bible studies form the basis of a book which is printed in the U.K. (1973).
September 27	Autograph party is held for *The Grace of Giving* recently published. It is

subsequently translated into Chinese (1976), Korean (1977), and Swedish (1978).

November 29   Stephen tenders his resignation to the congregation of Calvary Baptist Church. He agrees to remain with the church through June 30, 1973 and with "The Calvary Church Hour" until September 2, 1973, thus culminating 14 years with the church almost to the day.

1973

January 30-31   Stephen speaks at congressional breakfast in Washington, D.C. and addresses formal banquet at NRB Convention.

February 7   Autograph party held for the book, *Tell It From Calvary,* which contains biographical sketches of all of Calvary's pastors and a selection of outstanding sermons delivered by each of them.

February 28   The honorary title of "Minister Emeritus" is bestowed on Stephen by Calvary Baptist Church.

March 10   Stephen ministers at World Bible Conference in Israel, as part of its 25th anniversary year. He preaches main sermon at the reenactment of the feeding of the 5000 on the shores of the Sea of Galilee.

April 25   Stephen participates in autograph party for book, *Silhouettes,* which features chapters on Bessie and Heather Olford.

May 15   Booklet, *The Secret of Strength,* is published.

May 20   Farewell and recommissioning services for the Olfords at Calvary Baptist Church, New York City.

Calvary Baptist Church celebrates and receives an award for 50 years of radio broadcasting.

May 23-31	Stephen visits Trans World Radio in Monaco and holds ministers' meetings in Florence, Italy.
June 27–July 4	Stephen conducts "One Way for Manchester" Crusade in England. The Olfords celebrate their 25th wedding anniversary during the crusade.
September 2	Stephen preaches concluding message on "The Calvary Church Hour" broadcast.
September 10	Encounter Ministries, Inc. moves to Holmes Beach on Florida's west coast. Stephen becomes President and Minister-at-Large of the organization.

1974

January 28–February 1	Stephen speaks at first Keswick Convention on the island of Trinidad, West Indies. 300 young people respond to the call for missionary service.
June	USA edition of *The Christian Message for Contemporary Man* is published.
July 16-25	International Congress on World Evangelization in Lausanne, Switzerland. Stephen speaks four afternoons on the theme, "Evangelistic Preaching from the Pulpit."
September 21-29	Stephen conducts nine-day crusade in Messina, Sicily, sponsored by the West Indies Mission in cooperation with local pastors. During the crusade Guy Sotille and his family are converted.

1975

January 31	Bessie Olford peacefully passes into the presence of her Lord (Cardiff, Wales).
May 16	Stephen is awarded honorary Doctor of Humanities degree from Richmond College, Toronto, Canada.

July 9-10	Stephen speaks at Keswick Convention in Brighton, England.
July 12-25	Friends of Encounter tour British Isles and join Stephen for two weeks at English Keswick as part of Keswick's centennial celebrations.
September 6-14	Stephen and Dr. Mario DiGangi conduct second crusade in Messina, Sicily.
October 17	WPIX-TV, Channel 11, honors Stephen for 15 years of dynamic television. Over 400 "Encounter" telecasts have been produced.
October 26–December 18	The Olfords make an eight-week trip to Africa (his first since 1935), teaching and preaching in South Africa, Rhodesia, and Kenya. As a result Encounter Ministries South Africa is formed.
December 1	"Encounter" radio begins broadcasting twice a week over Trans World Radio, Swaziland, covering an area of three million square miles from the Equator to the Cape and reaching a potential of 130 million people.

1976

January	Two new booklets by Stephen are printed—*One Nation Under God* and the *Coming New World*.
Summer	A five-minute radio program called "Encounter With Truth" is launched and aired Monday to Friday on stations across America, as well as Bermuda, Ecuador, and the Caribbean. The program continues through 1979.
November 1-15	Under the auspices of the National Association of Evangelicals, Stephen visits leading seminaries across the U.S.A. to conduct "Preaching Seminars."

1977

July 25	Six mini-books by Stephen Olford are published—*Becoming a Child/Man/Servant of God* and *Encounter with Fear/Anxiety/Loneliness.*
November 19	Jonathan Olford and Catherine Matthews are married in Columbia, South Carolina.

1978

February 20–March 5	The Olfords make their first visit to Japan to speak at Keswick conventions in Osaka, Hakone and Tokyo. Co-speaker at each of the conventions is the Reverend George B. Duncan of Scotland, a familiar face and voice at English Keswick.
May 5	Stephen receives Doctor of Theology degree from Luther Rice Seminary in Jacksonville, Florida.
June 4-9	He and his son David visit the Philippines to take part in the 30th anniversary of the Far East Broadcasting Company. Dr. Robert Bowman asks Dr. Olford to be the English voice of Station FEBC, thus expanding Encounter's outreach to parts of Asia.
August	Jonathan and Catherine Olford leave for Africa to serve as dorm parents and teachers at Rift Valley Academy in Kijabe, Kenya, East Africa.
October 16-27	Stephen conducts second preaching tour to more colleges and seminaries under auspices of N.A.E.

1979

February	The board of Regents of Luther Rice Seminary International in Jacksonville, Florida establish the Stephen F. Olford Chair of Pastoral Ministries "to honor Dr. Olford and to seek to perpetuate in others the spiritual and effective standards and procedures for which his ministry is noted."

March 24–April 21	Stephen preaches 36 times in 20 days to almost 30,000 people on second trip to South Africa and Kenya.
May 24	"Encounter" radio celebrates 15 years of broadcasting.
August	Encounter Ministries, Inc. moves to Wheaton, Illinois where it is linked with the National Association of Evangelicals. Dr. Olford becomes Minister-at-Large for N.A.E. while maintaining the presidency of Encounter Ministries.
September 15-22	Stephen delivers morning Bible Readings (attendance over 6,000) at the 25th anniversary of Filey Holiday Crusade in England. Over 500 young people commit their lives specifically for overseas service.
November 17–December 19	The Olfords minister to missionaries, national staff and visitors at Radio Station ELWA, Monrovia, Liberia, West Africa, continuing on to Nigeria and Kenya for seminars and guest appearances.

1980

November 1	Institute for Biblical Preaching (expository sermon outlines) is launched.

1981

May	John M. Balmer, Jr. is first ministerial student to intern at Encounter.
October 17-22	Stephen is featured speaker at Jubilee celebrations (50th) of Radio Station HCJB in Quito, Ecuador.

1982

June 14	He addresses the largest pastors' conference in the history of the Southern Baptist Convention at the Superdome in New Orleans, Louisiana.

July 19-30	Stephen participates in "Renewal '82"—a nationwide revival program in the Philippines, holding meetings in Manila, Cebu City, and Davao.
1983	*Going Places with God* is published.
May 20	Dallas Baptist University in Texas confers honorary Doctor of Divinity degree.
July 12-21	Stephen addresses plenary session and conducts two workshops at International Conference for Itinerant Evangelists in Amsterdam, Holland, sponsored by the Billy Graham Evangelistic Association.
October 10	He receives Faith and Freedom Award from Religious Heritage of America for "outstanding and creative service in communicating the ethics and principles of our religious heritage."
October 25	The Olfords become grandparents with the arrival of Jeremy David in Kenya, East Africa.
1984	
April 11-May 19	The Olfords take a spiritual safari to New Zealand, Korea, Japan, and the Philippines.
April 30	Stephen sets forth the mandate and the model for preaching in a new booklet called *Preaching the Word of God*.
July–December	The Olfords take a six-month sabbatical "to seek the Lord's guidance concerning future ministry."
1985	
March 23-27	Stephen speaks at Keswick Convention in Halifax, Nova Scotia, Canada.
June	Encounter Ministries, Inc. moves its corporate headquarters to Memphis, Tennessee at the invitation of Dr. James Latimer and the board of Elders of Central Church.

June 15	David Olford joins the Encounter team as Vice President.

1986

April 12	David Olford marries Ellen Grogan in Memphis.
May 5-9	The first Biblical Preaching Institute is conducted at Central Church, Memphis, Tennessee. Over 90 people are involved, representing 24 states and one foreign country (Nigeria).
July 12-20	Stephen is keynote speaker and conducts a workshop at the second Conference for Itinerant Evangelists in Amsterdam, Holland.
October 12	A second grandson is born in Kenya—Justin Stephen.

1987

January 28	Down payment is made for purchase of property to be known as the Stephen Olford Center for Biblical Preaching.
February 3-4	Stephen receives the Distinguished Service Award from the National Religious Broadcasters for 27 years of radio broadcasting at ceremonies in Washington, D.C. The next day he speaks at the sixth National Prayer Breakfast in honor of Israel.
March 2-8	He speaks at Keswick Convention in Hong Kong.

1988

June 3-4	Stephen is feted at surprise banquet by friends, converts, board members and staff who come to honor his life, his 70th birthday (March 29), 40th wedding anniversary (June 30), and nearly 50 years in gospel ministry. The next day the Center is officially dedicated by Dr. Charles Stanley. Some 300 attend the reception that follows.

July 18	Encounter Ministries move into its new headquarters.
September 19-22	The first "Institute" held in the new Center focuses on "Worship in the Local Church." Special guest lecturer: Dr. Paul S. Rees.
October 13-15	First Practical Preaching Workshop is held at the Stephen Olford Center.

1989

March–May	Stephen conducts three memorial services—two in England and one at Moody Memorial Church, Chicago—for Dr. Alan Redpath who went to be with the Lord March 16.
November	Thomas Nelson Publishers release David Olford's book, *A Passion for Preaching.* These reflections on the art of preaching are contributed by today's best-known preachers in honor of Stephen Olford.

1990

January 7-12	The Olfords minister at the Keswick Convention in Grand Cayman, Cayman Islands in the Caribbean.
February 5-9	The Olfords, along with David and Ellen Olford, share in week-long Congress on Revival in Poland near the Soviet border.
May 22–June 4	The Olfords go to West Germany for the biennial conference of the Bible Christian Union. He speaks six times to several hundred missionaries from all over Europe. From there they travel to Cardiff, Wales for a one-day preaching institute.
November 16	The Olfords first granddaughter—Lindsay Gayle—is born to David and Ellen Olford.
November 23-25	The Olfords return to Japan to celebrate the 100th anniversary of Rev. Barclay Buxton's ministry in that country. Mr. Buxton was one of the lecturers at the

	Missionary Training Colony in England during the thirties.
1991	
February 15	A fourth grandchild is born—Joshua Jonathan.
March 24-26	The first series of messages—"Victory in Jesus"—are videotaped for Encounter's professional video library. More are to follow.
August	Library is renovated and a new study is built to house Stephen's books at the Center.
October 4	Stephen receives Honor Award from South Central Chapter, National Religious Broadcasters, for over 30 years of faithful presentation of Christ through the media.
October 15-25	The Olfords travel to Nairobi, Kenya, East Africa to conduct seminars for African pastors.
1991–1992	Baker Book House publishes eight books as part of the Stephen Olford Biblical Preaching Library.
1992	
July 1	Stephen speaks on "Social Relationships: Facets of Friendship" to 15,000 people during Bill Gothard's Institute in Basic Life Principles at University of Tennessee in Knoxville. Included in the audience are at least 1,000 principals and students from Moscow, Russia.
September 23-26	Stephen addresses Second Congress on Evangelism in Rome, Italy initiated by Guy Sotille for the purpose of reaching Italy for Christ by the year 2000.
February 14	Stephen preaches the Sunday Worship Service at the 50th Annual Convention of the National Religious Broadcasters in Los Angeles.

1993

March 29	Stephen turns 75 years of age. "I am resolved," he says, "in the years left to me to live and preach with one objective: the pursuit of God."
April 21-24	Stephen addresses the Nationwide Bible Conference held at Bellevue Baptist Church, Cordova, Tennessee.
May 6-26	The Olfords travel to the U.K., where Stephen speaks at several conferences in England and Northern Ireland, including the Spring Convention in Birmingham, England.
July 24-30	Stephen speaks at Home Missions Week for the Southern Baptist Convention in Glorieta, New Mexico.
September 6-10	Gaetano Sotille, of Italy for Christ, hosts a Preaching Institute in Naples, Italy, at which Stephen is a speaker.
November 13	Calvary Baptist Church in New York hosts Stephen for a One-Day Institute for Biblical Preaching.
November 18-20	Stephen holds a Biblical Preaching Institute at Criswell College in Dallas, Texas.

1994

January 28-29	David Olford is appointed by his father, Stephen, as the new president of Encounter Ministries. The Emmaus Lodge guest house and the Founder's residence are dedicated on the campus of the Stephen Olford Center for Biblical Preaching.
February 5-18	Stephen preaches at both the Trinidad Keswick Convention and the Barbados Keswick Convention.
March 8-10	At Beeson Divinity School, on the campus of Samford University, in Birmingham,

	Alabama, Stephen speaks at the William E. Conger, Jr. Lectures on Biblical Preaching.
June 8	Stephen delivers a message during Chapel for the Senior Tour Nationwide Golf Championship in Alpharetta, Georgia.
June 28 – July 1	The North American Conference for Itinerant Evangelists, at which Stephen is a speaker, is held in Louisville, Kentucky.
August 13-20	Stephen preaches at the 70th Anniversary of the Victorious Life Conference, America's Keswick, in Whiting, New Jersey.

1995

January 17	Stephen's book, *Not I, But Christ,* is released by Crossway Books.
January 22	The Olford's welcome their fifth grandchild, Stephanie, into the world. She is the daughter of David and Ellen Olford.
May 9-10	Stephen preaches at the Billy Graham School of Evangelism in Toronto, Canada.
June	The first edition of Stephen's biography, *Only One Life,* by Dr. John Phillips, is released by Loizeaux Brothers Publishing.
June 1-5	Sponsored by Italy for Christ, Stephen speaks at the Conference for Pastors, in Naples and Florence, Italy.

1996

February 6-11	Stephen, Heather, and David travel to Nassau, Bahamas, to conduct a Preaching Institute.
April 13-17	Stephen preaches at the Nova Scotia Keswick Convention in Halifax.
May 31-June 1	Encounter Ministries and The Stephen Olford Center for Biblical Preaching hold their 10th Anniversary Celebration on their campus in Memphis, Tennessee.

November 9-10	Stephen attends the 25th Anniversary of the New York School of the Bible, at Calvary Baptist Church, New York, New York.

1997

January 25	The Japanese edition of *Not, I but Christ* is released by Word of Life Press.
April 24-26	Olford Ministries International hosts its first Christian Life Convention in Memphis, Tennessee.
May 4	Stephen preaches at the 150th Anniversary Celebration at Calvary Baptist Church, in New York, New York.
July	Baker Book House publishes *Special-Day Sermon Outlines.*
September 15-17	The Olfords conduct a Preaching Institute at Tabernacle Baptist Church in Penarth, Wales.

1998

January 22	*The Way of Holiness* is published by Crossway Books.
February	*Anointed Expository Preaching,* written by Stephen and David Olford and published by Broadman & Holman, is released.
March	Baker Book House publishes *Sermon Outlines on the Cross.*
March 11-15	Stephen preaches at the International Conference on the Bible at Grace Community Church, Santa Clarita, California.
March 27	The National Black Evangelical Association Conference, at which Stephen is a speaker, is held at Mississippi Boulevard Christian Church in Memphis, Tennessee.
May 26-29	Stephen speaks at the Heart-Cry for Revival Conference at Willow Valley Retreat and

	Conference Center in Lancaster, Pennsylvania.
October 5-8	In affiliation with Dr. Charles Stanley, Stephen speaks at Pastor's Conferences in Birmingham and London, U.K.

1999

March	*The Christian Message for Contemporary Life: The Gospel's Power to Change Lives* is published by Kregel Publications.
May 9-13	The Olfords travel to Tokyo, Japan to speak at the Ochanomiza Christian Center.
June	Stephen's book, *A Time for Truth,* is published by AMG International.
August	Stephen Olford is diagnosed with Non-Hodgkins Lymphoma and treatment begins immediately.
October 19	The Bethany Ministry Center on the OMI campus is dedicated. This building includes a chapel/lecture room, library space, forty-three bedrooms, a studio, as well as other facilities.

2000

February 1	The Japanese edition of *The Way of Holiness* is released by Word of Life Press.
February 10-28	Stephen and Heather travel to Japan to preach at the Japan Keswick Conventions.
June 3-10	In affiliation with Italy for Christ, Stephen speaks to thousands in Rome (World March for Jesus) and Bari (KAIROS 2000), Italy.
June 12	Stephen preaches at Westminster Chapel for the Premier Radio Rally in London, England.
July 29-August 6	At the Amsterdam Conference for Itinerate Preachers (BGEA), Stephen preaches during a plenary session.

September 24-28	Stephen travels to Ontario, Canada to speak at both Tyndale College and Seminary and Heritage Baptist College.
October 3	Stephen preaches at the Tony Evans Preachers Conference in Dallas, Texas.

2001

January	Born from his bout with cancer, Stephen's book, *The Sword of Suffering,* is released by AMG International.
May 21-26	Stephen conducts a Pastors' Seminar in Honduras and Nicaragua.
July 12	E.K. Bailey Ministries presents Stephen with the 2001 Living Legend Award for "proclaiming the Gospel of Jesus Christ throughout the world and assisting African-American preachers in developing their skills for expository preaching."
September 1	*Windows of Wisdom: Fresh Views on Proverbs' Truths* is published by Ambassador Emerald.
September 3-6	Stephen preaches at the Penarth Institute in Penarth, Wales.

2002

January 18	Stephen speaks at the Beyond All Limits Pastors Conference in Orlando, Florida.
February 13-28	The Olfords participate in the Japan Keswick Conventions.
June 9-14	Stephen delivers a sermon at The Peoples Church in Willowdale, Ontario, Canada. He also preaches at the Essentials of Evangelistic Preaching conference in Cambridge, Ontario.
July 8-12	In Dallas, Texas, Stephen addresses the E.K. Bailey Expository Preaching Conference.
September 4-8	Stephen speaks at the Family Conference in Fiuggi, Rome, Italy.

| November 12-14 | Stephen preaches at Southeastern Baptist Theological Seminary in Wake Forest, North Carolina. |

2003

January 16-17	Stephen addresses the students at Mid-America Baptist Theological Seminary in Memphis, Tennessee.
April 21-24	Stephen speaks at the Ministers Bible Conference in Hume Lake, California.
July 1-3	The Frank Ray Expository Preaching Conference, at which Stephen is a speaker, is held in Memphis, Tennessee.
September	*Basics for Believers* is published by Cook Communications.
November 23	An ordination service is held at Calvary Baptist Church, New York, for Stephen's son, David. Ministry friends and staff, as well as family members, are in attendance as Stephen preaches the Ordination Message.

2004

February 6-29	Stephen and Heather travel to Japan, for the seventh time over twelve years, to minister at the Keswick Conventions.
March 8-11	At Southern Baptist Theological Seminary, in Louisville, Kentucky, Stephen addresses the National Conference on Preaching.
March 29- April 2	Stephen preaches at the Trinidad Keswick Convention.
July 15-16	Stephen, along with his son David, record what would be the last Encounter radio shows.
August 29	After a brief illness, Dr. Stephen F. Olford goes home to be with his Lord.

Numerous sermon and book manuscripts received careful attention during hours of hard work behind the desk in Stephen's study.

Published Works of Stephen F. Olford

For Stephen Olford, writing was not just a logical extension of his ministry; it was an act of worship. From his private devotional journals to his hymns, the depth of his personal relationship with the Lord was evident. It was through his desire to share that relationship with others that his preaching ministry was born. But the reach of Stephen's preaching extended beyond the borders of a single country or a solitary pulpit. Not only did he preach the Word globally in person, on television, and through radio, but he brought the same intensity and excellence to his writing ministry. His first publication, post-World War II, was the evangelistic booklet, *Becoming a Child of God.* Over the years he wrote journal articles, books, sermon outline series, and more. Many of his publications have been translated into a variety of languages. Stephen was unafraid to tackle the tough issues, whether it was tithing for laymen or the integrity of pastors. He was also undaunted by new methods of publishing. By the time of his passing in 2004, several of Stephen's books were available on the internet in the form of e-books. Stephen Olford's understanding of Scripture and clarity of expression have made his writings valuable and timeless. Today, through the efforts of Olford Ministries International, many of his writings are still available as they continue his call to "Preach the Word."

BOOKS IN PRINT

Anointed Expository Preaching. Broadman & Holman Publishers, 1998.

Basics for Believers. Cook Communications Ministries, 2003.

Christian Message for Contemporary Life, The. Kregel Publications, 1999.

Expository Preaching Outlines, Vol. 1-7. Encounter Ministries, Inc., 1980-1989.

Going Places with God. Master Design Ministries, 2000.

Heart Cry for Revival. Christian Focus Publications, 2005.

Not I, But Christ. Crossway Books, 1995.

Preaching the Word of God. Encounter Ministries, Inc., 1989.

Sword of Suffering, The. AMG International, 2001.

Tabernacle: Camping with God, The. Kregel Publications, 2004.

Way of Holiness, The. Crossway Books, 1998.

Windows of Wisdom. Ambassador Emerald International, 2001.

BOOKS OUT OF PRINT

Believing Our Beliefs. Baker Books, 1992.*

Biblical Answers to Personal Problems. Baker Books, 1991.

Christianity and You. Eerdmans Publishing, 1958.

Committed to Christ and His Church. Baker Books, 1991.

Fresh Lessons from Former Leaders. Baker Books, 1991.

Grace of Giving, The. Kregel Publications, 1990.*

I'll Take the High Road. Zondervan Publishing, 1973.

Inviting People to Christ. Baker Books, 1998.

Living Word, The. Moody Publishers, 1963.

Living Words and Loving Deeds. Baker Books, 1992.*

Proclaiming the Good News. Baker Books, 1998.

Pulpit and the Christian Calendar, The, Vol. 1-3. Baker Books, 1991-1992.*

Sanctity of Sex, The. Revell Publishing, 1974.

Secret of Soul-Winning, The. Treasure House, 1994.*

Sermon Outlines on the Cross. Baker Books, 1997.

Special Day Sermon Outlines. Baker Books, 1997.

Time for Truth, A. AMG International, 1999.*

E-BOOKS*

Answers to Personal Problems Outlines

Bible Character Sermon Outlines

Biblical Answers to Personal Problems

Fresh Lessons from Former Leaders

Heart Cry for Revival

Pulpit and the Christian Calendar, The

Sermon Outlines on the Cross

Special Day Sermon Outlines

BOOKLETS*

Manna in the Morning

Becoming a Child of God

Becoming a Man of God

Becoming a Servant of God

Encounter with Anxiety

Encounter with Fear

Encounter with Loneliness

SOFTWARE*

The Olford Expository Preaching CD, Version 1. Olford Ministries International, in conjunction with WordSearch Corp., 2002.

The Olford Expository Preaching CD, Version 2. Olford Ministries International, in conjunction with Logos Research Systems, 2004.

*These titles are available by calling Olford Ministries International at 1-800-843-2241 or by visiting www.olford.org .

Notes

PREFACE

1. John Phillips, *Only One Life* (Loizeaux: Neptune, New Jersey, 1995) 9-10.

CHAPTER 1 — THE BOY

1. T. Ernest Wilson, *Angola Beloved* (Neptune, NJ: Loizeaux, 1967) 102-103.

CHATPER 2 — THE BELIEVER

1. Stephen F. Olford, "When the Spirit Became Lord" from the book *My Most Memorable Encounter With God* David Enlow, ed. (Wheaton, IL: Tyndale House, 1977) pp. 149-157. See also John Pollock's authorized biography, *Billy Graham* (New York: McGraw Hill, 1966) 38-39.

CHAPTER 4 — THE FATHER

1. Quoted In *Pulpit Helps* (Chattanooga, TN: AMG International, June 1988) 17.
2. *The Evangel* vol. 39, no. 24, Calvary Baptist Church, Knoxville, TN, June 17, 1990.
3. *A Passion for Preaching: Essays in Honor of Stephen F. Olford.* Compiled by David L. Olford (Nashville: Nelson, 1989) 25.

CHAPTER 5 — THE SOUL WINNER

1. Stephen F. Olford, *The Secret of Soul Winning* (Shippensburg, PA: Treasure House, 1994) 9-12.

CHAPTER 6 — THE TRAVELER

1. Marvin R. Vincent, *Word Studies in the New Testament,* 4 vol. (Grand Rapids: Wm. B. Eerdmans Publishing Company) 822.
2. Elisabeth Elliot, ed., *The Journals of Jim Elliot* (Grand Rapids: Baker/Revell, 1978) 11-12.

CHAPTER 7 — THE EVANGELIST

1. Some of these men have been Stephen's partners in evangelism throughout the years: Noel Knight, a bank manager with a gift for publicity and programming; Clarence Jefferies, Chairman of the Board of his own business, and the Chairman of most crusade committees held in Manchester; Val Grieve, a solicitor and advisor in legal matters that inevitably arise in endeavors of this kind. These and more were men "whose hearts the Lord had touched" for His glory and the salvation of the lost. At Stephen's suggestion the committee arranged for seasoned speakers to visit Manchester every month to prepare Christians to expect great things from God.

2. Sanna Barlow Rossi, *Anthony T. Rossi, Christian & Entrepreneur: The Story of the Founder of Tropicana* (Downers Grove, IL: Intervarsity Press, 1986).

3. Guy Sottile, from "I Found a Friend" *Encounter* (vol. 4, no. 3: July-September 1977) 6-7.

4. From "The Proclaimer" vol. 1, no. 1 (Italy for Christ, January 1992) 1,3. All rights reserved.

CHAPTER 10 — THE TEACHER-PREACHER

1. Marshall, Morgan & Scott, 1952; now out of print. In his carefully researched treatment of the history and ministry of the Keswick movement, Dr. Barabas points out that in spite of the uninformed critics, the message and influence of Keswick have sent more men into the work of the Lord and more missionaries to the ends of the earth than any other agency within the religious life of the church. Dr. John Hudson Taylor recruited most of his task force for China through the Keswick Convention in England. One reason for this is the biblical and balanced sequence of truth that has been continuously followed by the speakers at the "Keswick Week," namely: the glory of God, sin in the believer's life, the provision for cleansing and victory, the lordship of Christ and the response of surrender, the Spirit-filled life, Christian service and the missionary call. Stephen Olford has captured this progression of truth in a hymn he wrote for the yearly Christian Life Convention at Calvary Baptist Church, New York City—"Lord, Meet My Need." Later it was accepted by the Keswick Council and incorporated into the authorized Keswick hymnbook.

CHAPTER 11 — THE CONTENDER

1. John R. W. Stott, *The Preacher's Portrait: Some New Testament Word Studies* (Grand Rapids: Eerdmans, 1961) 55, 57.

CHAPTER 12 — THE COUNSELOR

1. John Baillie, a *Diary of Private Prayer* (New York: Charles Scribner's Sons, 1949).

2. Leon Morris, *The Gospel According to St. Luke, Tyndale New Testament Commentaries, 3d ed.* (Grand Rapids: Eerdmans, 1976) 196.

3. H.C.G. Moule, *The Epistle to the Romans* (Grand Rapids: Zondervan, n.d.) 22.

CHAPTER 13 — THE MAN

1. Roger Willmore, as quoted by Anthony Wade, "Preaching legend Olford dies at 86", *The Alabama Baptist Online,* September 9, 2004, http://www.thealabamabaptist.org/ip_template.asp?upid=5613&ctid=8 2 (accessed April 14, 2006).

CHAPTER 14 — THE DREAMER

1. Stephen F. Olford, *Heart-Cry For Revival* (4th ed. Rev. Memphis, TN: *Encounter,* 1987) 14-19.
2. Vance Havner, *Threescore and Ten* (Grand Rapids: Baker/Revell, 1973) 72-73.
3. Adapted from the article "Growing Old Gracefully" by Martha Cruz-Griffith, *The American Baptist* (Valley Forge, PA, September 1991) 16.
4. "The Best Was Yet to Best," *Eternity* (Philadelphia, November 1978) 20.
5. *The American Baptist*, September 1991, 15.

CHAPTER 15 — THE AFTERWORD

1. Adrian Rogers, as quoted by Erin Curry, "Noted expository preacher Stephen Olford dies at 86," *Baptist Press,* Aug 30, 2004; http://www.bpnews.net/bpnews.asp?ID=18977 (accessed December 14, 2005).

Olford Ministries International

The mission and passion of Olford Ministries International is to provide biblical instruction and practical training to encourage and equip preachers and teachers to "rightly divide" the Word of truth in the power of the Holy Spirit. It is accomplished with a global concern to see the church revived and the world reached with the saving Word of Christ.

Through a variety of planned training events, biblical instruction and practical training are made available to those in the ministry, those preparing for ministry, and for all who seek to be better equipped to preach or teach the Word of God. Attendees come from all backgrounds and from all over the world to take part in:

- **Seminars** . . . on expository preaching and teaching, evangelistic preaching, church leadership, spiritual growth, and other related subjects. Video "streaming" of some training events will provide an on-going program and resource for ministry.

- **Workshops** . . . providing an opportunity for preachers and teachers to strengthen and enhance their gifts and skills in an open, constructive environment.

- **Conferences / Retreats** . . . designed for spiritual enrichment and renewal, focusing on such themes as holiness, revival, and personal spiritual growth.

- **Continuing Education** . . . Olford Ministries International offers its own *"Fellowship"* program for those wanting a structured training experience with accountability. Also, individual seminars can be taken for academic credit through affiliated seminaries.

- **Resources** . . . A wide variety of teaching tools and resources are available, from audiocassettes and videos, to CDs, sermon outlines and books, all designed to encourage and equip God's people for spiritual faithfulness and practical fruitfulness.

For more information or to obtain a brochure, please visit www.olford.org or write to us at: Olford Ministries International, P.O. Box 757800, Memphis, TN 38175-7800.